MULTIPLE-CHOICE & FREE-RESPONSE QUESTIONS WITH DBQ IN PREPARATION FOR THE AP EUROPEAN HISTORY EXAMINATION

(SIXTH EDITION)

Ellis A. Wasson
University of Delaware

D&S MARKETING SYSTEMS, INC.
1205 38th Street Brooklyn, NY 11218

w w w . d s m a r k e t i n g . c o m

ISBN # : 978-1-934780-36-7 / 1-934-780-36-7

PREFACE

The purpose of this book is to give you some pointers on how best to approach the AP European History examination and to help you practice and review for that exam. There is an introductory section, review outlines, multiple choice questions, examples of short-answer questions, document-based essays, long-essays, and two full-length sample exams.

Remember that the examination is always evolving. Check with your teacher about the most current information relating to the structure and content. **This review book is designed to meet the needs of students taking the revised AP European Exam first to be administered in May 2016**.

Based on more than three decades of teaching AP to students of wide-ranging ability as well as many years of grading the exam and serving on the committee that makes up the questions, I have tried to make this book as realistic as possible.

I have made a particular effort to include illustrations, charts, graphs, maps, cartoons, and quotations from historical documents, which you will find are a part of both the multiple choice, short-answer and essay portions of the examination. Work hard to acquire the skills necessary to master these problems of interpretation. Remember, even the factual section of the examination is not a mere exercise in memorization. You are being tested on your ability to think critically. Good Luck!

All communications concerning this book should be addressed to the publisher and distributor:

D & S Marketing Systems, Inc.
1205 38th Street
Brooklyn, NY 11218

Biography of Ellis Wasson

Ellis Wasson was a teacher and administrator in independent schools for 39 years during which time he always taught AP European history. He now teaches at the University of Delaware. He has served as a member of the Test Development Committee of the AP European History Examination, edited the College Board support website, and has been a Table Leader and Question Leader at the annual reading of the exam for several decades. He is the author of six books, including a standard college textbook on British history 1715 to the present.

TABLE OF CONTENTS

STUDENT SURVIVAL GUIDE

What are the big problems that face the world and what can I do to help? How do I distinguish between fact and opinion in learning about these issues (or when I'm buying a used car for that matter)? What do I believe in and why do I believe it? How can I express what I believe and what I have learned in a coherent and persuasive manner? These and many other questions can be at least partially answered by taking a course such as AP European History. Remember that you will be acquiring and honing skills of vital importance to success in college and in life. At the same time you will be learning about an important piece of the past.

It is fashionable at the moment to value all societies equally. In many ways this is a fair and reasonable approach to history. Every person should be equal; every society is deserving of respect. We should be familiar with the broad outline of all human development, and understand the basic beliefs of all large cultures. But Europe has a special place in the creation of the modern, technological society in which we live. Our language and our laws derive directly from the European experience. Philosophy, art, literature, economic theory, etc. are all part of this inheritance. The modern research university and modern mathematics and science come from Europe. Unfortunately, the Atlantic slave trade and modern racism also was a legacy of European civilization. If you wish to understand the good and the bad in American society you must first learn about Europe.

China, India, and Japan are important to the world economy and American strategic thinking, but Europe is still the largest and the richest economic force in the world and will remain so for a long time. The legacy of European imperialism in the Middle East helped to create the tragedy of September 11th and our military interventions in Iraq and Afghanistan.

To do well in this course you will have to commit yourself to hard work. Only dedication combined with intelligence can win you the highest score on the examination. But enjoy yourself. There is so much wonderful drama, so much grandeur and horror, so much that is human.

CONNECTING THE PAST

Your teacher will provide you with material about the curriculum prepared by the College Board. You can also go online and visit the College Board website. You will learn about the skills you are expected to master during the course of the year and the factual material that has to be covered. I find, however, that imposing an independent superstructure on the textbook you use and the Curriculum Framework being followed in this course often throws a fresh light on what you are studying and helps you to think more creatively and thus remember more easily. The skills are ones every good history teacher incorporates in every course they teach.

Five themes are helpful in connecting the mass of information that will threaten to overwhelm you unless some kind of organizational structure is imposed on it. Try to fit what you read into this model.

1. The rise and decline of great powers. This involves religion, the idea of the state, the conduct of war and diplomacy, the growth of nationalism, the development of economic systems, and the influence of great individuals on history.
2. The second theme is "equality vs. liberty." This balance remains as elusive today as it has always been. The growth and decay of ideologies and the conflict between them falls here. So too does the attempt to solve problems by reform and revolution. How the individual relates to society is one of the fundamental aspects of life.
3. The third theme is social structure and the transition from orders and estates to class. You must focus attention on the elites, middle level, and the lower orders or classes in the worlds of agriculture, urban life, and industrial society. (By the way, do not make the mistake of confusing royalty with aristocracy. Often the interests of kings and nobles were diametrically opposed.) Managing poverty and prosperity is one of the most difficult things that human beings try to accomplish.
4. Historians today like to talk about the "Great Divergence" between the West and the rest of the world. They argue about when the divide opened up and why, for a time, Europe and its settler outposts surged ahead in terms of economic and political power. The relationship between Europe and the other cultures of the planet is one of the most important aspects of modern history. And remember, this interaction was not a one-way street. It is not a story just about Europe "doing things" to others. Ideas, wealth, and people flowed back into the imperialist homeland transforming society there also.
5. The fifth theme is the history of culture: the visual arts, music, literature, science, philosophy, etc. The creators of culture shape our views of ourselves and of society. It is impossible to exaggerate the importance of Luther, Newton, and Darwin. Few have so profoundly understood the human condition as Count Tolstoy or Jane Austen. Historians like to impose a framework of "objective" knowledge vs. "subjective" ideas about the world, although that is a line often hard to discern.

One other theme to keep in mind: the history of the family—perhaps the most fundamental of all historical issues, involving the relationships between men, women, and children and the history of the home and the work place. The family is the building block of society. By the way, historians are in constant conflict with each other on virtually every kind of issue, but no area is faster moving or more fraught with misinformation at the moment than this one. Textbooks never give enough space to the topic and are obsolete almost immediately when it comes to family history.

Warning: Western Europeans and Americans, since the time of the Enlightenment, have been subject to what historians call the fallacy of the "Whig interpretation" of history. This is the notion that history moves onward and upward in a progressive trajectory that is inevitable and for the best. Ironically, Adam Smith and Karl Marx both suffered from this delusion. One would have thought that World War I and World War II and the nuclear bomb would have cured us of the idea, but alas we still believe in happy endings. That is our privilege, but do not assume that in the past positive change was inevitable or that every reform was an advance.

THE EXAMINATION

You should look at the material published on the College Board website (see: http://apcentral.collegeboard. com). In it a Curriculum Framework is provided of the material covered in the examination. Roughly a quarter each of the exam will cover four periods:

c.1450–1648

c.1648–1815

c.1815–1914

c.1914–to the present

Of course, history does not neatly divide itself into such categories. Questions relating to major themes stretch across those boundaries and so also will questions on the exam. Be prepared for a question that may test your ability to make connections over centuries. Sample questions are included with the Curriculum Framework, but this book will give you a wider and richer opportunity to test your mastery of the material.

The examination itself is outlined in the Curriculum Framework. Sixty percent of the exam is composed of short answer questions based around either pieces of historical evidence or topics of historical importance. The other forty percent consists of two essays.

MULTIPLE-CHOICE

You will have 55 minutes to answer 55 multiple choice questions covering the period 1450 to the present counting 40% of the examination score. It is important to remember that the questions are mixed up chronologically and in level of difficulty. Do not panic if you come to a couple of questions you cannot answer. There will be easier ones later. You should take a guess even if you are not sure about the correct answer. Move rapidly through the questions. Do not pause for long on difficult ones. Skip the puzzling ones and come back at the end.

There are three crucial things to know about the multiple-choice section.

1. You will do better if you practice. That is a key point of this book. Your teacher should give you some opportunities to answer multiple-choice questions during the year. Examples of multiple-choice questions have been published by the College Board. Use these to practice on in your final review for the examination.
2. There is no substitute for careful study and memorization. You cannot "wing it" and hope to do well on this section.
3. You can answer a number of questions incorrectly and still get a five on the examination. No course will cover all the material. Many different textbooks are used to prepare students for this test. You are competing against your peers, not against a set standard, and the final grade is a kind of curve.
4. The multiple choice questions are arranged in sets of 3 to 5 questions based on some kind of historical source. This can be a historical document (speech, letter, diary entry, poem, passage from a book, photograph, painting, cartoon, map, etc.), a set of statistics in the form of a graph, table, or other format, a modern map of a historical period, a passage written by a historian after the fact. The focus may be on one event or era or answers may require making connections between various periods of history. The questions are designed to test a variety of historical thinking skills and cover a variety of periods. You will not be able to rely entirely on your reasoning ability to figure out the answers. Some historical knowledge needs to be applied. On the other hand, perfect recall of every fact in the textbook will also not be required. Important information will be provided in the text you are analyzing.

SHORT-ANSWER QUESTIONS

This section consists of four questions with 50 minutes to complete. It consists of twenty percent of the exam score. These questions require you to write out your answers, but unlike with analytical essays you are not required to provide a thesis statement. The answers will require demonstration of historical thinking skills and mastery of factual knowledge. The questions will be based on a piece of historical evidence such as a quotation from a document, a map, or image. Quotations from contemporary historians may also form the basis of questions. Other questions will be based on general propositions in European history. Do not use bullet point. Write in full sentences. Keep your answer within the lined margins on the answer sheet.

THE REST OF THE EXAM

For a discussion of the Documents-Based Questions and Long Answer Questions, see the chapters designated under those headings that are located immediately after Chapter Twelve.

HOW TO USE THE OUTLINES

Each chapter contains an outline. These lists are intended to include the bare minimum of essential factual information needed to succeed on the AP European history exam. No outline can be totally complete. The exam is very comprehensive, and some information may be highlighted in a given year that does not appear in my outlines. The vast majority of the multiple-choice questions will involve information contained in these outlines.

I have included lists of causes and outcomes of major events. These lists are good preparation for answering the short-answer and long-essay questions. Rarely are questions framed in a way to evoke simple regurgitation of a list (e.g. "Discuss the causes of the Renaissance"). However, if the question—"Was the Reformation mainly an economic event?"—is asked, knowledge of all the possible causes of the Reformation will give a student the foundation on which to build a solid answer.

Do not wait until the night before the exam to read over these outlines. The best thing to do is to review over several weeks. Compare your class notes and textbook underlinings to the outlines. Write in missing or supplementary information either in the margins here or in your notebook, whichever works best for you. Once you have a consolidated outline, work particularly hard to review the sections that you found most confusing or have forgotten the most about.

Inevitably, in outlines of this kind, broad, sweeping trends over many countries or centuries and some big themes do not emerge clearly. Many essay questions may at first glance seem not to relate directly to "answers" in the outlines. However, if you are asked to write an essay on female monarchs or types of revolutions, you will find plenty of examples in the outlines on which you can draw.

The selection and ranking of important of facts and events can be controversial among historians. In some cases even terms such as "Counter Reformation" vs. the "Catholic Reformation" or the English "Civil War" vs. "Revolution" divide historians into opposing camps. What is purveyed here is not "the truth" but a collection of information that will help you organize a vast amount of data as efficiently as possible for the purpose of spending three hours taking the AP exam. I have included items in my lists because while some historians and teachers would reject them many others see them as important. Your teacher will make you aware of areas where current controversy is lively.

The outlines are no substitute for a solid textbook, hard work, study of the Curriculum Framework, and a good teacher. They are intended for review purposes only and presuppose much additional information that students should already know. Nor will they always work as review mechanisms for tests given by individual teachers who emphasize issues and events that seem important to them but may not appear on the AP exam. (Every good AP teacher emphasizes certain aspects of the course in which he or she has special interests and expertise.)

Many of the dates provided here are not necessarily crucial to remember. They are listed in order to help you place people and events in chronological context. It is much more important to remember the ORDER in which things happen than the year. Nonetheless certain dates must be memorized both to provide a skeleton upon which to organize the rest of the chronology and because they mark crucial moments in the human story that we should never forget. I have marked the ones that have great importance with an *.

CHAPTER 1

THE RENAISSANCE

This course begins during the fifteenth century when most historians accept a shift occurred in the direction of Western European civilization, which we call the Renaissance. Students should be aware of the principle characteristics of medieval life in order to understand the importance of the changes that followed.

The main characteristics of pre-Renaissance **medieval life** were a reliance on agriculture and the power of the Roman Catholic Church. Rank and order were central to the social hierarchy that ranged from the Pope and Holy Roman Emperor at the top through kings and sovereign princes down to the great nobles, lesser nobles, knights, merchants, artisans, independent peasants, laborers, and serfs. Massive poverty, overwhelming pandemics, illiteracy, and spirituality existed everywhere. Although a few Jews and Muslims lived on the fringes of society, virtually all people from Poland and Hungary westward were Roman Catholics (except southern Spain, which was Islamic). **Feudalism** was the principal system of political, social, and economic organization. Latin was the predominant written language among the literate, who largely came from the clergy. People tended to see themselves as part of large communities and organizations with little individual self-awareness, and were focused on life after death. Marriages were partnerships in which work was divided by gender, but the contribution of men and women were both critical to survival.

Change was fostered by the impact of the **Black Death** (1347), the increasing wealth of merchants who allied with monarchs against the great nobles, the Great Schism in the Church (1378–1417), the Crusades (1095 onwards), and technological advances in navigation and weaponry (especially the invention of cannons).

THE FIFTEEN CENTURY

FRANCE

Still internally fragmented by the 100 years war with England (1337–1453) with a powerful nobility that weakened the king.

1

SPAIN
Divided into numerous kingdoms including Castile and Aragon with the Muslims still in Granada until *1492. The marriage of **Ferdinand and Isabella** (1469) brought unity and strength, led to the conquest of the South, intensification of religious uniformity, and overseas exploration.

ENGLAND
The Wars of the Roses (c. 1455–85) kept the nobility preoccupied and divided and led ultimately to the growth of a strong monarchy under the **Tudors** (Henry VII 1485). Still a small, weak, and relatively unimportant country.

HOLY ROMAN EMPIRE (largely a Germanic Federation)
Hopelessly divided with the power of the Emperor (from 1452 on always a **Habsburg** of Austria) deteriorating (outside his personal domains) after concessions to the seven **electors** and the hundreds of minor autonomous princes and bishops were made at each "election" of a new monarch.

ITALY
Fragmented into many states, of which the most important were: the Papal territories, Venice, Milan, Rome, Genoa, Naples, and Florence. It is here that the Renaissance developed.

THE RENAISSANCE
A period from the later 14th to the mid–16th century whose name "Renaissance" ("rebirth") first gained wide currency after its use by the 19th-century Swiss historian, Jacob Burckhardt. A rich flowering of culture and revival of Classical ideas and learning, which began and flourished in Northern Italy. However, some historians see more continuity than change. The effects of the Renaissance were largely confined to high culture and urban elites.

CAUSES OF THE RENAISSANCE
- The **breakdown of feudalism** and the rise of a market economy in Northern Italy led to greater wealth and leisure, which could support the pursuit of culture and learning.

- The rise of international **banking**, which promoted **trade** and created prosperity. The location of Italy at the center of trade networks connecting the East and West made it an ideal place to dominate commerce.

- The rise of **city-states** with independent rulers and substantial urban populations. Rulers invested in cultural competition and in gaining popular support. This led to new architecture, painting, sculpture, and literary patronage and the rapid spread of ideas and styles.

- **Crusaders** returned from the Middle East with new wealth and ideas.

- An enlarged **merchant class** emerged that demanded more and better education and had wealth and leisure to enjoy art and literature.

- The **Great Schism** weakened respect for the authority of the Church, which allowed more secular ideas to emerge and survive.

- The rediscovery of **Greek and Roman (Classical) texts** brought by scholars fleeing from endangered Byzantium (Constantinople conquered by the Ottomans 1453) and by searches in neglected repositories in Western Europe. The teaching of Classical languages was revived and an interest in Classical art and architecture became popular.

- Absence of any single controlling authority in **Italy** made it difficult for a single religious or world view to be imposed, nor could rulers easily halt the spread of innovation and new ideas.

- A number of **individual geniuses** emerged, particularly in Florence, who interacted and competed with each other stimulating ever-greater achievements in the arts and literature.

CENTRAL IDEAS OF THE RENAISSANCE

The central idea of the Renaissance was **humanism**, which can be defined as enhanced liberal and secular learning, recovery and study of **Classical** texts, and moving the center of gravity in life towards human concerns. The Greek idea of "Man Is the Measure of All Things" became influential. For the literate and well to do engagement in civic life came to be regarded as noble and necessary. Not everything changed. The Roman Catholic Church remained predominant and spiritual life active. More than half of all Renaissance art involved Christian themes. The Popes were principal patrons of many artists. The subordination of women continued. Most poor people remained illiterate and their lives were harsh and difficult. The social hierarchy did not change. Many people had misgivings about the direction of Renaissance ideas. In Florence the monk **Savonarola** (d. 1498) preached against decadence.

| DIFFERENCES BETWEEN THE MIDDLE AGES AND THE RENAISSANCE ||
MEDIEVAL	RENAISSANCE
emphasis on the community	individualism and personal achievement
feudal rule by nobility	**civic humanism** and active participation in civic life
spiritual fulfillment through God	**Virtù**, reaching for perfection, shaping one's own destiny, fully developed mind and body
accept community standards and judgments	self-awareness, "know thyself"
dominance of Church hierarchy	secularism
focus on the afterlife	materialism in this life
rely on the Church and lords for guidance	be educated, refined and self-sufficient
educated people use Latin	educated people use **vernacular**
"Gothic" style, focus on the religious purpose of art	"Classical" values of balance, order, symmetry and secular uses of the arts
life is a mere stage on the road to Heaven	limitless opportunities for a good and improved life here and now

GREAT FIGURES OF THE RENAISSANCE

Certain figures in the arts stand out as specially associated with the Renaissance. Only a few of the most important can be listed here. In literature: **Dante** (d. 1321) was the first great master of vernacular literature (*Divine Comedy*). **Petrarch** (d. 1374) was the father of humanism and promoted the coexistence of Classical and Christian values. **Boccaccio** (d. 1375) was a pioneer of humanist studies and author of *Decameron*. **Pico della Mirandola** (d.1494) authored *On the Dignity of Man*. **Castiglione** (d. 1529) promoted the importance of education, good manners (author of the *Courtier*). **Machiavelli** (d. 1527), author of *The Prince*, a guide to politics, admired the heroism and patriotism of the Romans.

In sculpture and painting: **Brunelleschi** (d. 1446) designed the cathedral dome in Florence. **Donatello** (d. 1466) recreated "living" sculpture, most notably with his "David", the first free-standing nude statue since Classical times. **Botticelli** (d. 1510) was famous for his rendering of female beauty, notably in the "Birth of Venus". **Leonardo da Vinci** (d. 1519) known as the universal or "Renaissance" man, was a master in art and science. **Michelangelo** (d. 1564) perhaps the greatest master of all, glorified the human body and spirit. His masterworks were the Sistine Chapel ceiling at the Vatican and his "David" in Florence. **Raphael** (d. 1520) is noted for the "School of Athens" in the Vatican.

Among rulers, statesmen, and patrons of the arts the **Medici family** of Florence is usually regarded as the most notable. They were innovative and enormously successful bankers who used their wealth to become the rulers of the city-state. They were also noted for "Machiavellian" ruthlessness. The two best known were Cosimo (d. 1464) and Lorenzo the Magnificent (d. 1492).

Among the many notable popes of the period **Julius II** (d. 1513) stands out as both a warrior prince who expelled French invaders and a great patron of the arts.

OUTCOMES OF THE RENAISSANCE

- Weakening of the authority of the Church. Humanism and the Christian religion are ultimately incompatible, for one places God at the center and the other man.

- The "modern" frame of mind begins to emerge: skeptical, curious, individualistic, civic-minded, and self-aware. A critical and analytical outlook was encouraged. Serious study of history begins.

- A revival of the study of Classical Greece and its language and texts accelerates, and Latin and Greek become central to male education among the elite.

- A revival of Classical style in architecture and art develops.

- A huge body of great art was created employing new techniques to achieve realism through the use perspective and other means.

- An interest in exploring unknown areas of the globe, in part encouraged by improved ship technology, mapping, and navigation.

- A greater interest in the study of science begins, particularly in astronomy, physics, chemistry, and anatomy.

- The creation of modern banking and business techniques including double-entry bookkeeping develops.

- A rapid growth in the printing and distribution of books is launched by **Gutenberg's** (1450s) invention of moveable type for printing presses.

New styles of art emerge after the initial surge of the early to mid-Renaissance. In Italy **Mannerism** dominates from the1520s. Later in the seventeenth century the **Baroque** style was popular, while in the eighteenth century Rococo developed. All of them were Classical in their elements and drew on the innovation of the Renaissance.

THE NORTHERN RENAISSANCE

The ideas of the Italian Renaissance spread northward gradually in the fifteenth and sixteenth centuries, reaching France and the low countries first and then England, Poland, Hungary, and Germany, finally penetrating to Scandinavia. The Renaissance had less impact in Spain and little at all in Russia.

The Northern Renaissance was less secularizing than the Italian one. The ultimately unworkable idea of "**Christian Humanism**" emerged, most notably associated with the Dutch monk **Erasmus** (d. 1536). This was an attempt to reconcile knowledge of the Classical world and a more analytical approach to learning with Christian values and devotion. He believed in the freedom of the human will and critical scholarship, and resisted the Reformation. **Sir Thomas More** (d. 1535), author of *Utopia*, also resisted the Reformation, which cost him his life. He was a social liberal and a theological conservative. Greater literacy and education expanded, although the most widespread impulse for this development came from the Reformation (see Chapter II). The use of vernacular language encouraged a greater sense of national awareness and feeling among the educated elites. Much great art was produced in the Netherlands.

In the arts many notable figures are associated with the Northern Renaissance. These include the German painter and engraver **Dürer** (d. 1528), a German painter, the Flemish artist **Rubens** (d. 1640), and the Dutch master of unsurpassed sensitivity and penetration, **Rembrandt** (d. 1669). In literature the giant figure of **Shakespeare** (d. 1616) predominates. In business the German banking family, the **Fuggers** rivaled the Medici.

IMPORTANT DEFINITIONS AND IDENTIFICATIONS

- banking
- Baroque
- Black Death (the Plague)
- Boccaccio
- Botticelli
- breakdown of feudalism
- Brunelleschi
- Castiglione
- Christian humanism
- city-states
- civic humanism
- Classical learning
- Crusaders
- Dante
- Leonardo da Vinci
- Donatello

- Dürer
- electors
- Erasmus
- Ferdinand and Isabella of Spain
- feudalism
- Fugger family
- the Great Schism
- Gutenberg
- Habsburg dynasty of Austria
- Holy Roman Empire
- humanism
- Julius II
- Machiavelli
- Mannerism
- Medici family
- medieval life

- merchant class
- Michaelangelo
- Sir Thomas More
- Northern Renaissance
- Petrarch
- Pico della Mirandola
- Raphael
- Rembrandt
- Renaissance
- Rubens
- Savonarola
- secularism
- Shakespeare
- Tudor dynasty of England
- vernacular
- *virtú*

IMPORTANT DATES

1347 Black Death

*c.1350–1550 Roughly the time span of the Italian Renaissance

1378–1417 The Great Schism in the Roman Catholic Church

1450s Invention of the printing press with moveable type

1453 Constantinople falls to the Turks

1485 Tudor dynasty established in England

*1492 Ferdinand and Isabella send Columbus to the New World

Muslims expelled from Spain

15th–16th c. Roughly the time span of the Northern Renaissance

CHAPTER 1
MULTIPLE-CHOICE QUESTIONS

Questions 1.1–1.3 refer to the following passage.

A great quantity of money came from the donations of pilgrims visiting Rome in a holy year to the Apostolic See, and with this Pope Nicholas V commenced building in many places, and sent for Greek and Latin books, wherever he was able to find them, without regard to price. He gathered together a large band of writers, the best that he could find, and kept them in constant employment. He also summoned a number of learned men, both for the purpose of composing new works, and of translating such works as were not already translated, giving them most abundant provision for their needs meanwhile; and when the works were translated and brought to him, he gave them large sums of money, in order that they should do more willingly that which they undertook to do. He made great provision for the needs of learned men. He gathered together great numbers of books upon every subject, both Greek and Latin, to the number of 5000 volumes. So at his death it was found by inventory that never since the time of Ptolemy had half the number of books of every kind been brought together.

Vespasio da Bisticci, *Life of Nicholas V*, c. 1480.

1.1 According to Vespasio da Bisticci Pope Nicholas V (r. 1447–54) was

(A) Spending his money on luxuries and valueless objects
(B) Decorating his new palaces with books
(C) collecting Classical texts to form a great library
(D) Competing to equal ancient Egyptian pharaohs in spending

1.2 Many popes during the Italian Renaissance were noted for which of the following?

(A) Being patrons of religious and secular arts and literature
(B) Their ignorance about arts and literature
(C) Objections to secular arts and literature
(D) Banning artists from the Vatican Palace

1.3 The Roman Catholic Church in the Renaissance period accepted the teachings of Greek and Roman authors on which of the following subjects?

(A) Defining the nature of sin
(B) The conduct of Church ritual
(C) Astronomy and mathematics
(D) Church history

7

Questions 2.1–2.3 refer to the map below.

2.1 This maps depicts Italy at which of the following periods?

(A) The Renaissance
(B) The Reformation
(C) The Wars of Religion
(D) The French Revolution

2.2 Which of the Italian states shown on this map had a large overseas empire not depicted here?

(A) Naples
(B) Florence
(C) Venice
(D) Siena

2.3 The fragmented nature of the political system in Italy until the 19th century meant which of the following was true?

(A) The Ottoman Empire became the overlord
(B) Was intensely nationalistic
(C) Was subject to foreign invasions
(D) Easily converted to Lutheranism

Questions 3.1–3.3 refer to the following passage.

Cruelties can be exploited well or badly. Well committed may be called those (if it is permissible to use the word well of evil) which are perpetrated once for the need of securing one's self, and which afterwards are not persisted in, but are exchanged for measures as useful to the subjects as possible.

In taking a state the conqueror must arrange to commit all his cruelties at once, so as not to have to recur to them every day, and so as to be able, by not making fresh changes, to reassure people and win them over by benefiting them. Whoever acts otherwise, either through timidity or bad counsels, is always obliged to stand with knife in hand, and can never depend on his subjects, because they, owing to continually fresh injuries are unable to depend on him. For injuries should be done all together, so that being less tasted, they will give less offence. Benefits should be granted little by little, so that they may be better enjoyed.

A prince should therefore have no other aim or thought, not take up any other thing for his study, but war and its organization and discipline, for that is the only art that is necessary to one who commands, and it is of such virtue that it not only maintains those who are born princes, but often enables men of private fortune to attain that rank. And one sees, on the other hand, that when princes think more of luxury than arms, they lose their state.

Nicolo Machiavelli, *The Prince*, (compiled 1513, published 1532)

3.1 To the Renaissance writer Machiavelli the chief duty of a ruler is which of the following?

(A) Enjoy themselves at the expense of their rivals
(B) Build an overseas empire
(C) Provide prosperity to the people
(D) Provide order and protection to the people

3.2 According to Machiavelli a ruler should not be afraid to do which of the following?

(A) Be ruthless in the pursuit of his duty
(B) Extract as much wealth as they can through taxation
(C) Use torture on a regular basis
(D) Retreat in the face of opposing force

3.3 Which of the following best characterizes the Italian city states of the Renaissance?

(A) Enjoyed an unusual reign of peaceful relations
(B) Were in a constant state of warfare
(C) Flourished only when they were at peace
(D) Were dominated by the papacy by force

Questions 4.1–4.3 refer to the image of the Medici Palace (1444–84) in Florence.

4.1 This palace in Florence built by the Medici family draws on which architectural style?

(A) Baroque
(B) Classical
(C) Gothic
(D) Mannerist

4.2 The heavily fortified nature of the building at street level suggests what about Florence and the Medici?

(A) They ruled by violence
(B) They were never popular
(C) They did not like the people of Florence
(D) At times Florentine politics became rough

4.3 The Medici acquired political power by first establishing themselves as successful

(A) Generals
(B) Bankers
(C) Explorers
(D) Diplomats

Questions 5.1–5.3 refer to the 1530 painting of an unknown man appearing below.

5.1 This portrait of a man from the low countries was painted about 1530

(A) Shows that Renaissance ideas had not yet reached north of the Alps
(B) Is likely to have been idealized rather than portraying the sitter as he really was
(C) Shows how prosperous peasants had become
(D) Portrays a wealthy and educated man

5.2 The clothing and background depicted in the painting suggest that the sitter held what social rank?

(A) Merchant
(B) Nobleman
(C) Clergyman
(D) Serf

5.3 The portrait was a relatively new in European art in the sixteenth century. This represented what development?

(A) Artists with greater talent had emerged
(B) Houses were bigger and more wall space had to be covered
(C) The growth of interest and focus on the individual
(D) Museums wanted to collect portraits

SHORT-ANSWER QUESTIONS

Question 1

1. Using the c. 1480 painting by Andrea Mantegna titled "Lamentation of Christ" and your knowledge of European history answer both parts (A and B) of the question below.

    A)   Identify and explain TWO characteristics of the Renaissance represented by the work of the artist.

    B)   Identify and explain ONE reason why the artist chose a religious subject to depict.

CHAPTER 2

THE REFORMATION

The Protestant Reformation was a revolution in the Christian church that split Western Europe into Catholic and Lutheran communities, and ultimately led to the fragmentation of Protestantism into many sects. Humpty Dumpty fell off the wall and could never be put back together again.

THE LUTHERAN REFORMATION

In ***1517** the Catholic academic and monk **Martin Luther** (1483–1546) in the **95 Theses** publicly challenged the authority of the Pope over the sale of **indulgences** and other theological points. He was prompted to do so by a personal crisis of faith, but quickly found widespread support in Germany.

Emperor Charles V (r. 1520–58) was the most powerful figure opposed to Luther. He called the reformer to account for himself at the **Diet of Worms** (1521). Luther was put under an imperial ban and went into hiding, when he was protected by **Frederick of Saxony**, one of the princes who embraced Protestantism. During this period, he translated the New Testament into German. A **Peasant's War** prompted by social and economic grievances erupted in 1525, but Luther sided with the princes against the populist revolt, which was suppressed. In 1531 the **Schmalkaldic League**, a German Protestant alliance against Charles V and the Roman Catholics was formed. The initial wars of religion came to an end with the recognition that neither side had enough power to overcome the other. The **Peace of Augsburg (*1555)** established the principle—*cuius regio, eius religio* (he who rules, his will be the religion), but excluded Calvinists and Anabaptists. Thus it failed to find a permanent solution. For the most part Northern Germany became Protestant and Southern Germany remained Catholic. The Holy Roman Empire became little more than a legal fiction.

In England the marital problems of King **Henry VIII** in his pursuit of a male heir led to his breaking free of papal authority. Many Protestant reformers supported the formation of the **Church of England**, of which the King was the head. Parliament enacted the **Act of Supremacy** in 1534.

CAUSES OF THE REFORMATION

- Economic discontent among the wealthy in Germany over sending money to Rome focused on the **sale of indulgences** and Church taxes.

- **Economic and social discontent** among the peasantry due to price inflation and feudal obligations prompted challenges to established authorities.

- Greater emphasis on the individual's relationship with God arose from a medieval movement towards **mysticism** and flowed from the Renaissance. Early reformers like **Jan Hus** (d. 1415) paved the way to reform.

- The Renaissance also prompted a more critical spirit in receiving traditional teachings.

- Corruption in the Church (**simony**, **nepotism**, **pluralism**, and **vice** among the clergy) undermined the prestige of and trust in the Church.

- The prestige of the Papacy still suffered from weakness due to the **Great Schism** and poor leadership.

- Some rulers of **German principalities** saw the break with Rome as a means to challenge the authority over them of the Holy Roman Emperor, who stood loyal to the established Church. The war to defend the Reformation became a kind of war of independence from central political control.

- **Attacks by the French and the Turks** on the Emperor's realms distracted his ability to suppress the Reformation and allowed the Protestants to organize successful resistance.

- The invention of the **printing press** allowed the rapid and uncontrolled dissemination of Protestant tracts and news.

- The rise of a **capitalistic spirit** that emphasized personal restraint and the pursuit of wealth meshed well with Protestantism.

REFORMATION THEOLOGY

At the core of the Protestant Reformation was a challenge to the traditional teaching of the Roman Catholic Church. Luther began the process, and other Protestant leaders refined and altered the original ideas and practices. They claimed to be reaching back to the earliest teachings of Christ sloughing off the encrustations of institutionalized Catholicism.

PROTESTANT THEOLOGY	
Martin Luther (d. 1546)	**Justification by faith** (by God's grace) **Authority of Scripture** **Priesthood of the Believer** Renunciation of Papal authority Bible to be translated into vernacular Clergy can marry No Purgatory
Ulrich Zwingli (d. 1531)	No **transubstantiation** No altars, stained glass, statues, relics Pulpit in the front and center of the church No central processional aisles or use of incense No fasts or pilgrimages Reduced number of sacraments Abolition of monastic life
John Calvin (d. 1563)	No bishops The Church and civil society should be ruled by a democratic theocracy **Predestination** Emphasis on sermons and the text of the Bible
Anabaptists	Attempt to create a perfect Christian community Full immersion at Baptism
Henry VIII (d. 1547)	The King of England to be the supreme governor of the Church in place of the Pope **King James Bible** (1611) and Cranmer's (d. 1556) *Book of Common Prayer*

THE CATHOLIC REFORMATION

The response of the Roman Catholic Church to the Protestant reformation is sometimes called the Counter-Reformation. Some see it merely as a pushback against Luther. Others notice the significant reforms that were made. The **Council of Trent** (1545–63) reaffirmed the traditional teachings of the Church including clerical celibacy, the vulgate (Latin) Bible, papal authority, and even the granting of indulgences. But much was done to eliminate corruption, and the clergy became increasingly better educated and more respected. A renewed surge of enthusiasm and dedication characterized the Church. A **College of Propaganda** was established to propagate the faith. New orders such as the Society of Jesus (Jesuits) dedicated themselves to missionary work and education. The most notable figure in this movement was **Ignatius of Loyola** (d. 1556) who was famous for his passionate obedience to the Papacy. In Spain the notorious **Inquisition** persecuted all non-Catholics with ruthless cruelty.

THE OUTCOMES OF THE PROTESTANT REFORMATION

The Reformation reshaped Northern and Western Europe in profound ways.

- The end of a single, united Christian Church in Western Europe.

- Brutal and bloody wars of religion between nations and within France, Germany, the Netherlands, and Britain. However, religious and political conflicts become intermingled.

- Fierce religious persecution, especially in Spain.

- The disappearance of most of the remaining authority of the Holy Roman Emperor in Germany.

- Italy, Spain, Austria, Hungary, Poland, and Southern Germany remain Catholic

- England became Anglican (close to Catholic theology but separate from Rome)

- Northern Germany, the Baltic, and Scandinavia mostly Lutheran

- The Netherlands, much of Switzerland, Scotland, and a sizeable minority in France (**Huguenots**) became Calvinist.

- The Catholic Reformation refreshes and energizes the Roman Catholic Church.

- The growth of **capitalism** through an emphasis on thrift, sobriety, and the search for material success as a sign of Grace was encouraged. Moral discipline and individualism were highly valued.

- New values was placed on family and marriage, but marriages remained patriarchal, if more companionate. The Reformation challenged the cult of the Virgin Mary and women were seen more as temptresses. Women also lost autonomy where monastic life was ended, and males dominate all clergies. However, emphasis on literacy in order for the Bible to be read encouraged greater parity between the sexes in education.

- Latin gave way to the vernacular in the practice of religion in Protestant countries, and increasingly it lost its place as the universal language of the educated class.

- Protestantism encouraged more tolerance for Jews.

- Persecution encouraged Protestant settlements in Massachusetts and elsewhere in the New World.

- Confiscation of Church and monastic lands enriched rulers and landed elites.

- The Kings of France (**Gallican Church**) and Spain gained more independent control over the Catholic hierarchy in their respective countries, strengthening central power of the monarchy.

THE HABSBURG SUCCESSION

Emperor Charles V reigned over more territory than any previous European monarch. His empire included the Holy Roman Empire, Hungary, the Netherlands, Spain, parts of Italy and vast territories in the Americas. The far-flung nature of his lands turned out to be a handicap. He decided to break up the inheritance between his brother, Emperor Ferdinand, who inherited the imperial crown and the hereditary lands of the **Habsburg** dynasty Austria-Hungary, and his son Philip II, who became King of Spain, the Netherlands, parts of Italy, and the Spanish territories overseas.

GENEALOGY OF THE HABSBURG DYNASTY

Maximilian I, Holy Roman Emperor
(1459–1519)
m
Mary of Burgundy
↓
King Philip I of Castile
(1478–1506)
m
Joanna of Castile (daughter of Ferdinand and Isabella of Spain)
(1479–1555)
↓
Charles V, Holy Roman Emperor, King of Spain
(1500–58)
m
Isabella of Portugal
↓
Philip II, King of Spain
(1527–98)
(from whom descended the Kings of Spain)
(Charles V's brother, Ferdinand, succeeded him as Holy Roman Emperor)

IMPORTANT DEFINITIONS AND IDENTIFICATIONS

- Act of Supremacy
- Augsburg, Peace of
- Authority of Scripture
- John Calvin
- Capitalism
- Catholic Reformation
- Charles V, Holy Roman Emperor
- Church of England
- Diet of Worms

- Gallican Church
- Habsburg dynasty
- Henry VIII of England
- Huguenots
- Jan Hus
- indulgences
- Inquisition
- Jesuits
- Justification by faith
- King James Bible

- Ignatius of Loyola
- Martin Luther
- Peasant's War
- predestination
- priesthood of the believer
- printing press
- transubstantiation
- Council of Trent
- Ulrich Zwingli

IMPORTANT DATES

*1517   Protestant Reformation

1520–58   Reign of Emperor Charles V

1534   Act of Supremacy in England

*1555   Peace of Augsburg

1545–63   Council of Trent—Catholic Reformation

CHAPTER 2
MULTIPLE-CHOICE QUESTIONS

Questions 1.1–1.4 relate to the following passage.

One thing, and one thing alone, is necessary for life, justification, and Christian liberty; and that is the most holy word of God, the Gospel of Christ, as He says: "I am the resurrection and the life; he that believeth in me shall not die eternally" (John xi 25); and also (John viii 36) "If the Son shall make you free, ye shall be free indeed"; and (Matt. iv 4) "Man shall not live by bread alone, but by every word that proceedeth out of the mouth of God."

Let us therefore hold it for certain and firmly established that the soul can do without everything, except the word of God, without which none at all of its wants are provided for....

The first care of every Christian ought to be, to lay aside all reliance on works, and strengthen his faith alone more and more, and by it grow in the knowledge, not of works, but of Christ Jesus, who has suffered and risen again for him.

Good works must not be done with any notion that by them a man can be justified before God. True then are these two sayings: Good works do not make a good man, but a good man does good works. Bad works do not make a bad man, but a bad man does bad works.

Martin Luther, "Concerning Christian Liberty", 1520

1.1 The fundamental tenet of Lutheranism was which of the following?

(A) Do good works
(B) Believe and you will be saved
(C) Attend Mass every day if you wish to be saved
(D) God has already decided whether you will be saved

1.2 Luther believed which of the following?

(A) We have the free will to save ourselves or not
(B) Salvation is random
(C) Only Protestants will be saved
(D) There are no sacraments

1.3 Luther changed the teaching of the Roman Catholic Church on which of the following?

(A) Bishops were abolished
(B) The Trinity was overthrown
(C) Females could become priests
(D) Clergy could marry

1.4 What made Lutheranism so appealing to masses of people?

(A) The simplicity of its central doctrine of justification by faith
(B) Denying the authority of the Scripture
(C) Retaining loyalty to the Pope while changing the ritual
(D) Keeping Latin as the language of the Church

19

Questions 2.1–2.3 relate to the following passage.

The commissioners to dissolve monasteries came to this city in the summertime to execute their commission, and beginning first with the priory of St. Nicholas, after they had viewed the same they commanded a man to pull down the rood loft pertaining to Roman Catholic ritual in the church. In the meanwhile certain women and wives in the city minding to stop the suppressing of that house, came in haste to the said church, some with spikes, some with shovels, some with pikes, and some with such tools as they could get and, the church door being locked, they broke it open. And finding the man pulling down the rood loft hurled stones unto him. They pursued him so eagerly that he was enforced to leap out of a window and so to save himself. The women made fast the church doors and bestowed themselves in places meet as they thought to stand to their defenses.

John Hooker, Chamberlain of the City of Exeter, England, report, 1535

2.1 For what reason were the monasteries being dissolved?

(A) To convert them to ecumenical centers
(B) Cities needed the land they occupied to expand
(C) On the orders of Pope Julius II
(D) To bring an end to Roman Catholic practices

2.2 What does the passage tell us about the role of women in 16th-century English society?

(A) They were confined to activities in separate spheres
(B) They were active in civic life
(C) They were more likely to be Roman Catholics than their husbands
(D) They were so busy at work they had no time for anything else

2.3 In what way did the Reformation enhance women's lives?

(A) Encouraged to become literate in order to read the Bible
(B) Encouraged to become more active in business once usury was allowed
(C) Admitted to the army and police force
(D) Granted the right to suffrage

Questions 3.1–3.3 relate to the following passage.

There are many evil writings put forth of late occasion on account of the assembling of the peasants, to cast scorn upon the Gospel, saying: Is this the fruit of the new teaching, that no one should obey but all should everywhere rise in revolt, and rush together to reform, or perhaps destroy entirely, the authorities, both ecclesiastical and lay? The articles below shall answer these godless and criminal fault-finders, and serve in the first place to remove the reproach from the word of God and, in the second place, to give a Christian excuse for the disobedience or even revolt of the entire Peasantry. In the first place the Gospel is not the cause of the revolt and disorder, since it is the message of Christ, the promised Messiah, the Word of Life, teaching only love, peace, patience and concord. Thus, all who believe in Christ should learn to be loving, peaceful, long-suffering and harmonious. This is the foundation of all the demands of the peasants (as will be seen) who accept the gospel and live according to it. In the second place, it is clear that the peasants demand that this Gospel be taught them as a guide in life, and they ought not to be called disobedient or disorderly.

The Twelve Articles of the Peasants, Upper Swabia, Germany, 1525

3.1 Why is there such emphasis on obedience to religious belief in this preface to a list of grievances and demands?

(A) The peasants wish to appear less radical than they really were
(B) The peasants did not want to cause any trouble
(C) The peasants wanted to gain the support of the French king, who was very religious
(D) The peasants did not want to antagonize the Holy Roman Emperor

3.2 What was the Peasant Revolt about?

(A) Demands for democratic suffrage
(B) The overthrow of the Habsburg monarchy
(C) Demands for complete social equality
(D) Taxes and serfdom

3.3 What was Martin Luther's response to the Peasant's Revolt?

(A) He joined it
(B) He condemned it
(C) He ignored it
(D) He supported the Emperor

Questions 4.1–4.3 refer to the 16th-century woodcuts below.

4.1 These woodcuts illustrate the contrast between

   (A) Biblical morality and papal corruption
   (B) Capitalism as opposed to mercantilism
   (C) Calvinism against Zwinglism
   (D) Flagellants vs. the Albigensians

4.2 What in particular is depicted in the woodcut that led to a serious European-wide crisis in the sixteenth century?

   (A) The abuse of state power in the punishment of criminals
   (B) The sale of papal indulgences
   (C) War between the Papal States and Orthodox Christians
   (D) Persecution of Jewish worship

4.3 Why might printed illustrations be a useful form of propaganda to further a political or religious cause in the sixteenth century?

   (A) They were cheap and easy to produce
   (B) The mass of people were still illiterate
   (C) The Popes controlled all printed books
   (D) Moveable type had not yet been invented

Questions 5.1–5.3 refer to the 1523 portrait of Erasmus of Rotterdam painted by Han Holbein.

5.1 All of the following are true about this portrait of Erasmus EXCEPT.

(A) The realistic portrayal of his face reflects the artistic style of the 16th century
(B) He is portrayed in the simple dress of a member of the clergy
(C) He is surrounded by the lavish decoration suitable to his wealth and noble rank
(D) He is portrayed with the pen and paper suitable to his life as a humanist

5.2 Erasmus was best known as

(A) A Christian humanist who stayed loyal to the Roman Catholic Church
(B) A radical cleric who launched the Great Schism
(C) The priest who married Henry VIII to his second wife after the divorce with Catherine of Aragon
(D) A Protestant reformer in league with Zwingli

5.3 In his writings and teaching Erasmus was noted for

(A) Placing humanism above Catholicism
(B) Praising Luther for his break with Rome
(C) Attacking abuses in the Catholic Church
(D) Avoiding discussion of poisonous and social issues

SHORT-ANSWER QUESTION

Question 1

1. The Catholic Reformation (sometimes called the Counter Reformation) was the response of the Papacy and Catholic Church to Luther and other Protestant reformers. Using your knowledge of European history answer both parts (A and B) of the question below.

   A) Identify and explain TWO major developments forming part of the Catholic Reformation.

   B) Identify and explain ONE activity in which the practice of the Catholic and Protestant Churches were similar.

CHAPTER 3

EXPANSION AND WARS

Brutal civil and international conflicts arose over religion in the 16th and 17th centuries. **Emperor Charles V** (r. 1520–58) fought to restore his authority and uphold the unity of the Roman Catholic Church in Germany and failed. Regional princes fought to gain power over their own territories. Religious people fought to destroy the "devil's work"—whether they were for or against religious reform. France and the Low Countries were torn apart by war.

During this period four important changes took place:

- The modern state began to take on a recognizable form.

- Population rose dramatically.

- Europe expanded its power with overseas empires.

- The rise of a modern scientific outlook began to emerge.

THE ENGLISH REFORMATION

The **English Reformation** was precipitated by the Pope's refusal to grant a divorce to **Henry VIII** (r. 1509–47). His Catholic Queen, Catherine of Aragon, was Charles V's aunt. The Catholic Church could not afford to alienate its most ardent champion. Henry created a new English State Church (Church of England, later called the **Anglican Church**), which kept largely to Catholic doctrine but with the King replacing the Pope as Supreme Governor of the Church. Henry's son by a Protestant wife, Edward VI (r. 1547–53), encouraged a more advanced Protestant theology, but he died young. His older sister, **Mary I** ("Bloody Mary"—r. 1553–58), restored Roman Catholicism and married the great defender of the Roman faith, Charles V's son Philip II of Spain (1527–98). She also died after a brief reign, and was succeeded by her younger sister (also the child of another of Henry's Protestant wives—he married six times but produced only three heirs), **Elizabeth I** (r. 1558–1603)—a **politique**

25

—a ruler who balanced a personal predilection for Catholic theology with Protestant rule because it made her succession legitimate and brought political stability and economic prosperity. She was able to sustain a permanent Protestant settlement in England. Philip II tried to reclaim his English throne and overthrow Anglicanism with the **Armada** (1588) but was defeated by a superior English navy. Elizabeth sponsored revolt against Philip's rule in the Netherlands. She also secured the Protestant succession by executing the Catholic heir to the throne, her cousin, **Mary Queen of Scots** (d. 1587). Her son, James VI of Scotland (of the **Stuart** dynasty) was raised a Protestant and succeeded as King of England on Elizabeth's death.

GENEALOGY OF THE ENGLISH ROYAL FAMILY
(Tudor, Stuart, and Hanover dynasties)

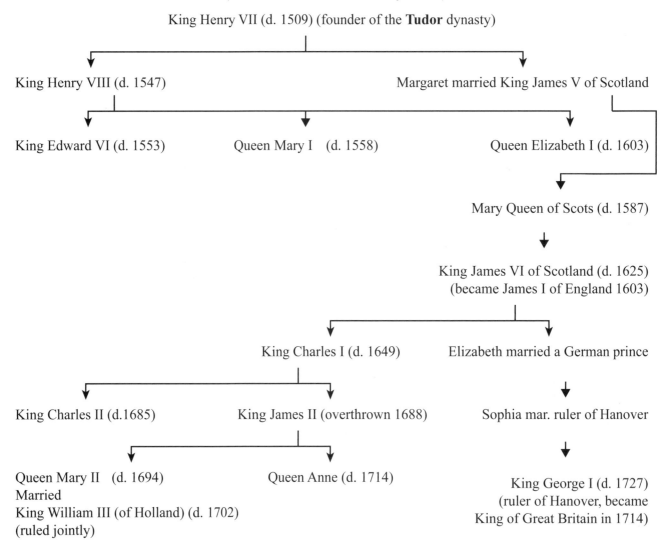

THE WARS OF RELIGION

Many aristocrats converted to Protestantism in France, and the Queen Regent, **Catherine de Medicis** (1519–89), although she initially tried to balance competing religious claims, ultimately sanctioned the **St. Bartholomew's Day Massacre** (1572) of Protestants in an attempt to secure the triumph of the ruling dynasty in the midst of civil war. This event created massive fear among Protestants across Europe. Eventually, the French throne fell to the **Huguenot** (Calvinist) leader, **Henry IV** (of Navarre) (r. 1589–1610), founder of the **Bourbon** dynasty, *a politique*, who converted to Catholicism to retain the throne and please the majority of his subjects. However, he granted toleration to Protestants in the Edict of Nantes (1598). He strengthened the monarchy and the economy.

Philip II of Spain (d. 1598) tried to centralize the power of the monarchy and restore Catholicism in Europe. He built a great monastery, which also served as his residence—**Escorial**. He fought a long war to suppress Protestantism in the Netherlands and failed. William the Silent (of Orange r. 1544–84), a *politique*, organized powerful resistance to Spanish/Catholic rule and helped found the United Provinces in the northern half of the Low Countries. England sent troops to support the Dutch. Although Philip successfully annexed Portugal, defeated the Turks in a contest for control of the Mediterranean (Battle of Lepanto—1571), and reaped great riches from the Americas, his incapacity to delegate and his religious obsession led to disaster.

THE THIRTY YEARS WAR

The **Thirty Years War** (1618–48) was precipitated by religious and national conflict in Bohemia (the modern Czech Republic) turned into a massive civil war in Germany, in which France, Denmark, and Sweden also played a notable role. It started as a religious war with political overtones and ended as a political war with religious overtones. The Protestant King **Gustavus Adolphus** of Sweden (r. 1611–32) carved out a large empire in Northern Germany but died in battle (1632). The war eventually turned into a struggle for power between Austria and France. The population and economy of Germany suffered tremendous losses. The struggles of the 17th century also ended the dominance of the Mediterranean states and economy in European affairs. Protestant Amsterdam emerged as the great financial center.

The War ended with the **Treaty of Westphalia** (***1648**). It outcomes included:

- **Calvinism** recognized as a co-equal religion with Catholicism and Lutheranism and Catholic claims to Protestant territory were abandoned in the Holy Roman Empire

- **Austria** emerged as separate from the Holy Roman Empire and became the focus of Habsburg rule

- **Bavaria** emerged as the leading Catholic power in S. Germany

- **Switzerland** was unified into cantons

- The **United Provinces** were officially recognized as a Protestant independent state

- **Sweden** gained territory in northern Germany

- **France** emerged as the "superpower" of Europe

- **Germany** lost virtually all central authority and the over 300 states became essentially independent states

- **Brandenburg-Prussia**, the leading Lutheran power in N. Germany emerged as stronger

- The **modern European state system** emerged

- War increased the **size and power of states**

THE WITCHCRAFT CRAZE

Magic was still a powerful force in the 16th and 17th centuries. Persecution of mainly female "**witches**" peaked in the century after 1550. The anxieties of the religious conflict, war and destruction, and individuals or communities taking advantage of the weak and the old led to the upsurge, predicated on misogyny and superstition.

Midwives were particularly vulnerable because infant mortality was so high. Eventually the elites themselves felt threatened (no one was safe from accusation) and the new level demanded for legal evidence fostered by the Scientific Revolution brought trials to an end in the 18th century.

THE AGE OF EXPLORATION

Europeans began to look outwards and explore unknown coasts in search for trade and wealth. Prince **Henry the Navigator** of Portugal (1394–1460) sponsored early voyages in the 15th century, as did Ferdinand and Isabella of Spain after *1492, and Elizabeth I of England in the 16th century. Geographical and economic advantages gave Europeans an ascendancy over other civilizations.

The Portuguese Bartolomeu Dias (c. 1451–1500) rounded the Cape of Good Hope at the southern tip of Africa in 1487. Vasco DaGama (c. 1460s–1524) reached India in the late 1490s. The Italian Christopher **Columbus** (c. 1450–1506) made voyages to the Caribbean beginning in 1492 sponsored by Ferdinand and Isabella of Spain. Spain and Portugal divided the Atlantic world between them by the Treaty of Tordesillas in 1494 brokered by the Pope and ignored by other powers. Ferdinand **Magellan** (c. 1480–1521) circumnavigated the globe 1519–22. Hernan Cortes conquered the Aztec Empire in Mexico 1519–21. Francisco Pizzaro destroyed the Inca Empire in 1531. The vast silver mines at Potosi were begun in 1545. The English made their first settlement in North America at Jamestown in 1607. The Mayflower brought Puritan refugees to New England in 1621.

CAUSES OF EUROPEAN EXPLORATION

- Monarchs desired **expanded territory** and income

- Merchants sought **trade routes** to India and China in order to avoid trading through middlemen in the Middle East, especially after the fall of Christian Byzantium (1453)

- **Renaissance ideas** fostered a spirit of inquiry and adventure and encouraged pursuit of individual goals and fame

- **New technology** in construction and operation of sailing ships

- **Adventurers** sought fame and fortune

- **Missionaries** sought to convert the non-Christians

OUTCOMES OF THE FIRST WAVE OF EUROPEAN IMPERIALISM

- Immense influx of **commodities**: precious metals and spices, and later silk, tea, coffee, chocolate, tobacco, and porcelain

- The rise of the **slave trade** between Africa and the Americas

- **Price rises** in Europe (inflation) partly due to the vast amount of new gold and silver and inefficient use of those metals; owners of land profit; bourgeois "rentiers" rose more rapidly into the upper classes through purchase of land

- Great new understanding of geography and the shape of the world oceans ceased to divide the world and the **sea became a highway**

- The **Commercial Revolution**—changes in investment and production—rise of the **domestic system**—new industries, new banking practices

- Rise of the **East India Companies** 1600 onwards

- Rise of the economic idea of **mercantilism**

  a) export more than you import

  b) trade as much as possible with colonies, taking in raw materials and exporting manufactured goods

  c) state sponsors manufacturing ventures

  d) accumulate as much gold and silver as possible

  e) object was to increase government revenue by increasing national wealth

- Encounters with unknown cultures of high levels of civilization that did not practice Christianity or even monotheism; **opened the European mind to new ways** of seeing and prompted criticism of traditional institutions and values

- The **Columbian Exchange**: new foods such as the potato and tomato brought to Europe while the horse and guns were brought to America; diseases were exchanged between continents, small pox in particular wiped out large proportions of some aboriginal peoples

- Promotion of **capitalism**, encouragement of new forms of investment and insurance

- The rise of the Atlantic World of trade, war, emigration, and ideas including Africa, the Americas, and Europe

EUROPEAN COLONIES

Vast Portuguese empire (Brazil, India, Africa, Macao)

Spain acquired most of South and Central America, some of N. America, islands and ports in the Caribbean and Africa, and the Philippines

The Dutch acquired the Cape of Good Hope, islands in the Caribbean, trading rights in Japan, and much of the East Indies (from Portugal)

England expanded in North America from the coast inwards and gradually took islands in the Caribbean, Atlantic, and Pacific, parts of India and eventually Australia and Canada

France acquired Canada, and moved through the interior down the river systems; islands in the Caribbean, parts of India

Most other European nations did not get much out of the scramble for colonies, although the Swedes made headway at first in America, the Danes got a few islands, and Russia expanded inexorably east and southwards, eventually taking Alaska and part of California

IMPORTANT DEFINITIONS AND IDENTIFICATIONS

- Anglican Church
- Armada (Spanish)
- Capitalism
- Charles V, Holy Roman Emperor
- Columbian Exchange
- Columbus
- Commercial Revolution
- domestic system
- East India Companies

- Elizabeth I of England
- English Reformation
- Escorial
- Gustavus Adolphus of Sweden
- Henry VIII of England
- Henry the Navigator
- Magellan
- Mary I (Bloody Mary) of England
- Mary Queen of Scots

- mercantilism
- Philip II of Spain
- *politique*
- slave trade
- Stuart dynasty
- Thirty Years War
- Treaty of Westphalia
- Tudor dynasty
- witch craze

IMPORTANT DATES

*1492 Columbus crosses the Atlantic

1558 accession of Elizabeth I of England

1572 St. Bartholomew's Day Massacre in France

1588 defeat of the Spanish Armada

1618–***1648** Thirty Years War—Peace of Westphalia (***1648**)

CHAPTER 3
MULTIPLE-CHOICE QUESTIONS

Questions 1.1–1.3 are related to the St, Bartholomew's Day Massacre of 1572 illustrated below.

1.1 The massacre on St. Bartholomew's Day 1572 in France may best be described as which of the following?

(A) German atrocities committed after the capture of Paris by the Holy Roman Emperor
(B) Queen Catherine de Medici's attempt to eliminate Protestant opposition to her rule
(C) A rising by Huguenots against the French monarchy
(D) Henry IV's attempt to murder all the Catholics in France

1.2 Which of the following best describes the response to the massacre in Western Europe?

(A) Spanish surrender to all demands made by France for territory in the New World
(B) Ended the predominance of the Roman Catholic Church in Italy and France
(C) Provoked an invasion of France by England and the Netherlands
(D) Renewed fear among Protestants of Roman Catholic attempts to achieve their total destruction

1.3 At what moment did a monarch expel or suppress all the Huguenots in France?

(A) Henry IV in 1598
(B) Louis XIV in 1685
(C) Napoleon I in 1804
(D) Louis Philippe in 1848

Questions 2.1–2.3 are related to the 1515 German woodcut by the Petrarra-Meister illustrated below.

2.1 Which of the following is depicted in this woodcut of 1515?

(A) The genealogy of the Holy Roman Emperor
(B) The importance of forestry in the European economy
(C) The social organization of Europe
(D) A Protestant Christmas tree

2.2 Who can be seen at the bottom of the tree?

(A) Kings
(B) Clergymen
(C) Soldiers
(D) Peasants

2.3 How would you describe the interactions between monarchs and their nobles in early modern Europe?

(A) Very friendly
(B) Occasionally hostile
(C) Pursuing different interests
(D) Always at war with each other

Questions 3.1–3.3 are related to the witchcraft craze. A pamphlet cover of 1566 entitled "Confession of Mother Waterhouse" is illustrated below.

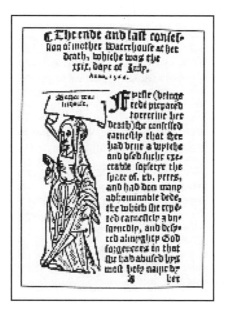

3.1 Why might a woman confess to being a witch?

(A) To get a divorce from her husband
(B) The legal system was too weak to be a problem
(C) To gain a sense of self-importance and attention
(D) To challenge Catholic leaders

3.2 All the following motives might prompt people to accuse others of witchcraft EXCEPT?

(A) The religious hysteria of the times
(B) Desire to take their property
(C) Win an election
(D) Because the "witch" was disliked or unpopular

3.3 What brought the "witch craze" to an end?

(A) More emphasis on empirical evidence and rational argument
(B) Women gained greater respect from society over time
(C) Too many cases became before the courts to be prosecuted
(D) The Protestant Reformation and the Catholic Reformation ended

Questions 4.1–4.3 relate to the following passage.

From New Spain are obtained gold and silver, leather cotton, sugar and other things; but from Peru nothing is obtained except minerals. The fifth part of all that is produced goes to the king, but since the gold and silver is brought to Spain and he has a tenth part of that which goes to the mint and is refined and coined, he eventually gets one-fourth of the whole sum, which fourth does not exceed in all four or five hundred thousand ducats, although it is reckoned at millions. Nor is it likely that it will long remain at this figure, because great quantities of gold and silver are no longer found upon the surface of the earth, as they have been in past years; and to penetrate into the bowels of the earth requires greater effort, skill and outlay, and the Spaniards are not willing to do the work themselves, and the natives cannot be forced to do so, because the Emperor has freed them from all obligation of service as soon as they accept the Christian religion. Wherefore it is necessary to acquire negro slaves, who are brought from the coasts of Africa and these are selling dearer every day.

Michele Soriano, *The Gold of the Indies*, 1559

4.1 What was the most important reason for the Spanish to important slaves from Africa to their Empire in South America?

(A) As military auxiliaries
(B) For conversion to Christianity
(C) To do labor the Spanish refused to do
(D) To do manufacturing work in cotton factories

4.2 The most valuable product coming from the Spanish Empire in the 16th century was which of the following?

(A) Sugar
(B) Slaves
(C) Minerals
(D) Cotton

4.3 The Gold and silver being exported from South America to Spain in the sixteenth century precipitated which of the following?

(A) Deflation
(B) Inflation
(C) Deficit spending
(D) Manufacturing

Questions 5.1–5.3 are related to the following document.

The threats which accompany this ban on me by the King of Spain are intended to shock you into leaving me. They make it seem that this war is being waged against me and not against you, just as the wolf would like to make the sheep believe that he intends to fight only against the dogs, and having killed them, would be on good terms with the herd, for it is the dogs who always start the fights.

The other thing they intend above all, is the extermination of the true religion. I will not discuss here, gentlemen, which is the true religion, the one in which God is truly served and invoked according to His Word. I leave this to people better trained in this area than I am, especially as every one can gather what my beliefs are from the profession I make. But I tell you frankly that the condition of your country is such that if the practice of the reformed religion is no longer allowed the country cannot survive for even three days. You see how miraculously the numbers of its adherents have increased and that the hatred of the pope has taken deep root in the hearts of all the inhabitants of the country because of the evil practices against the whole state have been so clearly exposed.

William the Silent, Prince of Orange, "Apology of His Serene Highness Against the Ban Published by the King of Spain", 1581

5.1 Why was being a prince useful to William the Silent in his battle with Philip II of Spain?

(A) It gave him the wealth needed to pay for an army and navy
(B) It meant he had experience as a general
(C) It gave him electoral experience
(D) His hereditary rank gave him stature to challenge a king

5.2 In his "Apology" how does William the Silent portray Philip II?

(A) Deceitful and untrustworthy
(B) Too powerful to oppose
(C) Wise and statesmanlike
(D) Sympathetic to Protestants

5.3 William the Silent succeeded in

(A) Assassinating Philip II
(B) Marrying Elizabeth I of England
(C) Turning the Netherlands into a Roman Catholic state again
(D) Establishing the house of Orange as hereditary rulers of Holland

SHORT-ANSWER QUESTION

This section consists of four questions with 50 minutes to complete. It consists of twenty percent of the exam score. These questions require you to write out your answers, but unlike with analytical essays you are not required to provide a thesis statement. The answers will require demonstration of historical thinking skills and mastery of factual knowledge. The questions will be based on a piece of historical evidence such as a quotation from a document, a map, or image. Quotations from contemporary historians may also form the basis of questions. Other questions will be based on general propositions in European history. There may be some element of choice within the questions.

Question 1

1. The sculpture above, "The Ecstasy of Saint Theresa" (1645–52) by Gianlorenzo Bernini illustrates the "baroque" style. Using the image and your knowledge of European history answer both (A and B) questions below.

   A) Identify and explain TWO characteristics of the "baroque" style illustrated by the example above.
   B) Explain ONE way in which the "baroque" style differs from the artistic character of the Renaissance.

CHAPTER 4

WAR AND STATE 1648–1789

The shape of European society was transformed by the wars of religion. Internal turmoil intertwined by economic, social, political, and religious forces produced different outcomes in different countries.

THE "ENGLISH CIVIL" WAR

Great Britain emerged as a richer and more influential nation during the seventeenth century. The Scottish **Stuart** dynasty succeeded to the English throne in 1603 (though the countries were quite separate except for the union of the crowns until 1707). Mary Queen of Scots' Protestant son, James VI, became **James I** (r. 1603–25) authorized "King James" version of the Bible in 1611) of England on the death of his childless cousin and last Tudor, Elizabeth I (the "Virgin" Queen). He and his son, **Charles I** (r. 1625–*1649), attempted to strengthen the power of the monarchy at the expense of Parliament and believed in the Divine Right of Kings. This led to civil war in 1641 and the execution of Charles I, the first occasion in modern history when a monarch was put on trial and executed for crimes against his people. Parliament was largely supported by small landowners, merchants, and Puritans (Protestants who felt the Church of England was too Roman Catholic and leaned towards Calvinism), in London and the South. The King found more support among the high aristocracy, Anglicans, and in the North and Wales. The Scottish Calvinists allied with the English Parliament against the King while in Ireland many Roman Catholics sided with the monarchy.

CAUSES OF THE CIVIL WAR (1641–49)

Once called the "English" **Civil War** many historians now see a war between the various kingdoms in the British Isles. The complex conflict developed in several phases.

- Monarchs could not acquire enough tax income (which could only be granted by Parliament) to operate the government, especially in times of war—plus large debt left by Elizabeth I

- Parliament attempted to force the monarch to accept religious, foreign, and other policy initiatives in exchange for more income—fear of absolutism and Catholicism

- Charles I attempted to rule without Parliament

- Conflicts in Scotland and Ireland provoked crises in England

- **Archbishop Laud** (d. 1645) imposed strict "high" church Anglican doctrine and practice in England and Scotland and harshly punished Puritan resistors

- Charles I imposed "illegal" tax—**ship money**

- Charles I seen as sympathetic to Catholics in Ireland, and had a Catholic wife who was distrusted by the Puritans

- Charles I pursued foreign and domestic policies that provoked **Puritan** opposition in Parliament

- Charles I punished opponents brutally and failed in a personal attempt to arrest leading opponents on the floor of the House of Commons

- Resentment against "corruption" at Court, granting of monopolies and other favors to aristocrats close to the throne

- Possible resentment by lesser **gentry** towards richer elites

- Character of **Charles** I—in many ways a decent man in private—who lacked political skill and came to be seen as dishonest and unreliable

Phases of the Civil War included Parliament's attempt to assert control over the King's powers in the **Petition of Right** (1628); the Scottish invasion of England provoked by an attempt to impose Anglican ritual on the Calvinist Church (1638); the King rallied his supporters in a military force against Parliament (1641); gradually the leadership of the "Roundheads" (Parliament) fell under the control of the brilliant military commander, **Oliver Cromwell** (r. 1649–58); several attempts to negotiate a settlement with the King failed because he felt he was not bound by coerced promises; Charles I was executed in 1649; a "Commonwealth" was formed under the quasi-King Cromwell, who was called the Lord Protector. He gradually stripped Parliament of most of its power. After Cromwell's death, Charles I's son was brought back from exile to rule as **Charles II** (r. 1660–85) in the **Restoration**. He was a *politique* who tried to put things back the way they were before the Civil War but did not entirely succeed in turning back the clock.

OUTCOMES OF THE CIVIL WAR

- The "**Commonwealth**" was established by military force led by Cromwell while a coercive dictatorship was needed to sustain his power, which made the regime unpopular

- Parliament was temporarily pushed aside

- Puritan restrictions were imposed against the arts and entertainment

- Toleration granted to the Jews

- Successful wars were fought against the Dutch and a strong navy was built

- Rebellions in Ireland were suppressed brutally and land was taken from Catholics and given to a new Protestant elite

- Radical groups such as the Levelers and Diggers frightened the elites with their extreme religious and political agendas

- Restoration of the monarchy with little retribution or constitutional change took place in 1660

- Restoration of the Anglican religion as the state church

- The execution of the King by Parliament in 1649 could never be entirely forgotten and emboldened Parliament to overthrow Charles I's son, James II, in 1688 forever changing the balance in the British political system

THE GLORIOUS REVOLUTION (1688–89)

Charles II had no legitimate children and hence was succeeded by his brother, **James II** (r. 1685–88). Within a few years the new King managed to alienate a large portion of the landowning elite who dominated in both houses of Parliament. Historians still debate whether the word "revolution" is appropriate in that the social composition of society was unaffected, and those who exercised power before the event were still in authority afterwards.

CAUSES OF THE GLORIOUS REVOLUTION

- The incompetence of James II, who antagonized his own supporters with his Roman Catholic faith and absolutist policies

- The birth of a son to James II by his second, Roman Catholic wife meant that the royal succession would return to a permanent Catholic line in a country that had become predominantly Protestant

- James's daughters, born when he was still a Protestant and raised as Protestants, offered an alternative line of succession

- The ambition of **William of Orange** (r. as William III 1689–1702), the husband of James's eldest daughter, **Mary II** (r. 1689–94), who was the stadholder of the Netherlands and leading Protestant opponent of King Louis XIV of France

- King James's friendly treatment of Roman Catholics in Ireland

- Fear of an alliance between the King and **Louis XIV** of France (a secret Treaty of Dover between England and France did exist)

- The brutality used in the suppression of opposition to James II

- The decision by great landowners that the King could not be trusted and that they were the true guardians of the nation's liberty

- The issuance by James of the **Declaration of Indulgence** (1687) granting religious toleration to Roman Catholics and Calvinists—can the King suspend laws of Parliament on his own authority?

OUTCOMES OF THE GLORIOUS REVOLUTION

- Succession of the Protestant joint monarchs **William III** and **Mary II** (1689)

- All future monarchs must be Protestant

- Alteration of legitimate line of succession by Parliament finally destroys idea of "Divine Right"; succession to Crown now lay with the legislature not the royal family

- Defeat of James II and the Catholic forces in Ireland at the Battle of the Boyne (1690), Protestants set to rule Ireland

- The **Bill of Rights** (1689) enacted to protect individual liberties and prevent arbitrary royal acts

- Ascendancy of Parliament dominated by the great landowners

- Emergence of **Whig** and **Tory** parties

- Victory of the United Provinces over France and the building of alliances that would halt the expansion of Louis XIV into Holland and Spain

- The Netherlands much weakened by its "victory", which gave Britain a commercial advantage in the future

- Parliament pursued an imperial and commercial policy that promoted trade and mercantile interests

- **Union** of English and Scottish parliaments (1707)

- Succession in 1714 of the German **Hanoverian** dynasty after the death of the last Stuart, Queen Anne

ABSOLUTISM IN FRANCE AND THE WARS OF CONQUEST BY LOUIS XIV

France took a different course from that of England in the 17th century. Monarchs were more astute and successful in gaining and retaining power. Henry IV, Louis XIII's great minister **Cardinal Richelieu**, and above all King **Louis XIV** (r. 1661–1715) centralized power in their hands and gradually weakened the power of the nobility. The latter group was much larger than the equivalent in England, and few individuals were as rich as many of the great dukes and earls across the Channel. During the **Fronde** (1648–53) the nobles tried to reassert their authority, but failed. The **Estates General**, the French equivalent of the English Parliament, did not meet at all between 1615 and 1789. Under the "**Sun King**" France enjoyed a golden age in culture under absolutist rule.

WHY WAS LOUIS XIV SO SUCCESSFUL?

- Political acumen and hard work—a single-minded focus on his goals

- Effective use of bourgeois "**intendants**" or local officials who owed their careers and hence their loyalty to the King and not to local lords

- Appointment of able ministers such as the finance minister **Colbert** (in office 1665–83)

- Ideological underpinnings of absolutist rule supported by **Bishop Bossuet** (d. 1704) who supported Divine Right monarchy

- Successful **mercantilist** economic policies including building canals, improving roads and ports, and state sponsored enterprises, mainly due to Colbert

- Focus on military reform, and exerting greater centralized control over the army (Louvois d. 1691 and Vauban d. 1707), uniforms, etc.

- Use of the Court at the Palace of **Versailles** to weaken powerful nobles.
  a. the "place" to be for fun
  b. source of favors and rewards
  c. rituals emphasizing royal stature—"*lever*"
  d. under the King's watchful eye

WHY LOUIS XIV FAILED

- He loved war too much; he pursued expensive military campaigns that did not yield true value to France or ended in defeat

- He reigned too long (60 years) and grew old and tired

- His weakening of the nobility separated them from their estates, left them without a sense of duty or purpose, and built up resentment and desire to rule without a sense of responsibility or experience to do so

- Colonial policy that did not include plans for large settlement by French people, which left French rule insecure

- Leaving a successor who was less fit to rule (**Louis XV** r. 1715–74)

- Suppression of **Jansenists**

- **Revocation of the Edict of Nantes** (1685) led to the expulsion of many talented Huguenots who went to Germany, the Netherlands and Britain where they prospered and helped their new countries in commerce and war

- Excessive ambition in hoping to combine the French and Spanish Empires under his sole rule

- Left his successors ever-worsening financial problems due to inefficient taxation

THE WAR OF THE SPANISH SUCCESSION (1701–13)

On the death of King Charles II of Spain (1700), the last of the Spanish Habsburg male line, Louis XIV succeeded, by virtue of his marriage to a Spanish Habsburg princess, in placing his grandson **Philip V** (r. 1700–24) on the throne in Madrid. The titanic struggle that ensued became a global war. Britain helped organize a coalition of opponents to French mastery in Europe and the Americas. Above all the British wanted a balance of power in Europe that prevented any single state from overwhelming the rest, a policy it continued to pursue until the end of the Cold War in the 1990s. The war ended with the **Peace of Utrecht** (1713–14).

OUTCOMES OF THE WAR OF SPANISH SUCCESSION

- The French prince, Philip V, was recognized as King of Spain. However, if the male Bourbon royal line became extinct in France, the Spanish Bourbon line could not succeed to both crowns

- Great Britain gained the rock of **Gibraltar** at the southern tip of Spain, which gave it control over access in and out of the Mediterranean (becomes the British "lake")

- Savoy (between southern France and northern Italy) acquired Sardinia, and the dukes become Kings of **Sardinia**

- Spanish territory in Italy (Milan, Naples, Sicily) passed to Austria

- The Spanish Netherlands (Belgium) was acquired by Austria

- France ceded Newfoundland and Nova Scotia to Britain (which gave the latter control over the mouth of the St. Lawrence River and hence the interior of N. America)

- Dutch independence secured

- The Elector of Brandenburg recognized as King (Prussia)

- *Asiento* (trading privileges) granted to British in Spanish colonies

- French preeminence in Europe blocked, although it retained conquests along the northern border

- Dutch weakened further and decline from the status of a great power

- Great Britain poised to become a global great power

THE BRITISH AND FRENCH POLITICAL SYSTEMS IN THE 18TH CENTURY		
	GREAT BRITAIN	FRANCE
Executive	Hereditary King but restricted to Protestants selected by Parliament. Can only act through ministers who can achieve a majority of votes in the House of Commons.	Hereditary King with almost unlimited power.
Legislature	Parliament divided into two houses Commons and Lords. The House of Lords consisted of bishops and the hereditary aristocracy . The House of Commons was elective, but filled largely by gentry and relatives of members of the House of Lords controlled all taxation and government spending. Can make or break governments and even Kings.	Estates General divided into three orders who voted separately. Not called by the King in the 18th century until 1789. Until then enough income had been granted on a permanent basis to operate the government.
Judiciary	Judges appointed for life by the King on the advice of officials.	Regional *parlements* largely composed of nobles who could rule the King's decrees unlawful. Louis XIV had gained ascendancy over them, but his successors lost this.
Church	State Church with the King selecting bishops on the advice of officials.	Roman Catholic Church headed by the Pope who had conceded the selection of bishops to the king.
Elite	A few hundred very rich nobles who gained automatic access to the House of Lords and dominated the Commons as well. Lived in London and the countryside, where they were active in local government.	Hundreds of thousands of nobles, many of whom were poor. Tended to live in urban areas with only occasional visits to their estates. Often unpopular.

THE RISE AND FALL OF GREAT POWERS IN THE 17TH AND 18TH CENTURIES		
WINNERS	MIXED	LOSERS
Great Britain Prussia Russia	Austria France	Sweden Spain Holland Holy Roman Empire Ottoman Empire Poland

CHARACTERISTICS OF SUCCESSFUL AND UNSUCCESSFUL STATES	
WINNERS	Strong leadership Strong central government, effective bureaucracy Effective sources of income Flexibility Diversified economies Large, modernized armies/navies Monarchy and aristocracy work out a mutually satisfactory relationship
LOSERS	Poor leadership Weak governmental institutions Rigidity Fragmented regions, intense local loyalties Narrowly focused economies Ineffective cooperation between monarchs and nobles

THE ONCE MIGHTY THAT DECLINED

SPAIN

- Virtually no exports or manufacturing

- Resources of empire depleted

- Empire too far flung and fragmented to be ruled successfully by the system in place

- Massive noble class many of whom were poor, not interested in government, and rigidly old fashioned (**Hidalgos**)

- Profligate spending of national resources without adequate returns

POLAND

- Perhaps the most disastrously organized state in Europe

- Dysfunctional elective monarchy

- Dysfunctional parliament (diet)—***liberum veto***

- Surrounded by ravenous and powerful states with no natural frontiers for protection

- Nobility too numerous (8% of population) and mostly poor

- Antiquated agricultural system and little commerce

- Gradually gobbled up by neighbors in a series of "**Partitions**" 1772, 1793, 1795

SWEDEN
- Empire too far flung

- Weak economy cannot sustain huge army

- Nobility and monarchy in conflict

- No successful ruler after **Gustavus Adolphus** (d. 1632)

- Recklessness of **Charles XII** (d. 1718)—defeated by Peter the Great of Russia—**Battle of Poltava** (1709)

HOLLAND
- Regional identities very strong

- Religious divisions

- Stagnation of industries

- London replacing Amsterdam as European economic center

- Exhaustion and damage after prolonged conflicts with England and France

- **Dutch East India Company** pushed out of India

- Weak leaders after the death of William III

- Stadholdership still elective and cumbersome and powers limited by the jealousy of the mercantile elite

- Remained divided between Protestants and Catholics

- British outstrip in naval technology and trade competition

HOLY ROMAN EMPIRE
- Central institutions, including the emperorship crippled

- **Habsburgs** increasingly focus on their Austrian territories

- **War of the Austrian Succession** (1740)

- Divided into over 300 mini-states, with big states such as Prussia trying to expand territories at the expense of others

- Economy and population devastated by **Thirty Years War** (1618–48)

- Divided religiously and culturally

OTTOMAN EMPIRE
- Complicated and inefficient system of succession

- Too fragmented and far flung

- Deep conservatism strangled innovation

- Bordered aggressive Russia and Austria

- Over-reached in attempting conquests of central Europe (at gates of Vienna 1529 and 1683)

STATES THAT EXPERIENCED ADVANCES AND SETBACKS

AUSTRIA

- Involvement in the affairs of the Holy Roman Empire divert attention from more essential issues

- Female heir of **Charles VI** (d. 1740) leads to sacrifices made in the **Pragmatic Sanction**

- Ottoman Sultan conquers southern territories and reaches Vienna 1683

- Frederick the Great seizes the rich province of Silesia in 1740

- Hungary regained 1687, but the nobles remained restive under Habsburg rule

- **Habsburgs** continue to hold their empire together, and gain territory from Poland and in Italy and the Balkans

- Habsburgs do well in the **War of Spanish Succession** (1701)

- Most of the population unified in the Roman Catholic faith

- Protestant nobles removed and land used to reward nobles loyal to the Habsburgs

- Strong lines of internal communication

- Some innovation and growth in the economy

FRANCE

- Weak leadership in last years of **Louis XIV** and under his successors, **Louis XV** and **Louis XVI**. Corruption and vice at Court

- **Mississippi Bubble** hurts economy and undermines central banking structure (1720). Hard to organize credit

- Costs of wars high; leads to huge public debt

- Indecisiveness in deciding about who was the most serious enemy—leads France to compete on sea and land against multiple opponents, which divided resources and led to defeats

- Clumsy censorship weakens respect for government without effectively stifling criticism

- Nobility wanted power and were given it by the Regent Orleans (d. 1723), but they were largely ineffective as governors

- Large resources and many effective government officials, but antiquated, cumbersome, unproductive tax system; inefficient budgetary and accounting apparatus

- Unified in the Roman Catholic faith after **Revocation of the Edict of Nantes** (1685), but weakened by the flight of talented Protestant exiles

- Innovative society with a large and influential intelligentsia

- Valuable colonial empire, which, however, was under-populated

- Strongest army in Europe

- Paris the grandest city in Europe—huge popularity of French language and culture

STATES THAT EMERGED AS GREAT POWERS

BRITAIN
- More tightly held together after Union with Scotland 1707

- Parliamentary system and a largely free press allowed public opinion to play a significant role in shaping policy

- Absence of a standing army and enactment of the Bill of Rights (1689) forced monarchs and Parliament to rule rationally and help build commercial prosperity

- Economy and central banking system (**Bank of England**) weathers **South Sea Bubble crisis** (1720)

- Efficient tax and excise system

- Government stability allows it to borrow cheaply to finance wars

- London became the money market of Europe

- Navy gained supremacy at sea around the world

- Empire expanded and prospered

- Hanoverian dynasty became a popular symbol of nationalism under **George III**

- Aristocrats governed responsibly and effectively

- Flexible economy and politicians—gifted leadership: **William III**, **Marlborough**, Walpole, the **elder and younger Pitts**, etc.

- **Robert Walpole** (d. 1745) first "prime minister" (1721–42)

- Social and political system open to men rising by merit

- Protestant Church of England became the dominant state church

PRUSSIA

THE EXCEPTIONAL LEADERS OF THE HOHENZOLLERN DYNASTY
The "Great" Elector Frederick William (d. 1688) King Frederick I (d. 1713) King Frederick William I (d. 1740) King Frederick II the "Great" (d. 1786)

- Added territory that contained resources, urban populations, and commercial and manufacturing activity in the Rhineland and Silesia

- Exceptionally strong army disproportionate to the size of the state

- Strong royal bureaucracy organized to support the army

- Subsidies from Britain to fund military operations

- Rulers enjoyed large income aside from taxes

- Society tolerant in religion and welcomed French **Huguenots** (Protestants)

- High literacy rate

- Effective cooperation between **junker** landowners and monarchs. The kings allow them to keep strict control over their serfs but subordinates the nobles within the military command structure

- Becomes a major European state under Frederick II, who almost doubled the size of the country during the **War of Austrian Succession** (1740-48)

RUSSIA

- No influence of the Renaissance or Roman Catholic Church

- Time of Troubles (1604–13), a period of chaos followed by the establishment of the **Romanov** dynasty

- Vast size, resources, and population

- Peasants effectively enserfed during 17th century (1649) and **Tsars** allow nobles strict control over their peasants

- Vigorous leadership from **Peter the Great**, Elizabeth, and **Catherine the Great** (some intervals of weak leadership)—Peter's system of succession faulty

- Frequent peasant uprisings weaken state

- Strong absolutist government developed

PETER THE GREAT'S (r. 1682–1725) ACHIEVEMENTS
took Baltic territories from Sweden, pushed south towards the Black Sea
built **St. Petersburg**—access to the West
Westernization of manners, customs, society
Gained strict control over the Orthodox church
built strong modern army and navy
imposed strict control over nobility (**boyars**)
destroyed opposition—Old Believers/**streltzy**
built a stronger economy
Russia became a major European state

THE RULING HOUSES OF EUROPE

Europe was profoundly monarchical in its systems of government until 1918. Not only did individual monarchs from Charlemagne of the Holy Roman Empire (r. 800–14) to Kaiser Wilhelm II of Germany (r. 1888–1918) influence social, political and economic developments, but also the institution of monarchy established a mental framework and established boundaries that encouraged stability but restrained political change.

EUROPEAN DYNASTIES	
Scotland	Stuart (Stewart)—merged with England 1603
England	Tudor 1485–1603 **Stuart** 1603–1714 **Hanover** 1714—(becomes Windsor 1917)
France	Valois to 1589 **Bourbon** 1589–1792 1814–30 Orleans 1830–48 Bonaparte 1804–1815 1852–1870
Holy Roman Empire	**Habsburg** to 1806
Austria-Hungary	Habsburg to 1918
Prussia	**Hohenzollern** to 1918
Germany	Hohenzollern 1871–1918
Russia	Rurik to 1604 **Romanov** 1613–1917
Spain	Habsburg 1516–1700 Bourbon 1700–1931 1975–
Sardinia/Italy	Savoy—kings of Italy from 1861–1946
The Netherlands	**Orange** 1572–(as elected stadholders until 1796)
Poland	(the monarchy was elective)
Portugal	Braganza 1640–1910
Sweden	Vasa 1521–1818 Bernadotte 1818–

THE STRUGGLE FOR GLOBAL POWER

Britain emerged as enormously successful politically and economically during the course of the 18th century, in spite of the loss of the American colonies in 1783. **Sir Robert Walpole** and **William Pitt the Elder** helped develop success in trade and empire. Two attempts by the Stuarts to restore their rule (supporters were called **Jacobites**) failed in 1715 and 1745. Britain's principal rival, France, was formidable but chose the wrong strategy and was crippled by ineffective leadership.

The **War of the Austrian Succession** (1740–48) and the **Seven Years' War** (French and Indian War in North American 1756–63) engaged most of the great powers. Prussia seized Silesia (nearly doubling its size and wealth in one stroke) and succeeded in holding it against all comers. **Frederick the Great** of Prussia was fighting France, Austria, and Russia simultaneously. Even possessing interior lines of communication, British subsidies, and a king of military genius almost failed to be enough. Fortunately for Prussia, the succession of Tsar Peter III in Russia (1762) led to the latter's withdrawal from the war. The French strategy of fighting both in a major continental war and in a global conflict overseas proved beyond its powers and led to a huge debt, loss of India (**Battle of Plassey** 1757—**Robert Clive**) and Canada, and serious decline in prestige.

IMPORTANT DEFINITIONS AND IDENTIFICATIONS

- *Asiento*
- Bank of England
- Bill of Rights (1689)
- Bishop Bossuet
- Bourbon dynasty of France
- Boyars
- Catherine (II) the Great of Russia
- Charles I of England and Scotland
- Charles II of England and Scotland
- Charles VI of Austria
- Robert Clive
- Colbert
- the Commonwealth
- Cromwell
- Declaration of Indulgence
- Dutch East India Company
- English Civil War
- Estates General
- Frederick William (the Great Elector) of Prussia
- Frederick I of Prussia
- Frederick William I of Prussia
- Frederick II (the Great) of Prussia
- the Fronde
- Gentry
- George III of Great Britain
- Gibraltar
- Gustavus Adolphus of Sweden

- Habsburg dynasty of Austria
- Hanoverian dynasty of Great Britain
- Hidalgo
- Hohenzollern dynasty of Prussia
- Huguenots
- *Intendents*
- Jacobites
- James I of England and VI of Scotland
- James II of England and VII of Scotland
- Jansenists
- junkers
- Archbishop Laud
- *liberum veto*
- Louis XIV of France
- Louis XV of France
- Louis XVI of France
- Duke of Marlborough
- Mary II of England
- Mercantilism
- Mississippi Bubble crisis (France)
- Partitions of Poland
- Peace of Utrecht
- Peter the Great of Russia
- Petition of Right
- Philip V of Spain
- William Pitt the Elder
- William Pitt the Younger

- Battle of Plassey
- *Politique*
- Battle of Poltava
- Pragmatic Sanction
- Puritans
- the Restoration (1660)
- Revocation of the Edict of Nantes
- Cardinal Richelieu
- Romanov dynasty of Russia
- St. Petersburg
- Sardinia
- Seven Years' War
- ship money
- South Sea Bubble crisis (England)
- Streltzy
- Stuart dynasty of Scotland and England
- "Sun King"
- Thirty Years War
- Tory Party
- Tsar
- Palace of Versailles
- Sir Robert Walpole
- War of the Austrian Succession
- War of the Spanish Succession
- Whig Party
- William III of England (of Orange) (William and Mary)

IMPORTANT DATES

1613   Romanov dynasty established in Russia

1641–49   English Civil War

*1649   Execution of Charles I of England

1660   the Restoration of the monarchy in Britain

1683   Ottomans besiege Vienna

1685   Revocation of the Edict of Nantes

1688–89   the Glorious Revolution

1701–13   War of the Spanish Succession (Peace of Utrecht 1713–14)

1709   Battle of Poltava

1714   Hanoverian Succession in England

1715   Death of Louis XIV

1740–48   War of the Austrian Succession

1756–63   Seven Years' War

1772–95   Partitions of Poland

CHAPTER 4
MULTIPLE-CHOICE QUESTIONS

Questions 1.1–1.3 relate to the following passage.

The English cannot sail at present to Poland and Prussia, because the Danish Straits are blocked against them. In Germany, at Hamburg, Lubeck, and other ports, for example, they are detested; because the German merchants still claim their ancient privileges of their exchange house in London, of which they were deprived by Queen Elizabeth a few years ago, merely with the view to foster English and restrict foreign commerce. The Venetians have suffered in the same way.

Then inside the Straits of Gibraltar, how can the English be endured, seeing that under the guise of merchants they plunder in the very vitals of foreign dominions all the shipping they find?

Hence both those who command, and those who execute here in England, see quite clearly how great, how universal, and how just is the hatred which all nations, nay all peoples we might say, bear to the English, for they are the disturbers of the whole world. The Kings of England, down to Henry VII and Henry VIII, were wont to keep up a fleet of one hundred ships in full pay as a defense, now the Queen's ships do not amount to more than fifteen or sixteen, as her revenue cannot support a greater charge; and so the whole strength and repute of the nation rests on the vast number of small privateers, which are supported and increase to that dangerous extent which everyone recognizes; and to ensure this support, the privateers make government officials partners in the profits, without the risk of a penny in the fitting out, but only a share in the prizes. To such a state has this unhappy Kingdom come that from a lofty religion has fallen into the abyss of infidelity.

Venetian diplomat in London, letter to the Venetian Senate, 1603

1.1 How accurate do you believe this account of the English in Europe in 1603 to be?

(A) Grossly exaggerated
(B) Reasonably accurate
(C) False
(D) Inaccurate

1.2 Why did the English government pursue a policy of attacking the merchant ships of other countries?

(A) The limited income of the state meant they could not afford a large navy or pay their officials adequately
(B) The English navy was destroyed by the Spanish Armada
(C) Queen Elizabeth needed money to build more palaces
(D) They did not understand how resentful Venice and other countries would become

1.3 Which of the following best characterizes the strategy the British would pursue over the next century?

(A) Continuous war with Poland and Prussia
(B) Block access of Mediterranean countries to the Atlantic
(C) Colonize all of North Africa
(D) Focus most of their trade in the Mediterranean

Questions 2.1–2.3 relate to the document below.

Whereas Charles Stuart, king of England, is and standeth convicted, attainted, and condemned of high treason, and other high crimes; and sentence upon Saturday last was pronounced against him by this Court, to be put to death by the severing of his head from his body; of which sentence, execution yet remaineth to be done; these presents are therefore to will and require you to see the said sentence executed in the open street before Whitehall, upon the morrow, being the thirtieth day of this instant month January, between the hours of ten in the morning and five in the afternoon of the same day, with full effect. And for so doing this shall be your sufficient warrant. And these are to require all officers, soldiers, and others, the good people of the nation of England, to be assisting unto you in this service.

Signed, Oliver Cromwell and others, 29 January 1649

2.1 For what reason was a sentence of death imposed on King Charles I?

(A) His refusal to recant his Puritan faith
(B) He failed repeatedly to keep his promises
(C) He embezzled from the Treasury
(D) His disrespect for religion

2.2 Charles was notable in European history for being the first king to

(A) Have no heir
(B) Cross the Atlantic
(C) Be tried for treason
(D) Be put to death

2.3 For which of the following is Oliver Cromwell well known?

(A) Moving to New England with other Puritans
(B) Becoming a military dictator
(C) Claiming India for England
(D) Converting to Roman Catholicism

Questions 3.1–3.3 are related to the document below.

In view of the sympathy which we ought to, and do, feel for our brethren of the reformed evangelical religion in France, who have been driven by persecution to leave their homes and settle in other countries, we, Frederick William, etc., desire by this edict to offer them free and safe refuge in all our lands and possessions and to specify what rights, privileges, and prerogatives we are graciously minded to grant them.

We command herewith that when any of the said French people of the reformed evangelical religion make their appearance, they shall be well received and every opportunity and assistance shall be given them in establishing themselves there. They shall, moreover, be free to establish themselves in any place in our lands and dominions outside the above-mentioned towns which shall seem to them more convenient for the purposes of their trade or calling.

If any of them shall desire to establish manufactories of cloth, stuffs, hats, or other articles, we will not only bestow on them all the necessary permissions, rights, and privileges, but will further aid them, so far as is in our power, with money and requisite materials.

Frederick William, Elector of Prussia, proclamation, 1685

3.1 The main reason the Elector of Prussia admitted Huguenots into his country after the Revocation of the Edict of Nantes in 1685 was?

(A) Entice enough Protestants to Prussia to outnumber Roman Catholics in the country
(B) Strengthen what was a poor, agricultural state with manufacturing and trade
(C) Provoke a war with Louis XIV in order to gain French territory
(D) Find new recruits for the Prussian nobility

3.2 The Huguenots brought which of the following with them to Prussia?

(A) Military expertise
(B) Agricultural skills
(C) Democratic ideals
(D) Commercial experience

3.3 The dominant force in Prussian society was which of the following?

(A) The junker nobility
(B) Peasants
(C) The middle class
(D) The clergy

Questions 4.1–4.3 relate to the 17th-century Dutch painting of a dentist illustrated below.

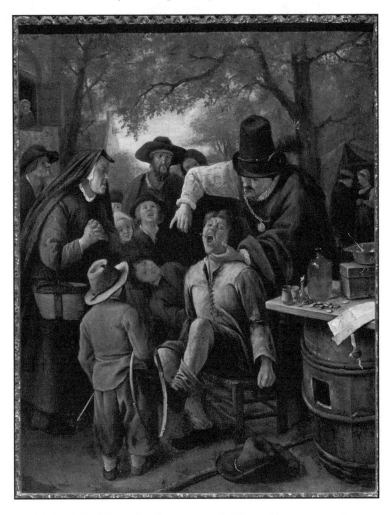

4.1 This scene illustrates which of the following?

 (A) Scientific equipment being used
 (B) Daily life among the Dutch in the seventeenth century
 (C) The importance of magic in seventeenth-century Holland
 (D) The mistreatment of children in the seventeenth century

4.2 The likely purchaser of such a painting would have been?

 (A) A Protestant clergyman
 (B) The Prince of Orange
 (C) A middle-class businessman
 (D) A peasant

4.3 The mid-seventeenth century is sometimes referred to the Dutch "Golden Age". What prompted this use of the term?

 (A) They Dutch seized the Spanish mines in Mexico and Peru
 (B) The Dutch East India Company found gold in Java
 (C) Business and the Arts reached their highest points
 (D) The Prince of Orange was elected Holy Roman Emperor

Questions 5.1–5.3 relate to Tsar Peter the Great and his construction of a new capital at St. Petersburg illustrated below.

5.1 The image above of Peter the Great of Russia watching the construction of the new Russian capital of St. Petersburg on the Baltic is intended to convey which of the following messages?

  (A) His disapproval of the haphazard nature of its construction

  (B) The versatility of serf labor

  (C) His indifference of aesthetic considerations

  (D) The importance he placed on building the new city

5.2 Peter imported Western European architects and engineers to build St. Petersburg because?

  (A) He thought Western Europeans made better serf laborers

  (B) He focused all his energy only on building the grandest royal palace in Europe

  (C) He hoped to copy Western European buildings slavishly

  (D) Russia was technologically less advanced than Western Europe

5.3 Peter founded St. Petersburg to achieve what goal?

  (A) Create an entry for contact with Western Europe in trade and culture

  (B) Establish the first year-round warm water port in Russia

  (C) Build a launching pad for a naval invasion of Western Europe

  (D) Challenge the French and British in the Atlantic trade of slaves and sugar

Questions **6.1–6.3** relate to the reign of Empress Catherine II (the Great) of Russia, whose portrait is reproduced below.

6.1 Empress Catherine the Great of Russia had herself portrayed in the painting

(A) To appear as feminine as possible
(B) To appear to be an intellectual
(C) To meet the expectations of a male dominated world
(D) To attract French *philosophes* of the Enlightenment to Russia

6.2 Catherine II (the Great) was well known for which accomplishment?

(A) Expanding the borders of Russia at the expense of Poland and the Ottoman Empire
(B) Freeing the serfs
(C) Waging successful wars against France and England in North America
(D) Crushing rebellions led by the Russian nobility

6.3 To what degree were Catherine the Great's reforms influenced by the Enlightenment?

(A) To an extreme degree
(B) Moderately
(C) The Enlightenment had no impact on her reforms
(D) Not as much as her son's reforms

SHORT-ANSWER QUESTIONS

Question 1

Between 1648 and 1789 England, Prussia, and Russia expanded their wealth and power while Holland, Spain, Poland, and the Ottoman Empire declined. A few experienced mixed success. Using your knowledge of European history answer the questions (A and B) below.

A) Identify and explain TWO reasons why some countries met with economic and political success during this period.

B) Identify and explain ONE reason why some countries declined economically and politically during this period.

CHAPTER 5
THE ANCIEN REGIME: SOCIETY, SCIENCE AND THE ENLIGHTENMENT

The **ancien regime** (old regime) is a term used to describe European society in the 17th and particularly the 18th century, before the French Revolution of *1789.

CHARACTERISTICS OF THE OLD REGIME

- Emphasis on tradition and established rights and privileges

- **Hierarchy**, ranks, orders, rigid social conventions

- **Aristocracies** assertive

- All countries monarchies except for Switzerland and the Netherlands

- Agricultural economy, life governed by scarcity and the seasons

- **Family economy**—few large scale economic units
  all members of the family work
  father is the head
  marriage crucial to economic stability
  role of women: bring dowry, economic partners of the men, raise children, housework, high infant
  mortality rate, high birth rate

- Change is slow, most people find it difficult to imagine a different social or political organization

- Large numbers of servants

- Massive poverty

- Many children born out of wedlock; foundling hospitals

- More commercialized sex

- In the East serfdom—Russia, Prussia, Austria-Hungary (*robot*—compulsory unpaid labor)

- In the West more complex rural social structure with independent landowning peasants, share croppers, wage laborers, scavengers—in England few peasants, mostly wage laborers

- Most land owned by the Crown, church, aristocrats, and rich merchants

- Aristocracies divided into many levels—the smallest and richest in England, the largest and poorest in Poland

- Growing literacy, especially in Prussia, France and England, but majority of the population still uneducated

- Comparatively small armies fighting wars with limited objectives and few battles (although those were very bloody)

- Violence endemic—both judicial and criminal

- Religion still very important, both among followers of traditional, organized Catholic and Protestant churches, and new upwellings such a John Wesley's "**Methodism**" (later 18th c.)

- Rise of popular, often popular "emotional" and **pietistic** movements—reactions to "rationalist" religion

- **Bourgeoisie** increasingly prosperous in Western Europe, consumers on a large scale, interested in "polite" manners and culture

- Great age of classical music: **Mozart** (d. 1791), **Haydn** (d. 1809); **Beethoven** (d. 1827)

- Rise of the **novel**: Richardson's *Clarissa* (1747); Fielding's *Tom Jones* (1749)

CHALLENGES FACING THE OLD REGIME

- Cities growing larger

- **Demographic change**, populations expanding rapidly

- Increasing **secular** spirit

- Bourgeois wealth increases to great size

- The secular and **meritocratic** ideas of the **Enlightenment**

- Separation between high and low cultures growing

- Separation in social, economic, and political structures between Easter and Western Europe increasing

- Commencement of **industrialization** and invention of new technologies

- The **American Revolution** presents a functional alternative example of a meritocratic, secular, and democratic state to existing conditions in Europe

- Dynamic global economy reorders the ranks of wealthy states and introduces new products and ideas

- **Mercantilism** beginning to give way to ideas of a **free market** and free trade

- Emergent **nationalism** breaks down old traditions and loyalties

- Easier and more rapid travel which increases the tempo of economic and political life

- Increasing literacy gives more and more people access to "**the public sphere**" of open discussion of political affairs

REVOLUTIONS IN THOUGHT

Ideas play an influential role in history. Such was the case in the shift from the world of the *ancien regime* to the modern era. Today many historians question the notion of a unitary, discrete "revolution" in science and see confining the shift in scientific thinking and the emergence of "enlightened" ideas to the West as Eurocentric. Undoubtedly, important ideas we now see as part of modern "science" or "enlightened" arose in a fragmented way and all over the globe. Nonetheless the terms remain useful ones in part simply to organize sprawling events into something that students can study and discuss in a manageable way and because the revisionist arguments are still being vigorously contested and are by no means universally accepted. That a massive shift took place in the way Europeans looked at the political, economic, social, and natural worlds in the centuries before the French Revolution is incontestable, even though, as with the industrial "revolution", the story is now seen as much more complicated and multifaceted than was once thought.

THE SCIENTIFIC REVOLUTION

During and after the Renaissance a gradual expansion of scientific knowledge and understanding about the physical world began to take place. Astrology became **astronomy**. Progress was more rapid in some fields than others. The supreme achievement was Newton's synthesis of earlier work that led to a profound understanding of the mechanics of the universe: **gravity**, **interplanetary motion**, and a sense of mastery over the mysteries of nature that unleashed the modern world, (although in more recent times **Newtonian physics** has itself been overturned). Acceptance of new ideas was often halting. Many Catholic and Protestant leaders united in their criticism of scientific advances, although secular rulers, scenting economic advantages, were more likely to be supportive.

THE NEWTONIAN SYNTHESIS

Because Newton was such a towering figure, the path to his achievements are sometimes referred to as the "Newtonian synthesis" ("I stood on the shoulders of giants".)

Copernicus – (d. 1543) **heliocentric** solar system which challenged the Ptolemaic earth-centered theory

Brahe – (d.1601) Danish astronomer who collected massive amounts of accurate data at his observatory

Kepler – (d. 1630) Brahe's assistant, who used the data to develop mathematical laws predicting the elliptical orbits of the planets

Galileo – (d. 1642) invented the telescope, **law of inertia**, mathematical uniformity of motion

Newton – (d. 1727) invented calculus, studied optics, laws of **gravity**, argued strongly for religion, key figure in establishing the **Royal Society** (1662) as the premier scientific organization in Europe – granted a royal charter by Charles II

OTHER IMPORTANT ACHIEVEMENTS IN SCIENCE AND MATHEMATICS

Bacon
(d. 1626) human improvement was the practical purpose of science, empirical research, **scientific method**, **induction**

Descartes
(d. 1650) analytical geometry, scientific method, **deduction**, *cogito ergo sum*—"I think, therefore I am" -renounce all previous assumptions and go back to the drawing board

Pascal
(d. 1662) combine reason and science with faith

Harvey
(d. 1657) blood circulation

Boyle
(d. 1691) laws of gases

EFFECTS OF THE "SCIENTIFIC REVOLUTION"

EMPIRICAL VIEW OF THE WORLD

- A new skepticism and the application of mathematics to the study of nature

- **Empiricism** and the scientific method

- A new view of the universe—the world is not random or chaotic

- New tools for research such as the microscope and telescope

HUMAN DIGNITY

- Mankind gains a new sense of mastery of its own fate, we can penetrate the mysteries that surround us

- New self-confidence and the **idea of progress**

- New emphasis on manners, delicacy, rational behavior; popular culture gradually tamed

- Laws more rational and just, rules for evidence in court more rigorous

- Attempts increase to relieve poverty and "improve" the poor

- Some women become scientists and intellectual leaders (Paris salons important 17th and 18th centuries)

SECULARIZATION

- Awe and fear at the vastness and impersonal nature of the universe

- Weakening of superstitions (belief in witchcraft) and of irrational traditions, more emphasis on merit than blue blood

- Increased weakening of organized religion, new skepticism in biblical studies, more toleration

- New concepts of natural law

ECONOMIC OUTCOMES

- New technologies to help with mining, navigation, construction, ballistics—stimulus to business and trade

- Increased emphasis on education and research

- Accurate maps and navigation aids

CULTURAL DEVELOPMENTS

Cervantes
(d. 1616) *Don Quixote*, satire of chivalric romance

Shakespeare
(d. 1616) conservative, patriotic, psychological penetration

Milton
(d. 1674) *Paradise Lost*, man responsible for his own fate

Bunyan
(d. 1688) Puritan piety

Hobbes
(d. 1679) man is base and materialistic, life brutish and short, to preserve order accept the will of a strong central authority—*Leviathan* (1651)

Locke
(d. 1704) *tabula rasa*—man is a blank slate—the natural human state is perfection, purpose of government is to cultivate human goodness, rebellion may be necessary under seriously unjust or incompetent rule:

constitutions—the rational way to construct governments, property owners (stake-holders) rule. "Life, Liberty, Property"

THE ENLIGHTENMENT

The Enlightenment consisted of the spread of ideas during the 18th century that grew out of the spirit of the Scientific Revolution. Emphasis on rational thought (the **Age of Reason**), **secularism**, and the spread of education and knowledge (the Age of Improvement). These ideas were articulated and spread by the *philosophes*, writers and thinkers interested in improving the world. Paris salons, often led by women, help spread ideas among the elite.

INFLUENTIAL THINKERS
Locke
(d. 1704) with Newton the real father of the Enlightenment; a more original and creative philosopher than most *philosophes*. Promoted more rational government and an understanding of human psychology

Voltaire
(d. 1778) deism, freedom of thought, popularized Newton, secularizer, historian

Montesquieu
(d. 1755) climate and circumstances affect types of government, separation of powers good

Diderot
the *Encylopédie* (1751–72)

Rousseau
(d.1778) politics, education, psychology, feelings, the *Social Contract*, the general will

Beccaria
(d. 1794) criminologist, against torture

Adam Smith
Scottish *physiocrat* (economist), advocated *laissez faire* economics (least possible state intervention), *The Wealth of Nations* (1776), the "invisible hand"

Hume
(d. 1776) Scottish Enlightenment, religion is mere superstition

Kant
(d. 1804) German Enlightenment, *Critique of Pure Reason*, categories of understanding

ENLIGHTENED ABSOLUTISM

Enlightened Absolutism (Despotism) is a term used to describe the rule of a number of monarchs who more or less attempted to incorporate some of the ideas of the Enlightenment into their governments. One can argue that far from being "reformers" or liberals, they were enhancing their own power. **Frederick the Great** set up state run elementary schools so his soldiers would be better able to follow orders. Louis XV and Louis XVI of France also presided over enlightened reforms but were not creative forces. Monarchs in smaller countries often emulated the reforms of the great figures.

CHARACTERISTICS OF ENLIGHTENED ABSOLUTISM	
Infrastructure	building canals Improving roads and bridges Building orphanages, asylums, hospitals Building factories and establishing state run businesses
Commerce	Introducing new products to manufacture Favor large trading companies such as the East India companies Mercantilist policies
Legal Reforms	Enacting legal codes enhancing absolutist power by abolishing traditional privileges and rights Abolish or reduce the use of torture and barbaric punishments Reform or abolish serfdom
Education	Encouraging educational institutions, literacy, etc.
Secularization	Encouraging religious toleration Weakening the power of the church
States Finance	Increase revenues of state through new tax laws and more efficient collection Acquire new territory and expand tax base
Military Power	Increase the size of armies and navies Expand empires in Europe and overseas
Propaganda	Portray monarch as a "servant" of the state and/or heroic figure Befriend *philosophes*

NOTABLE ABSOLUTISTS

Maria Theresa
(d.1780) Empress of Austria, fails to regain Silesia, but holds the rest of the empire together; devout Catholic; moderate reformer; improved economy, alleviated serfdom

Frederick (II) the Great
(d. 1786) King of Prussia, started the War of Austrian Succession; consorts with *philosophes*; codified laws; frees Crown serfs

Joseph II
(d.1790) Emperor of Austria; impatient and furious reformer; equal taxation; toleration; free press; Jewish nobles; improves commerce; suppressed monasteries; German language to be universal; secret police; land to serfs

Leopold II
(d. 1792) Emperor of Austria, rolls back many of Joseph's reforms to reduce outrage of nobles, but a moderate reformer in his own right

Catherine (II) the Great
(d. 1796) Empress of Russia codified laws; consorts with *philosophes*; expands Russian territory to south and west; puts down **Pugachev's Rebellion**; has a French *philosophe* educate her grandson and heir; allows nobles more power over serfs and in status

IMPORTANT DEFINITIONS AND IDENTIFICATIONS

- Age of Reason
- American Revolution
- *ancien regime*
- aristocracy
- astronomy
- Bacon
- Beccaria
- Beethoven
- Bourgeoisie
- Boyle
- Brahe
- Catherine the Great of Russia
- Cervantes
- *cogito ergo sum*
- Copernicus
- deduction
- demography
- Descartes
- Diderot
- empiricism
- The *Encyclopédie*
- Enlightened Absolutism
- the Enlightenment

- family economy
- Frederick the Great of Pussia
- free market
- Galileo
- gravity
- Harvey
- heliocentric
- hierarchy
- Hobbes
- Hume
- Idea of Progress
- induction
- industrialization
- interplanetary motion
- Joseph II of Austria
- Locke
- Maria Theresa of Austria
- mercantilism
- meritocratic
- Methodism
- Milton
- Montesquieu
- Mozart

- Nationalism
- natural law
- Newton
- Newtonian physics
- the novel
- Pascal
- *philosophes*
- *physiocrats*
- Pietistic
- public sphere
- Pugachev's rebellion
- *Robot*
- Rousseau
- the Royal Society
- the scientific method
- secularization
- serfdom
- Shakespeare
- Adam Smith
- *The Social Contract*
- *tabula rasa*
- Voltaire
- *The Wealth of Nations*

IMPORTANT DATES

1543   Copernicus published *On the Revolution of the Heavenly Orbs*

1687   Isaac Newton published the *Principia Mathematica*

1690   John Locke published *Essay Concerning Human Understanding*

1751–72   Publication of the *Encyclopédie*

*1789   French Revolution

CHAPTER 5
MULTIPLE-CHOICE QUESTIONS

Questions 1.1–1.3 refer to the following passage.

But if this manner of procuring and treating Negroes is not consistent either with mercy or justice, yet there is a plea for it which every man of business will acknowledge is quite sufficient. Here also the slave-holder fixes his foot. 'If it is not quite right, yet it must be so; there is an absolute necessity for it. It is necessary we should procure slaves; when we have procured them, it is necessary to use them with severity, considering their stupidity, stubbornness, and wickedness.'

Here are several mistakes. For, First, wealth is not necessary to the glory of any nation; but wisdom, virtue, justice, mercy, generosity, public spirit, love of our country. Better is honest poverty, than all the riches bought by the tears, and sweat, and blood, of our fellow-creatures.

[Slave-holders], what pains have you taken, what method have you used, to reclaim [the slaves] from their wickedness? Have you carefully taught them, that there is a God, a wise, powerful, merciful Being, the Creator and Governor of heaven and earth?

John Wesley, *Thoughts Upon Slavery*, 1774

1.1 On what grounds does the Rev. John Wesley, founder of the Anglican off-shoot, Methodism, most fundamentally ground his opposition to slavery?

(A) Theological arguments against slavery based on Biblical texts
(B) Classical economics derived from the work of Adam Smith
(C) The ideals of the Enlightenment developed by Voltaire and Rousseau
(D) It is a barbaric and uncivilized institution

1.2 The slave trade was most vital to which British colonies in the 18th century?

(A) The West Indies
(B) Georgia and the Carolinas
(C) Newfoundland and Nova Scotia
(D) New England

1.3 The Methodist movement in 18th century England can best be characterized as

(A) Politically radical and in sympathy with the French Revolution
(B) More significant than the Quakers in leading the anti-slavery campaign
(C) Teaching sobriety, morality, and piety in private life
(D) A national movement to establish choral societies signing the Wesley's great hymns

69

Questions 2.1–2.3 relate to English families in the 18th century such as the one illustrated below.

2.1 This eighteenth-century picture of an English family suggests which of the following?

(A) Girls were treated better than boys
(B) Children were seen as miniature adults
(C) Men and women dressed alike
(D) People in the eighteenth century dressed simply

2.2 This family was likely to members of which social group?

(A) Gentry
(B) Middle class
(C) Urban poor
(D) Peasants

2.3 The English elite derived their position and authority from which of the following?

(A) Shipping and insurance
(B) Banking
(C) Landed estates
(D) Manufacturing

Questions 3.1–3.3 relate to the map of Europe in 1780 provided below.

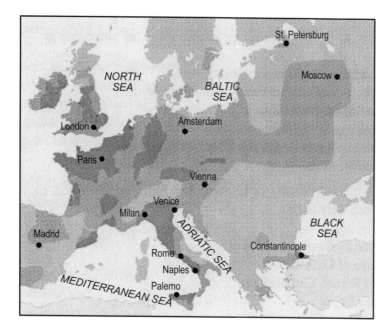

3.1 This map of Europe in 1780 indicates which of the following?

(A) The darkest areas were mainly Calvinist
(B) The lightest areas were Roman Catholic
(C) The darkest areas were the most heavily industrialized
(D) The darkest areas were the most heavily populated

3.2 This map of Europe in 1780 indicates which of the following?

(A) Darker areas still subject to famines
(B) Lighter areas still affected by the Plague
(C) Darker areas most affected by warfare in the eighteenth century
(D) Darker areas the most urbanized

3.3 Europe had become divided between East and West in the eighteenth century by which important factor?

(A) Serfdom in the West and free peasantry in the East
(B) Serfdom in the East and free peasantry in the West
(C) Monarchy in the East and republics in the West
(D) Protestant in the East and Catholic in the West

Questions 4.1–4.3 relate to the following passage.

Every individual is continually exerting himself to find the most advantageous employment for whatever capital he can command. It is his own advantage, indeed, and not that of the society, which he has in view. But the study of his own advantage, naturally, or rather necessarily, leads him to prefer that employment which is most advantageous to society.

Every man, as long as he does not violate the laws of justice, is left perfectly free to pursue his own interest his own way, and to bring both his industry and capital into competition with those of any other man, or order of men. The sovereign is completely discharged from duty, in the attempting to perform which he must always be exposed to innumerable delusions, and for the proper performance of which no human wisdom or knowledge could ever be sufficient; the duty of superintending the industry of private people, and of directing it towards the employments most suitable to the interest of the society.

Adam Smith, *The Wealth of Nations*, 1776

4.1 According to Adam Smith which of the following is most accurate?

(A) Deficit spending by the government benefits all
(B) The pursuit of self-interest leads to prosperity
(C) All history is the history of class competition
(D) Controlling the currency allows the government to manage the economy most effectively

4.2 Adam Smith was part of what intellectual movement?

(A) The Romantics
(B) The Enlightenment
(C) Utopian Socialism
(D) Utilitarianism

4.3 Adam Smith's greatest legacy over the centuries following his death came in the form of

(A) Free trade
(B) Mercantilism
(C) Pump priming
(D) Tariffs

Questions **5.1–5.3** relate to knowledge about the natural world, exemplified by the 1543 frontispiece to Vesalius's On the Structure of the Human Body illustrated below.

5.1 The research conducted on the human body by Vesalius contributed to what important development?

(A) The Enlightenment
(B) The Industrial Revolution
(C) The Reformation
(D) The Scientific Revolution

5.2 The major breakthroughs in knowledge about the natural world in the sixteenth and seventeenth centuries took place in which field?

(A) Astronomy
(B) Biology
(C) Geology
(D) Anthropology

5.3 Useful medical knowledge in the 16th century was largely confined to which area?

(A) Blood circulation
(B) Botany
(C) Anatomy
(D) Pharmacology

SHORT-ANSWER QUESTION

Question 1

Important differences arose between the economies and societies of Eastern and Western Europe that became marked by the eighteenth century. Using your knowledge of European history answer the following questions (A and B) below.

A) Identify and explain TWO major differences between countries in Eastern and Western Europe in the eighteenth century.

B) Identify and explain ONE of the factors shared by Eastern European countries described in question A above using at least two countries as specific examples.

CHAPTER 6

THE FRENCH REVOLUTION

Revolution convulsed France and Europe between 1789 and 1815*. Although urban workers and peasants played important roles at certain moments in the revolution, it was initially provoked by a struggle between the royal government and the **parlements**, noble-dominated courts that were used to resist increased taxation and encroaching monarchical power. Nobles continued to play a key role in the early stages of the revolution, and even **Napoleon** was a minor noble. All revolutions since have been influenced by the events in France during these years. Controversy among historians over interpretations of the Revolution has been and remains vigorous. Marx saw the Revolution as a triumph of the bourgeoisie over the second estate, a view that has had to be radically revised even by Marxist historians.

Chronology is key in understanding the French Revolution. Make sure to understand the sequence of the events.

CHRONOLOGY OF THE FRENCH REVOLUTION	
June 1789	**Louis XVI** calls the **Estates General** into session for the first time since 1614 **Tennis Court Oath** resolves crisis of voting by orders by declaring a National Assembly
14 July	**Fall of the Bastille**, symbol of royal authority in Paris, to a mob **The Great Fear** Enactment of the **Declaration of the Rights of Man and Citizen** *Émigrés*—princes and nobles who fled France to raise foreign opposition and assistance
1790	**Civil Constitution of the Clergy**—church nationalized and clergy became employees of the State; deeply antagonized the Pope, the clergy, the King, and many good Catholics of all classes; key factor in escalation of the revolution
1791	**Constituent Assembly**—(1789–91) drew up new constitution: unicameral legislature; limited monarchy; all new personnel for new assembly; active and passive citizens; periodically influenced by mobs of working people in Paris, *sans-culottes* *Le Chapelier* Law against organized labor, typical of bourgeois attitudes of revolutionaries in legislature *Assignats*—bonds issued by government, later used as currency; led to high inflation **Flight to Varennes**—Royal family attempted to escape **Declaration of Pilnitz**—Leopold II of Austria promised to participate in an anti-revolutionary war, hedged by qualifications that made the promise worthless; used as an excuse for war by revolutionaries
1792	**National Convention**—new legislature; declared war on Austria; committed to spread revolution abroad **Brunswick Manifesto**—invading Austrians promised revenge if royal family harmed; helped rally support for the revolution **September Massacres**—first executions due to war, precursor of the Terror
1793	**The Vendée**—counterrevolutionary uprising in west central France; brutally suppressed by Robespierre **The Terror**—(1793–94) organized to suppress counter-Revolution; spiraled out of control and eventually destroyed **Robespierre**; 70 % of the victims were from the lower orders; use of guillotine **The Committee of Public Safety**—(1793–94) organized the Terror; led by **Robespierre**
1794	**The Thermidorian Reaction**—reaction to the extremism of Robespierre; ended the Terror; established the Directory
1795	**The Directory**—(1795–99) continued revolution in a more conventional way; led by bourgeois; new constitution; continued the war

CAUSES OF THE REVOLUTION IN FRANCE

POLITICAL

- Incompetence of **Louis XVI** (r. 1774–92)

- Distrust and hatred of Queen **Marie Antoinette**

- National humiliation in war leading to the loss of India, Canada, and Atlantic trade

- Noble resistance to being taxed and fear of renewed royal incursions on their privileges

- Noble aspirations to emulate the powerful role of the aristocracy in Britain

- Long disuse of the **Estates General** leaving the nation out of practice with a legislative system

ECONOMIC
- Series of poor harvests in the 1780s

- Bankruptcy of the government due to war debts and inability to tax the nobility sufficiently (nobles paid some taxes)

- **Tax farming** system encouraged extreme measures in collecting taxes, but rendered less income to the state than direct collection would have

- Heavy tax burdens on the poor—the *taille*

- Decade-long recession

SOCIAL
- **Bourgeois** dissatisfaction with their role in society and politics and tension between them and the nobility

- Unpopularity of the Court nobility who often were detached from management of their estates and hated by the peasantry

- Continued retention of feudal privileges, *banalités*

- Unpopularity of church hierarchy and church economic and political privileges

IDEAS
- Example of the **American Revolution**

- Ideas and criticisms of the **Enlightenment**

- Ineffective **censorship** and expansion of the "**public sphere**" of political discussion

- Rising cycle of extreme rhetoric and violence, especially once war was declared, made the revolution veer towards an extreme path to dictatorship

LEADING FIGURES
- **Louis XVI**
(r. 1774–92) nice man out of his depth and incapable of the ruthlessness necessary to suppress a rebellion

- **Marie Antoinette**
(d. 1793) inept and insensitive to public opinion and a foreigner (Austrian)

- **Necker**
(d. 1804) royal financial official

- **Tom Paine**
English defense of the Revolution—*The Rights of Man* (1791)

- **Olympye de Gouges**
The Rights of Women (1791)

- **Mary Wollstonecraft**
Vindication of the Rights of Women (1792)

- **Edmund Burke**
English critic—*Reflections on the Revolution in France* (1790)—made the case for caution in political reform

- **Marat**
Jacobin leader, murdered by counter-revolutionary woman 1793

- **Danton**
(d. 1794) Jacobin leader; executed by Robespierre

- **Robespierre**
(d. 1794) Jacobin leader; becomes head of the **Committee of Public Safety** and for a while the dictator of France: incorruptible and a monster

- **Pitt the Younger**
(d. 1806) British organizer of alliances against the forces of revolution and Napoleon

- **Napoleon Bonaparte**
(r. 1799–1815) revolutionary general who supported the **Directory** and then overthrew it

IMPORTANT TERMS

- **Jacobins**
radical revolutionaries

- **Girondins**
more moderate than Jacobins, advocates of war with Austria

- *Enragés*
extreme radicals, the "Mountain" party

- *Levée en masse*
use of large numbers of fervidly patriotic troops to overcome disadvantage in training and organization of anti-revolutionary armies; precursor of Napoleon's mass armies

OUTCOMES OF THE REVOLUTION

POLITICAL

- Overthrow of the monarchy; executions of the King and Queen

- Power of the nobility seriously weakened

- France divided into a new administrative structure of departments with uniform legal systems

- More equality before the law

- Indiscriminant use of political violence and the rise of two competing ideas of the state—libertarian and monolithic—left France unstable and unreconciled

- Radical reorganization of the military

- Expansion of borders, wars of the Revolution

- The rise of Napoleon's imperial system

- France finally subordinated in a global order dominated by Britain

ECONOMIC
- Peasants secured tenure to much land

- Many noble families diminished in wealth

- Introduction of the metric system

- Calendar changed to a decimal system (later abolished)

- Serious economic losses in the West Indies

RELIGION
- Secularization of the state (at one point France was de-Christianized and a state religion worshipping "reason" was established); Napoleon later reconciled with the Roman Catholic church

SOCIAL
- Reform of family, divorce, and property law; end of primogeniture

- Egalitarian ideals entered the mainstream of Western society

NAPOLEON
One of the most complex and astonishing figures to bestride the European stage. Bred in a minor Corsican noble family of Italian origins, he rose due to opportunities afforded young officers during the French Revolution. He seized control of the state by force in the **coup d'État of 1799**, served a leader of the **Consulate** 1799–1804, declared himself Emperor in 1804, conquered much of Europe in masterful military campaigns where he won great victories such as **Austerlitz** (1805) and **Jena** (1806), and was finally defeated and exiled in *1815. He conquered the Netherlands, Italy, Dalmatia, Switzerland, Germany, Poland, Spain, Portugal, and placed a French marshal on the throne of Sweden. He invaded Egypt and Russia.

Much debate continues to surround Napoleon centered on questions such as the degree to which he was a revolutionary or an Enlightened Despot and whether he was a good or bad man.

NAPOLEON—FOR AND AGAINST	
FOR	AGAINST
• **Concordat**—(1801) restored partial independence of the Roman Catholic Church • Demolished the Holy Roman Empire (1806) • Wins many great military victories • Enacts **Napoleonic Code** reforming the laws of France which influenced legal systems throughout Europe • Abolished guilds and serfdom in conquered territories • Promoted soldiers and officials based on merit, making the son of a butcher field marshal and King of Sweden • Held **plebicites** and imposed constitutions, made himself Emperor "of the French", not "of France" • Promoted education and built infrastructure • Left many revolutionary reforms in place • Sold Louisiana to the USA • Did not allow tax exemptions by birth • Created **Bank of France** • Ended traditional practices and noble privileges in conquered territories • Spread the **metric system** across Europe	• **Invasion of Egypt**—(1798) Bonaparte's crazy expedition that ended in disaster, which he claimed was a victory • **Josephine**—the love of his life; jettisoned when she could not produce a male heir • **Continental System**—(1807) economic warfare against the British; failed to stop British trade and alienated French allies • **Bonaparte Family**—Napoleon's brothers and sisters, placed on various thrones • Outwitted diplomatically by British Prime Minister **William Pitt the Younger** who organized coalitions against him • Unable to defeat Britain (navy permanently disabled by British Admiral **Nelson** at the Battle of **Trafalgar**—1805) • Tries to outwit Tsar **Alexander I** at **Tilsit** (1807) but is outwitted by the Tsar in the disastrous invasion of Russia (1812) • Defeated at the Battle of Nations (**Leipzig** 1813) and again by the **Duke of Wellington** at the Battle of **Waterloo** (1815) • Creates a new hereditary nobility and a new monarchy • Invaded many countries without provocation and incorporated them into his empire and was responsible for hundreds of thousands if not millions of deaths in unnecessary wars • Napoleonic Code authoritarian and paternalistic • Established secret police and imposed censorship (Fouché) • Murdered the duc d'Enghein, Bourbon prince though an innocent man, in order to prevent disloyalty among his followers • Married a Habsburg Archduchess • Restored Catholic Church to a privileged position • Self-glorification

CONGRESS OF VIENNA 1814–*1815

Peace conference ending the wars of revolution. Established a general peace in Europe that lasted a century. It evoked little bitterness in France, ended long colonial rivalries. Issues of Germany and Poland were deferred. It restored the balance of power. The chief architects of the Treaty were **Prince Metternich** of Austria (flexible, conservative, shrewd), **Viscount Castlereagh** of Britain (conservative but with a eye to stability and British dominance), and **Prince Tallyrand** of France (crafty but moderate). The Congress was briefly interrupted by a come back by Napoleon (the **100 Days**) that fizzled out.

- Bourbons restored in France
  Louis XVIII—had learned some lessons from the revolution and upon his restoration in 1814 accepted parliamentary government, the Napoleonic Code, and abolition of feudalism

- Napoleon was exiled and his heir taken to Vienna, where he died (Napoleon II)

- **Quadruple Alliance** (Austria, Prussia, Russia, Britain) to last 20 years

- British confirmed in possession of South Africa (taken from the Dutch)

- Britain gained possessions in the Mediterranean and West Indies

- France rapidly restored to company of great nations

- Germany left divided among a much reduced (39) number of small states but with little central authority

- The Netherlands and Belgium combined into a large buffer state to contain France (broke apart 1830)

- Austria regained Tuscany and Lombardy and also absorbed Venice

- Spanish, Portuguese, and Sicilian monarchies restored

- **Polish-Saxon Question: Alexander I** wanted to be king of a reunited Poland in exchange for giving Saxony to Prussia. France, Austria, and Britain resist. Russia and Prussia only gained a fraction of their desired goals

- Sweden gained Norway

- Sardinia gained Nice and Genoa

- **Slave trade** condemned

- Agreement to hold future congresses of the great powers to resist revolutionary ferment (the **Congress System**)

- **Holy Alliance** formed by **Alexander I** vaguely in favor of peace and religion (Russia, Prussia, Austria—Britain does not join and Metternich did not take it seriously)

The French Revolution, Napoleon, and the associated wars precipitated by both spread revolutionary and **reformist** ideas across Europe, a process that could be curbed by not extirpated. They also encouraged a spirit of **nationalism** not only in France, and, inadvertently, aroused powerful anti-French nationalism in Spain, Italy, Britain, Russia, and Germany.

IMPORTANT DEFINITIONS AND IDENTIFICATIONS

- 100 Days
- Alexander I
- American Revolution
- *Assignats*
- Battle of Austerlitz
- *banalités*
- Bank of France
- *Bastille*
- Bonaparte family
- Bourgioesie
- Brunswick Manifesto
- Burke
- Viscount Castlereagh
- Censorship
- *Le Chapelier* Law
- Civil Constitution of the Clergy
- Committee of Public Safety
- the Concordat
- Congress System
- Constituent Assembly
- the Consulate
- Continental System
- Danton
- Declaration of Pilnitz
- Declaration of the Rights of Man and Citizen

- the Directory
- *Émigrés*
- the Enlightenment
- *Enragés*
- Estates General
- *coup d'État*
- Invasion of Egypt
- Girondins
- Olympye de Gouges
- the Great Fear
- Holy Alliance
- Jacobins
- Battle of Jena
- Empress Josephine
- Battle of Leipzig
- *levée en masse*
- Louis XVI
- Louis XVIII
- Marat
- Marie Antoinette
- metric system
- Prince Metternich
- Napoleon I
- Napoleonic Code
- National Convention
- Necker

- Admiral Nelson
- *parlements*
- Tom Paine
- William Pitt the Younger
- plebicites
- Polish-Saxon Question
- the public sphere
- Quadruple Alliance
- nationalism
- reformism
- Robespierre
- *sans-culottes*
- The September Massacres
- slave trade
- *taille*
- Prince Tallyrand
- Tax farming
- Tennis Court Oath
- The Terror
- Thermidorian Reaction
- Treaty of Tilsit
- Battle of Trafalgar
- The *Vendée*
- Battle of Waterloo
- Duke of Wellington
- Mary Wollstonecraft

IMPORTANT DATES

*1789   The French Revolution

1790   Civil Constitution of the Clergy

1795   The Directory

1799   Napoleon takes power

1804   Napoleon become Emperor

1805   Battle of Trafalgar

1812   Invasion of Russia

*1815   Napoleon defeated at Waterloo

Congress of Vienna

CHAPTER 6
MULTIPLE-CHOICE QUESTIONS

Questions 1.1–1.3 relate to the 1789 drawing by Jacques-Louis David titled "The Tennis Court Oath" reproduced below.

1.1 The scene above depicted by the great French artist, Jacques-Louis David, is of what event?

(A) The first Olympic Games held in Paris
(B) The first meeting of the National Assembly
(C) A riot protesting against a royal decree against sports
(D) The declaration of Napoleon Bonaparte as Emperor of the French

1.2 The artist in this drawing

(A) Was sympathetic to what the people he was portraying were doing
(B) Was hostile to what the people he was portraying were doing
(C) Attempted to make the people he was portraying look foolish
(D) Played down the drama of the event

1.3 The radical Jacobins of the French Revolution asserted their authority

(A) At the Tennis Court Oath
(B) In the Committee of Public Safety
(C) By concluding a peace with Austria
(D) When denouncing the "Terror"

Questions 2.1–2.3 relate to the following passage.

If it suffices here to have made it clear that the pretended utility of a privileged order for the public service is nothing more than a chimera; that with it all that which is burdensome in this service is performed by the Third Estate; that without it the superior places would be infinitely better filled; that they naturally ought to be the lot and recompense of ability and recognized services, and that if privileged persons (nobles) have come to usurp all the lucrative and honorable posts, it is a hateful injustice to the rank and file of citizens and at the same time a treason to the public welfare.

Who then shall dare to say that the Third Estate has not within itself all that is necessary for the formation of a complete nation? It is the strong and robust man who has one arm still shackled. If the privileged order should be abolished, the nation would be nothing less, but something more. Therefore, what is the Third Estate? Everything; but an everything shackled and oppressed. What would it be without the privileged order? Everything, but an everything free and flourishing. Nothing can succeed without it, everything would be infinitely better without the others.

Emmanuel Joseph Sieyès, delegate to the Estates General, "What is the Third Estate?", pamphlet, 1789

2.1 This passage was written by which of the following?

(A) An opponent of the French Revolution
(B) A supporter of the French Revolution
(C) A courtier at Versailles
(D) A bishop and delegate of the Second Estate

2.2 Which of the following were members of the Third Estate in France in 1789?

(A) The nobles
(B) The clergy
(C) Military officers
(D) The bourgeoisie

2.3 The Third Estate was represented in the Estates General, which met in 1789. What happened to the French parliament in that year?

(A) It was reconstituted as the National Assembly
(B) It remained the French parliament until 1871
(C) It elected General Napoleon Bonaparte Emperor of the French
(D) It ordered the execution of King Louis XVI

Questions 3.1–3.3 relate to the following passage.

Your literary men, and your politicians, and so for the whole class of the enlightened among us, essentially differ in these points. They have no respect for the wisdom of others; but they pay it off by very full confidence in their own. With them it is a sufficient motive to destroy an old scheme of things, because it is an old one. As to the new, they are in no sort of fear with regard to the duration of a building run up in haste; because duration is no object to those who think little or nothing has been done before their time, and who place all their hopes in discovery. Their attachment to their country itself is only so far as it agrees with some of their fleeting projects; it begins and ends with that scheme of polity which falls in with their momentary opinion.

Edmund Burke, *Reflections on the French Revolution*, 1790

3.1 Burke saw the main error of the Enlightenment philosophes as being which of the following?

(A) They were stuck in outmoded ideas
(B) They believed in constitutions
(C) They distrusted tradition
(D) They put too much faith in kings

3.2 Burke regarded the French Revolution as

(A) A terrible mistake
(B) A glorious triumph
(C) Necessary and timely
(D) A matter of indifference

3.3 In Great Britain the Enlightenment may best be characterized as which of the following?

(A) More liberal than the French Enlightenment
(B) The most radical in Europe
(C) The most conservative in Europe
(D) Pragmatic and moderate

Questions 4.1–4.3: France, Napoleon, Metternich

At the audience he gave me at St. Cloud, when I delivered my credentials, I found Napoleon standing in the middle of one of the rooms, with the minister of Foreign Affairs and six other members of the Court. He wore the Guards uniform, and he had his hat on his head. This latter circumstance, improper in any case, for the audience was not a public one, struck me as misplaced pretention, showing the *parvenu* (social climber).

His attitude seemed to me to show constraint and even embarrassment. His short, broad figure, negligent dress, and marked endeavour to make an imposing effect, combined to weaken in me the feeling of grandeur naturally attached to the idea of a man before whom the world trembled. In subsequent meetings in his freaks, in his fits of passion, in his brusque interpellations, I saw prepared scenes, studied and calculated to produce a certain effect on the person to whom he was speaking.

The pains which he took to correct the faults of his nature and education only served to make his deficiencies more evident.

Prince von Metternich, Austrian Ambassador to France 1806–09, *Memoirs*, published 1880

4.1 What was the most important factor shaping Metternich's view of Emperor Napoleon I?

(A) His aristocratic birth and heritage
(B) His prejudice against military officers
(C) His dislike of the French
(D) His Roman Catholicism

4.2 How did Austria fare in its relations with France in the years before Napoleon was overthrown?

(A) A series of easy military victories
(B) A series of humiliating military defeats
(C) Loyal allies
(D) Election of Napoleon as Emperor of Austria

4.3 In 1815 Prince Metternich did which of the following?

(A) Joined Napoleon on St. Helena
(B) Let Louis XVIII decide Napoleon's fate
(C) Gave Napoleon a choice about where to go after he was defeated at the Battle of Waterloo
(D) Coordinated the dismantling of Napoleon's empire at the Congress of Vienna

SHORT-ANSWER QUESTION

Question 1

Using your knowledge of European history answer the questions below (A and B).

A) Identify and explain TWO of the most important social or economic causes of the French Revolution.

B) Identify and explain ONE theory of history that might lead a modern historian to designate a particular factor as the fundamental cause of the French Revolution.

CHAPTER 7

THE INDUSTRIAL REVOLUTION

Historians disagree about the origins of this immensely complex phenomenon, and especially about when it can be said to have begun. A conventional date is around 1780* (Watt's steam engine came into use from the 1770s), although a fully industrialized machine-powered economy did not emerge in Britain until after 1850. There is also disagreement about the number of "stages"—first, second, etc. Again the conventional wisdom is that textiles and railways composed the first stage and electricity, chemicals, internal combustion engine, etc. was the base of the "second" one. One also has to remember that much pre-industrial activity (the **domestic system**, for example) continued long into the "industrial" era. Britain was the epicenter of the first Industrial Revolution and stayed in the lead until the late 19th century. Its finance and service (insurance, shipping, etc.) economy remained larger than any other until the 1940s. Some technologies spread very rapidly, such as the railways, even to countries that were otherwise very slow to change.

Belgium followed Britain, then Northern France, the Rhineland, Silesia, and eventually Bohemia, Northern Italy, and the USA. Although pockets of industrialization developed elsewhere, such as around St. Petersburg in Russia or Belfast in Ireland, many areas remained primarily agricultural until the 20th century.

CAUSES OF INDUSTRIALIZATION

Few other questions are more contested by historians than why industrialization happened and why Britain was first, with the added dimension of why Europe accelerated past China and India ("the Great Divergence") both of which possessed many of the elements that ignited the British economy. It is fair to say that there is no consensus among historians at present on these issues, which makes it all the more exciting and important to study them. The most significant factors leading to British industrialization are listed below.

- **Agricultural Revolution** increased productivity and created large amounts of excess capital. Food for an expanding population and money for increased investment. More efficient production also freed labor for other occupations

- The unique British system of landownership concentrated land in the hands of a small number of noble families. They rented the land in substantial blocks to rural entrepreneurs with incentives to innovate. The vast incomes of the great families were used in part to invest directly in mining, construction of infrastructure (harbors, roads, canals, tunnels, bridges) and more indirectly in manufacturing

- New technologies were developed both in agriculture (seed drill, crop rotation, animal breeding) and in industry (cotton manufacturing, steam power, iron-making, railways)

- Inventive geniuses—Hargreaves, Cartwright, Arkwright, **Watt** (d. 1819) efficient steam engine, **Stephenson** (d. 1848) railways

- Emergence of a **consumer culture** and the economies of production

- **Enclosure** of common fields drove some workers off the land and into cities and made agriculture more efficient and profitable—more workers mobile

- Stable political system that encouraged some degree of shared decision-making in an island that proved impregnable to foreign invasion—all of which encouraged long term investment and the security of property

- Strong central banking system for capital allocation (**Bank of England** founded 1694)

- Large capital market

- Sophisticated financial mechanisms to share risk both via purchase of stocks and insurance

- Abundant mineral resources, especially coal and iron ore often located close together and close to inexpensive water transportation. For a variety of reasons inexpensive coal became the principal source of energy earlier than in any other country

- No place in England was distant from navigable waterways

- Effective patent system and a legal system that worked reasonably effectively to protect contracts and business operations

- Low rates of taxation

- Britain tended to rely on the Royal Navy for protection of the homeland and expansion over seas. A large army was used infrequently and temporarily. Navies were cheaper to maintain than armies and sustaining both drained national resources away from other investments in France

- The ideas of **the Enlightenment** shaped approaches to understanding the natural world fostering the rise of new technologies and attitudes towards commerce

- The Parliament controlled by landed aristocrats responded to commercial and business needs, employed the power of the state to expand markets and protect British business at home and abroad

- **Aristocracy** resilient and willing to make large concessions to other groups in society in order to maintain social stability and economic prosperity (Reform Act of 1832, Repeal of the Corn Laws, Factory Acts)

- Colonial system provides raw materials, additional markets and a place for excess population to work

- Britain largest free trade area in Europe

- Experienced business and merchant class

- Capital from the slave trade, the *asiento*, and world trade generally

INDUSTRIALIZED SOCIETY

- Movement of population from countryside to large cities—**Manchester** (the "shock city", Birmingham, Leeds, Sheffield)

- Gradual impoverishment of domestic weavers

- Regimentation of life—no longer responsive to seasons or hours of sunlight, the factory whistle: long working hours, boring and dangerous work even by small children

- Boom—bust cycles became more dramatic and painful for workers

- End of famine in industrialized societies

- Poor housing, alienation from support of local village life

- Gradual improvement of living standards and wages after the ("Hungry") 1840s

- Cheap, easily cleaned, quick-drying clothing (cotton)

- Eventually hours reduced, child labor regulated, schooling increased

- Clergy/churches slow to keep up with urban growth, although Sunday Schools were ubiquitous

- Industrial fortunes eventually began to match or outpace aristocratic ones

- Gradual extension of the franchise to working men in the **Second** (1867) and **Third** (1884–5) **Reform Acts**

- Growing importance of organized labor in **trades unions**

- Expanded material culture

- Withdrawal of many women from the workplace once a single workman's salary could support a family

- Global trade expanded

IMPACT OF THE RAILWAYS POST–1830
a) national time
b) national newspapers distributed rapidly
c) food, goods transported cheaply and rapidly
d) suburbs—commute by train
e) vacations/tourism—travel by train, even the poor
f) social leveling—all classes travel in same way, suitable clothes for train travel similar for all
g) professional sports—teams can travel, scores rapidly disseminated
h) huge increase in employment both to build the tracks, bridges, viaducts, stations, and make the rolling stock and to operate the system with engineers, conductors, porters, clerks, etc.
i) stimulated other industries—demand for steel and coal, rapid and cheap transportation of raw materials and finished goods

PROS AND CONS OF URBAN INDUSTRIAL LIFE	
PROS	CONS
• more opportunities to advance	• lose sense of community
• more social activities	• less extended family support
• greater marriage opportunities	• unhealthy and confined living spaces
• more personal freedom	• factory regimentation/ boring work
• eventually higher wages	• boom/bust—much unemployment
• eventually better schooling	• injuries and death with machinery/ in mines
• more things to buy	• lack of a sense of personal accomplishment
• eventually a political voice for men	• more prostitution
• professional police forces set up	• urban crime increases
• cheaper clothes and goods	• women less partners with men, more subordinated when man sole breadwinner

THE INDUSTRIAL AGE

During the mid-19th century industrialization gradually spread beyond Britain to other parts of Europe. Life for the majority of laborers in Western Europe began to change as larger and larger numbers moved to the cities and entered urban life. However, many people remained on the farms and millions of others worked as servants and not in factories. Particularly difficult times were encountered in the "Hungry 40s" when potato blight provoked a catastrophic **famine in Ireland** and food crises in many continental countries. Wages were low and living conditions harsh in the cities. Gradually, from that time forward things began to improve.

REACTIONARY CONSERVATIVISM

Many see the period after the French Revolution as an age of "**reaction**", of which some later Romantics (see Chapter Eight) can be seen as a part. Certainly, the Congress of Vienna put many things back the way they were. However, even **Prince Metternich** implemented some imaginative and non-traditionalist policies.

CONSERVATIVE ATTITUDES AND BELIEFS

- Support monarchy, the church, and the aristocracy

- Active government, intervention in the economy

- Paternalistic

- Single national religion

- Censorship

- Generally they feared nationalism and liberalism

- Upheld hierarchy, the military, and "honor"

- Some were Romantics

- "Burkean" distrust of rapid change

- Supporters generally upper class or clergy

THE CONGRESS SYSTEM

- Congress of Aix-la-Chapelle 1818—Allies withdraw forces from France; international force against changes by violence discussed; Atlantic slave trade discussed

- Congress of Troppau 1820—Russia, Austria, Prussia agreed to suppress revolution in Naples. Britain refused to agree to collective international action

- Congress of Verona 1822—intervention in Spain authorized and no support for Greeks against the Ottomans

THE TRIUMPH OF REACTION

RUSSIA

Although raised by *philosophe* tutors, and at first a reformer, Tsar **Alexander I** became a conservative, especially after 1822. His domestic policies were increasingly reactionary after 1803. He pressed for a "**Holy Alliance**" of monarchs against modernity at Vienna. He was succeeded in 1825 by even more reactionary **Nicholas I** (d. 1855), who suppressed the **Decembrist Revolt**. Russia moved into an era of autocratic rule not matched in any Western state; Polish revolt suppressed in 1830

AUSTRIA

Leopold II's successor, **Francis II**, along with the dynamic and far-sighted **Metternich,** charted a conservative course. The latter worked against constitutionalism and nationalism, dual threats to Habsburg authority. Press censorship and secret police were implemented. The **Carlsbad Decrees** (1819) suppressed student liberalism and nationalism. The "**Congress System**" established at Vienna helped suppress rebellions in Spain and Italy

GREAT BRITAIN

Lords Liverpool and **Castlereagh** pursued a conservative foreign policy (although they withdrew from the Congress System); at home they suppressed movements for reform (**Peterloo** and the **Six Acts** 1819); growth of Methodism dampens protest from below; Luddites suppressed

FRANCE

Louis XVIII restored in 1814 and again in 1815 tried to pursue a moderate course, and left a considerable amount of Napoleon's reforms intact. However, **Charles X** (1820–30) tried to turn the clock back. His extreme conservatism provoked a revolution that placed a cousin, **Louis Philippe**, Duc d'Orleans on the throne in 1830 (July Monarchy)

SPAIN

Ferdinand VII was restored to the throne in 1815, dissolved the Cortes, and ruled as an absolute monarch. French intervention during a revolt in 1823 saved his throne. Revolutions in Latin America won independence from Spain in 1820s

ITALY

Remained divided. Austrian intervention in 1822 and 1826 to repress revolts

PRUSSIA

Monarchy, aristocracy, and military restablized after the defeat at Jena (1806). Radical reforms by Scharnhorst and Gneisenau strengthen the army, Stein and Hardenberg strengthen the state, serfdom lessened; German nationalistic movements suppressed

OTTOMAN EMPIRE

Greek independence movement starts 1821; Russo-Turkish War; Battle of Navarino—Turks defeated: great powers recognize Greek independence 1829; other Balkan states recognized as autonomous; Turks weaker and weaker ("Sick Man of Europe")

LIBERALISM, REFORM, AND REVOLUTION

Revolutionary uprisings motivated by nationalism and liberalism did break out during the 1820s and 1830s with varying degrees of success.

LIBERAL ATTITUDES AND BELIEFS
("liberalism" first used in the 1820s to convey the following)

- Enlightenment values of rationalism and freedom of the individual

- Distrust of the military

- Republicanism or constitutional, limited monarchy

- Dislike hereditary privilege and many distrust aristocracy

- Believe in constitutions

- Distrust religious organizations and clerical powers

- Want a secular state

- Free speech and free press

- Anti-slavery (Britain abolished trade 1807 and slavery in the empire in 1834)

- Legal equality

- Promotion by merit

- Laissez-faire economics, anti-tariffs

- Supporters largely middle class, businessmen, etc.

- Many accepted Benthamite concepts of "**Utilitarianism**" (greatest good for the greatest number)

- The most influential statement of Classical Liberalism was made by **John Stuart Mill**, *On Liberty* (1859)

Nationalism is a term that came to describe aspirations for national independence or unification. It threatened to break up multi-national empires such as Austria and pull together fragmented states such as Germany and Italy. Nationalists believed that true nations usually shared:

- Common history

- Historic geographical area

- Common language

- Common religion

- Shared culture

- Common enemies

Nationalists in particular countries tended to overlook inconvenient historical events and inconvenient problems with religion or language differences. They locked onto a vision of history that suited their ideological position. Nationalism tended to go beyond patriotism into the realm of arrogance and hatred. It gave a "moral" underpinning to racism.

NATIONALIST AND LIBERAL UPRISINGS

Although no continent-wide war or revolution took place between the Congress of Vienna (*1815) and the outbreak of the First World War (*1914) numerous risings and revolts occurred. Although both liberalism and nationalism played a role in most of these events some were predominantly motivated by one or the other of the two ideologies.

LIBERAL
Spain (1822)—unsuccessful liberal revolt against **Ferdinand VII**, put down by French
Decembrist Revolt (Russia 1825)—uprising led by officers exposed to liberal ideas while visiting the West 1814–15. Occasioned by confusion over the succession after the death of **Alexander I**. Ruthlessly suppressed by **Nicholas I**
France (1830)—successful liberal revolt against Charles X (Bourbon), established liberal constitutional monarchy under **Louis Philippe** (Orleans)—"July Monarchy"
Reform Act of 1832* (Great Britain)—liberal (Whig) party led by aristocrats imposes liberal reform of the electoral system doubling the number of voters and giving representation in Parliament to industrial cities; eliminate many "rotten" boroughs. Other reforms including reduction in use of capital punishment
NATIONALIST
Greek Independence (1820s) Nationalist (Greek Orthodox) uprising against Ottoman (Islamic) rule. Successful due to intervention by Russian and British forces.
Poland (1830)—nationalist uprising against Russian control, suppressed by **Nicholas I**
Belgium (1830)—successful nationalist revolt against rule by the Dutch
MIXED
South America (1820s)—Nationalist and liberal uprising against Spanish rule—successful due to weakness of the mother country after Napoleonic wars. Brazil broke free from Portugal (1822) but retained Portuguese emperor

IMPORTANT DEFINITIONS AND IDENTIFICATIONS

- Agricultural revolution
- Alexander I of Russia
- Aristocracy
- Bank of England
- Carlsbad Decrees
- Viscount Castlereagh
- Charles X of France
- Congress System
- Conservatism
- consumer culture
- Decemberist Revolt (1825)
- domestic system
- enclosure
- the Enlightenment
- Ferdinand VII of Spain

- Francis II of Austria
- Greek Independence
- Holy Alliance
- industrial revolution
- Irish Famine
- *laissez-faire*
- liberalism
- Louis XVIII of France
- Louis Philippe of France
- Earl of Liverpool
- Manchester (England)
- Prince Metternich
- John Stuart Mill
- nationalism
- Nicholas I of Russia

- ***On Liberty*** (1859)
- Peterloo
- Polish Revolt (1830)
- "reaction"
- Reform Act of 1832 (Britain)
- Second Reform Act (1867—Britain)
- Six Acts (1819)
- Stephenson
- Third Reform Act (1884–5—Britain)
- trades unions
- Utilitarianism
- Watt

IMPORTANT DATES

1770s Watt steam engine

1780 Conventional approximate date of the beginning of the industrial revolution in Britain

1830 Passenger railways began operation

July Monarchy overthrows Charles X in France

Polish Revolt

1832 First Reform Act (Britain)

CHAPTER 7
MULTIPLE-CHOICE QUESTIONS

Questions 1.1–1.3 refer to the statistical table below.

Value Added in British Industry, 1770–1831 (£ millions)

Sector	Product	1770	1801	1831
Textiles	Cotton	0.6	9.2	25.3
	Wool	7.0	10.2	15.9
	Linen	1.9	2.6	5.0
	Silk	1.0	2.0	5.8
Coal and Metals	Coal	0.9	2.7	7.9
	Iron	1.5	4.0	7.6
	Copper	0.2	0.9	0.8
Building	Buildings	2.4	9.3	26.5
Consumer Goods	Beer	1.3	2.5	5.2
	Lather	5.1	8.4	9.8
	Soap	0.3	0.8	1.2
	Candles	0.5	1.0	1.2
	Paper	0.1	0.6	0.8
Total		22.8	54.2	113.0

1.1 The graph above demonstrates which of the following was true 1770–1831?

(A) The construction sector suffered serious setbacks
(B) The Napoleonic War had a large impact on the British economy
(C) Textiles were the biggest area of growth
(D) Most growth came from exports

1.2 The graph above suggests which of the following statements was true 1770–1831?

(A) The lack of demand for candles was due to the growth in the availability of electric light
(B) Home grown cotton boosted the textile industry
(C) More traditional industries were overtaking new ones
(D) The factory system was beginning to boost production of manufactured goods

1.3 Widespread application of steam power to manufacturing, which marked mature industrialization, was

(A) Still to be fully accomplished by 1831
(B) Fully in place by 1600
(C) Fully in place by 1770
(D) Overtaken by hydroelectric power by 1850

98

Questions 2.1–2.3 refer to the statistical table below.

Total Industrial Potential, 1750–1980, As a Percentage of Global Total

	1750	1800	1830	1860	1880	1900	1913	1928	1938	1953	1963	1973	1980
Developed	26.8	32.0	39.7	63.3	79.1	88.9	92.5	92.8	92.8	93.5	91.5	90.1	88.0
UK	1.6	4.1	9.8	19.9	22.8	18.5	13.6	10.0	10.7	8.4	6.4	4.9	4.0
Germany	3.2	3.4	3.8	4.9	8.4	13.1	14.8	11.7	12.7	5.9	6.4	5.9	5.3
France	3.9	4.1	5.4	8.0	7.8	6.8	6.1	6.0	4.4	3.2	3.8	3.5	3.3
Italy	2.4	2.7	2.2	2.7	2.5	2.6	2.5	2.7	2.7	2.3	2.9	2.8	2.9
Russ./USSR	4.7	5.4	5.4	7.1	7.8	8.9	8.3	5.3	9.0	10.7	14.8	14.4	14.8
USA		0.7	2.7	7.1	14.7	23.7	31.9	39.3	31.4	44.7	35.1	33.0	31.5
Japan	3.9	3.4	2.7	2.7	2.5	2.4	2.7	3.3	5.2	2.9	5.1	8.8.	9.1
Third World	73.2	67.3	60.9	36.7	20.9	11.1	7.5	7.2	7.2	6.5	8.5	9.9	12.0
China	33.1	33.3	29.9	19.5	12.5	6.3	3.5	3.4	3.1	2.3	3.5	3.9	5.0
India/Pakistan	24.4	19.7	17.9	8.4	2.8	1.7	1.4	1.9	2.4	1.7	1.8	2.1	2.3
World	100	100	100	100	100	100	100	100	100	100	100	100	100

2.1 The data included in the table above indicates which of the following?

(A) The Industrial Revolution did not reach a rapid pace until the 1840s and 1850s
(B) Germany and France did not industrialize until the 1920s
(C) Russian industrialization never fully developed
(D) Italy maintained a steady pace of industrial expansion

2.2 When compared to Europe industrialization in China

(A) Kept pace technologically with Italy until the 1950s
(B) Had a more modern economy than France until 1880
(C) Diverged from the path to modernization in the early 19th century
(D) Was as powerful as Britain until the 1860s

2.3 This table can create a false impression when countries are compared to each other because?

(A) It exaggerates the success of the United States by leaving out Austria-Hungary and Spain
(B) Does not show East and West Germany after World War II
(C) Data are not calculated on a *per capita* basis
(D) Provides no data for the USA for 1750

Questions 3.1–3.3 relate to the following passage.

Here, then is the "curs" of our factory-system: as improvements in machinery have gone on, the "avarice of masters" has prompted many to exact more labour from their hands than they were fitted by nature to perform, and those who have wished for the hours of labour to be less for all ages than the legislature would even yet sanction, have had no alternative but to conform more or less to the prevailing practice, or abandon the trade altogether. This has been the case with regard to myself and my partners. We have never worked more than seventy-one hours a week before Sir John Hobhouse's Act was passed. We then came down to sixty-nine; and, since Lord Althorp's Act was passed, in 1833, we have reduced the time of adults to sixty-seven and a half hours in the week, and that of children under thirteen years of age to forty-eight hours in the week. The overworking does not apply to children only; the adults are also overworked. The increased speed given to machinery within the last thirty years, has, in very many instances, doubled the labour of both.

John Fielden, *The Curse of the Factory System*, 1836

3.1 According to John Fielden how has technology affected the hours of labor of factory workers?

(A) Increased them
(B) Left them the same
(C) Reduced them
(D) Created unemployment

3.2 What might a historian find surprising about John Fielden's views?

(A) He seems to welcome legislation reducing working hours
(B) He calls for wages to be raised
(C) He is against the idea of factories
(D) He sees no difference between children and adults

3.3 Factory legislation was likely to be supported by

(A) Factory owners
(B) Politicians
(C) Unions
(D) Peasants

Questions 4.1–4.3 refer to the chart reproduced below.

European Railways 1835-1905						
Length of the railway (■ - 2000 km)						
Austria	France	Germany	UK	Sweden	Italy	Russian Empire
1835			▮			
—	141	6	544			
1855 ■	■■▮	■■■■	■■■■■ ■		▮	▮
1588	5037	7826	11,744	—	1207	1049
1875 ■■■■■ ▮	■■■■■ ■■■■▮	■■■■■ ■■■■	■■■■■ ■▮	■▮	■■■■	■■■■■ ■■■■▮
10,331	19,357	27,970	23,365	3679	8018	19,029
1895 ■■■■■ ■■■▮	■■■■■ ■■■▮	■■■■■ ■■■■■ ■■■■■ ■■■▮	■■■■■ ■■■■▮	■■■■■ ■■■	■■■■■ ■■■	■■■■■ ■■■■■ ■■■▮
16,420	36,240	46,500	28,986	9756	15,970	37,058
1905 ■■■■■ ■■■■■ ▮	■■■■■ ■■■■■ ■■■■■	■■■■■ ■■■■■ ■■■■■ ■■■▮	■■■■■ ■■■■■ ▮	■■■■■ ■▮	■■■■■ ■■■▮	■■■■■ ■■■■■ ■■■■■ ■■■■■ ■■■■■ ■■■■■ ▮
21.002	39,607	56,739	31,456	12,647	17,078	61,085

4.1 This chart indicates which of the following?

(A) Russia was the most industrialized country in Europe
(B) Britain always had a greater length of track than any other state
(C) Proportionate to its size Austria had the largest rail system in 1905
(D) The rapid acceleration of German industrial growth

4.2 Proportionate to its population, which country appears to have been the least industrialized?

(A) Russia
(B) Italy
(C) Sweden
(D) Austria

4.3 In which year were the European railway lines largely complete?

(A) 1875
(B) 1905
(C) 1918
(D) 1945

SHORT-ANSWER QUESTION

Question 1

We argue that international trade was a key reason why the British Industrial Revolution was different. The argument comes in two parts. First, a given domestic stimulus to growth, such as the new technologies of the Industrial Revolution, led to a greater rise in incomes as a result of opportunities afforded by international trade. By helping the economy escape from resource constraints, trade ensured that technological change translated into a more sustained growth experience than would otherwise have been possible. Second, the extent of technological change itself depended at least to some extent on the openness of the economy to trade.

> Ronald Findlay and Kevin H. O'Rourke, *Power and Plenty: Trade, War, and the World Economy in the Second Millennium*, 2007 [Princeton University Press, Princeton 2007, p. 339]

. Based on your knowledge of European history and the quotation from a book by two modern historians answer the following questions (A and B).

A) Identify and explain ONE technological innovation of the kind mentioned by Findlay and O'Rourke critical to the Industrial Revolution.

B) Identify and explain TWO alternative explanations for the rise of industrialization not mentioned by Findlay and O'Rourke.

Question 2

We ought not then to begin first, by considering who ought to be electors, and then who ought to be the elected; but we ought to begin by considering who ought to be elected, and then constitute such persons electors as would likely to produce the best elected.

> Earl of Liverpool, debate in the House of Lords, 1793

Based on your knowledge of European history and the quotation from Lord Liverpool's speech above answer the following questions (A, B, and C).

A) Identify and explain ONE reason why the topic of electoral reform of the British Parliament might be under discussion in the later eighteenth century.

B) Identify and explain ONE reason why Parliamentary Reform in Britain was enacted in 1832.

C) Identify and describe the social class of most of the new electors enfranchised in 1832.

CHAPTER 8

THE NINETEENTH CENTURY

*1848: THE YEAR OF REVOLUTIONS

Only *1789 and *1989 reverberate in quite the same way as *1848 in the history of modern Europe. One famous historian wrote that is was the turning point in history in which history failed to turn. With a few notable exceptions after 1848 relative social peace reigned until 1917.

CAUSES OF THE REVOLUTIONS OF *1848
Food shortages
Weakness in factory production
Low wages, unemployment
Poor living conditions worsened in cities
Discontent among peasants
Nationalism
Liberal reformism
Domino effect

FRANCE

Dissatisfaction with corruption and the inefficiency of Louis Philippe's leadership plus a sense of national humiliation in foreign affairs precipitated overthrow of the July Monarchy. Serious conflict broke out between middle class liberals and the workers leading to violence in the **Bloody June Days**. The 2nd Republic marked the triumph of property owners and constitutionalism. The election of Napoleon's nephew (**Prince Louis Napoleon**—became **Emperor Napoleon III**, r. 1852–70) as President was caused by fear of disorder and search for the return of military glory.

AUSTRIA

Metternich was driven into exile and the incompetent Emperor was replaced by a younger one (**Franz Joseph** —r. 1848–1916). Revolts in various parts of the Habsburg dominions were successfully repressed by the policy of keeping insurgents divided. Perhaps the most serious was the outbreak of nationalism in Hungary repressed by Russian troops called in by Vienna. **Nicholas I** was happy to oblige. Rural reforms pacified the peasantry and military conquest put down the Italians.

BRITAIN

Chartist (working class movement demanding the vote and other constitutional reforms) protest a flop. Alliance of middle and upper classes with the monarchy held firm.

PRUSSIA

Frederick Wilhelm IV (r. 1840–61) forced to make some constitutional concessions.

GERMANY

Liberal nationalists call unofficial meeting of the **Frankfurt Parliament**. Plans to unify fall into two categories. The Grossdeutsch solution included the Austro-Hungarian empire, thus bringing millions of non-Germans along. The **Kleindeutsch** solution excluded Austria, which left millions of Germans out of the state and made illiberal Prussia the dominant force. The imperial crown was finally offered to the King of Prussia, who declined it because he would be limited by a liberal constitution and have to accept the throne from middle class liberals. Thus, perhaps the last chance for a peaceful unification of Germany was lost.

ITALY

Uprisings in the Austrian north and in the Papal States. Republican nationalist, **Joseph Mazzini** (d. 1872), founder of "Young Italy", led a revolt in the Papal States that forced the Pope to flee Rome. Repressed by Austrian intervention. **Pius IX** returned to the Vatican a confirmed reactionary.

THE CRIMEAN WAR (1853–56)

Often overlooked but important. A conflict between Russia on the one hand and Great Britain, France, and the Ottoman Empire on the other. It was fought mainly on the Crimean peninsula in the Black Sea, hence the name given to the war. Austria stayed neutral, to the indignation of **Nicholas I**, who had bailed **Franz Joseph** out of difficulty in Hungary in 1849.

CAUSES

- Russian foreign policy was to assert as much power as possible in the Balkans, destroy or subordinate Ottoman authority, gain free passage of shipping through the Dardanelles (and thus permanent warm water ports for commerce, and a naval presence in the Mediterranean.

- **Napoleon III** of France was intent on winning military achievements to match his uncle's and gain popularity

- Britain regarded the Mediterranean as their lake, and thus a Russian naval presence as an unacceptable intrusion

- Ottomans were trying to stave off collapse; they were already "The Sick Man of Europe"

- Technical dispute over religious authority in Jerusalem, really only a pretext

- Sardinia enters war against Russia to gain leverage with France for unification of Italy

GREAT FIGURES

- **Florence Nightingale** (d. 1854)—addressed the inadequate medical treatment accorded British soldiers. Helped found the modern nursing profession. One of the first women not a monarch or writer to achieve international fame for work in the public realm

- **Alexander II** of Russia (r. 1855–81)—succeeded his father, Nicholas I during the war. Negotiated peace and instituted reforms

OUTCOMES

- Implacable enmity by Russia towards Austria due to its failure to come to its aid during the war

- Sardinia gains a place at the negotiating table allowing **Count Cavour** to work with **Napoleon III**

- Russia reforms and rearms, becoming much more formidable

- Russia was blocked from acquiring access through the **Dardanelles**

- Military embarrassments (e.g. charge of the Light Brigade) and extraordinary number of deaths made engaging in continental warfare very unpopular in Britain. Hence it stood aside during the unifications of Italy and Germany, an ill-judged isolationist policy

- Ottomans staggered on for another half century, although they lost most of their Balkan territories in the years to come

- Balance of power preserved

UNIFICATIONS OF ITALY AND GERMANY

ITALY

Nationalist aspirations for the unification of Italy (**The Risorgimento**) were stimulated during the occupation of the pennisula by Napoleon I. Movements were repressed during the next few decades by the Congress system and Austria in particular. The attempt by **Mazzini** to establish an Italian republic failed in 1848. **Count Camillo di Cavour**, liberal Prime Minister of Sardinia (also called Piedmont or Savoy), a kingdom in northwest Italy, then organized the gradual conquest of the entire peninsula during the late 1850s and early 1860s. By the time of his death in 1861 all but the Pope's territories around Rome and the *irredenta* (unredeemed) in the northeast retained by Austria had been incorporated into a united Kingdom of Italy under the rule of the Sardinian King.

STAGES

1. Cavour entered the Crimean War and gained the alliance of Napoleon III, ever on the lookout for military glory and territorial expansion. Cavour promised Nice and Savoy in exchange for military assistance against Austria
2. Cavour provoked war with Austria and gained Lombardy, but the withdrawal of Napoleon's support left Venetia in Austrian hands (1859)
3. Cavour helped the northern duchies of Modena, Parma, and Tuscany to overthrow their rulers and join the new Italy
4. Cavour assisted rabid nationalist **Garibaldi** (d.1882) invade Sicily and Naples where he overthrew the Bourbon monarchy and marched north towards Rome
5. Cavour blocked Garibaldi's advance on Rome "protecting" the Pope, negotiated absorption of the Kingdom of the Two Sicilies and most of Papal territories into Italy
6. Gained Venetia from Austria during the **Six Weeks War** in 1867
7. Napoleon III had garrisoned Rome to protect Pius IX's remaining land. He was forced to recall these troops during the war with Prussia in 1870 when all but the Vatican itself was incorporated into Italy.

Thus Cavour, the leader of a small, weak country, was able to overcome opposition from France, the Pope, Austria, and the kings and princes of the Italian states. He also overcame the republicanism of Garibaldi and Mazzini. Britain did not intervene due to its isolationist policy despite its great interests in the Mediterranean.

OUTCOMES

- A liberal, constitutional monarchy ruled a united Italian state, though suffrage was limited until 1913

- The North conquered the South, and henceforward the North became the beneficiary of public spending and investment at the expense of the South (most emigrants from Italy fled the poverty of the South)

- The Papacy became a hostile prisoner in the Vatican until finally recognizing Italy in 1929; loses prestige

- The *irredenta* remained a festering wound that played a key role in World War I and the rise of Mussolini

- Italy remained weaker economically and militarily than its size suggested, crippled by corruption and an ineffective political structure

- Cavour never got the credit his work deserved, most of the public praise being given to the King

GERMANY

Nationalist aspirations for the unification of Germany were stimulated by the occupation by Napoleon I, who combined much of central Germany into a new Kingdom of Westphalia. Metternich and other German princes and kings helped dampen the nationalist movement until 1848, and Frederick William IV of Prussia rejected the imperial crown offered by the Frankfurt Parliament. An economic agreement (**Zollverein**) established by Prussia in 1834 made the advantages of unity more obvious.

The Prussian Prime Minister, **Count Otto von Bismarck** (later Prince, d. 1898) a conservative **junker** and Prussian patriot decided the only way to preserve Prussian power was to conquer the rest of Germany and absorb it into a gigantic Prussian state. Like Cavour, he was a master of **Realpolitik**.

STAGES

1. Bismarck provoked war with Denmark in alliance with Austria to seize the border duchies of **Schleswig-Holstein**
2. Bismarck provoked war with Austria, which was defeated rapidly by **Count Helmuth von Moltke** (d. 1891) at the battle of **Sadowa** (1867). Austria was knocked out of contention as leader of a united Germany. The Catholic southern German states that allied with Catholic Austria were not punished, but northern Protestant Hanover was seized and the king overthrown
3. Bismarck goaded **Napoleon III** into war in 1870 (**Franco-Prussian War**). The pretext involved possible **Hohenzollern** succession to the Spanish throne (**Ems Telegram**). Southern German states allied with Prussia against France. Napoleon III was defeated and captured on the battlefield
4. Bismarck persuaded the King of Bavaria, the largest southern Catholic state, to offer the imperial crown to **William I**, King of Prussia, who became **German Emperor** (Deutches Kaiser) in *1871 (ceremony held in the Hall of Mirrors at Versailles)
5. Harsh peace imposed on humiliated France including heavy reparations and confiscation of two border provinces, **Alsace and Lorraine**. France became a perpetual enemy, thus ensuring the continued loyalty of the southern states to Prussian leadership

Thus Bismarck overcame the opposition of Austria, Denmark, the German Princes and Kings, and France to achieve unification. Russia was persuaded to remain neutral and Britain remained in isolation.

OUTCOMES

- German Empire established *1871 headed by **Hohenzollern dynasty** in a federal state where smaller kingdoms and principalities retained their monarchs but in which Prussian power and the authority of the Emperor (Kaiser) predominated

- Bismarck a national hero who retained tight control over the state until his dismissal in 1890

- German Empire built on military victory

- France deeply aggrieved and sought revenge

- Italy gained Papal states and Venetia

- Austrian weakness offers the Hungarians an opportunity to gain more autonomy in the *Ausgleich* (1867) when the **Dual Monarchy** was established sharing a ruler, military, and diplomatic corps, but with a separate parliament and domestic government in Budapest

- **Napoleon III** overthrown and France returned to republican government (**Third Republic**, 1871–1940)

- Bismarck pursued a pacific foreign policy thereafter

- Bismarck established a long-term alliance with Austria, while other states on the periphery increasingly sought security with each other, especially France and Russia, which seemed like encirclement to the Germans and aroused their anxiety

- Bismarck banned the Socialist Party but enacted social legislation to win loyalty of the working class

- Bismarck pursued vendetta against independent sources of power outside his authority, such as the Catholic church—***Kulturkampf***

THE LAST YEARS OF THE CENTURY

The map of Europe in *1871 was simpler in aspect than it ever had been or ever would be in modern times. Four huge empires bestrode the center and east: Russia, Germany, Austria-Hungary, and the Ottomans (most of the Balkans was still technically theirs). In the west Great Britain, France, and Italy controlled most of the territory, along with Spain, Portugal, and the three Scandinavian countries. The only small states were the Benelux countries, Switzerland, Greece, and Montenegro.

FRANCE

Second Empire (Napoleon III) combined progressive economic policies, aggressive foreign policy, and authoritarian institutions. Concessions were made to the working class

The **Paris Commune** (1871)—city felt betrayed by monarchists in the National Assembly, and anarchists and socialists exploited the chaos of defeat by Prussia to establish a radical regime. Suppressed violently

The **Third Republic**, although it lasted from 1871 to 1940 was plagued by instability. Orleanists, Bonapartists, Legitimists (Bourbon line), Socialists, Communists, all lacked loyalty to the established political structures. Only the Liberals were pleased, but they distrusted the military and rightly feared reactionary influences.

Maintenance of the tricolor flag (orig. French Revolution) provoked monarchist antagonism and refusal of the throne by Henry "V", the Bourbon pretender

Military officers, clergy and aristocracy disaffected

Dreyfus Affair (1894) involving espionage charges against an innocent Jewish officer opened up such serious rifts in French society that the Republic barely survived; Zola, "*J'accuse*"

The one shared value was hatred for Germany

French population growth much slower than most other Western countries due to system of land tenure. France lagged in the industrial sector, although its empire in Africa and Asia grew large

AUSTRIA

Austria-Hungary (after 1867) held together by the Habsburg bureaucracy and personal loyalty to **Franz Joseph**

"Dual Monarchy" after *Ausgleich* 1867

Composed of many different nationalities (Poles, Germans, Czechs, Ukrainians, Hungarians, Romanians, Croats, Slovenians, Italians, Serbs, etc.) Some of these groups had aspirations for independence (e.g. Poles) while others yearned to be joined with fellow countrymen already independent (e.g. Serbs).

Competing for territory and influence with Russia as Ottoman authority in the Balkans evaporated

Hungarian zealots repress other nationalities under their control

Vienna a center of medical and cultural excellence; the city center was rebuilt on a grand scale; vicious anti-Semitism aroused there

RUSSIA

Alexander II—(d. 1881) was a modernizing, Westernizing Tsar
- a) serf emancipation (***1861**)
- b) established trial by jury and other legal reforms
- c) established *zemstvos*, local elected councils
- d) military reforms
- e) planed constitution limiting the autocracy

Although serfs were freed from the landlords, the *mir*, a system of shared land tenure tied them to each other; they also were given poor quality land, and had to pay off long-term mortgages to compensate landowners

Smaller gentry also hurt by the serf abolition program, and most were struggling seriously financially or bankrupt before the 1917 revolution began

Secret police and censorship were retained and expanded in the wake of populist and nihilist terror campaigns; numerous attempts made to kill officials, royalty

Limited industrialization

Polish rebellion 1863 crushed

Massive illiteracy and small middle class

Tsar assassinated by terrorists 1881

Alexander III (r. 1881–94) succeeded his murdered father and instituted aggressive and effective repression; halted reforms. He vigorously attempted to impose Russian language and culture on non-Russian peoples in the Empire

Nicholas II (r. 1894–1917) tried to follow his father's policies but was inept and incompetent. He barely survived an attempted **revolution in 1905** after the loss of the **Russo-Japanese War**. He was forced to grant a parliament (**Duma**), but renéged on his promises when he could. His minister, **Stolypin**, introduced land reform, but was assassinated in 1909. **Count Witte** fostered further industrialization, which only created a greater threat to autocracy. Trans-Siberian railway.

Terrible **pogroms** were directed by the state against the Jewish population under Alexander III and Nicholas II

BRITAIN

Queen Victoria (r. 1837–1901) embodied a stricter moral code emanating from the top of society, gloried in the expansion of empire, symbolized stability and grandeur of "Victorian" Britain; Empress of India

Increased moves towards democracy: **Second Reform Act** 1867, expanded electorate; secret ballot 1872; **Third Reform Act** 1884 moved close to universal male suffrage

"**Tory Democracy**"—**Benjamin Disraeli** led the Conservative Party towards electoral reform and paternalistic legislation to win votes from the working class—included public health, sanitation, workers housing, and protection for trade unions

William Gladstone led the Liberal Party in reform legislation; with the Education Act (1870) the government took responsibility for elementary schools; competitive exams for the civil service; reformed universities; free trade

Irish politicians agitated for Irish autonomy (Home Rule) and disrupted British politics; Gladstone accepted **Home Rule** and split the Liberal Party. Home Rule finally granted in 1914, but was deferred by the First World War

House of Lords emasculated by Parliament Act of 1911

Sun never sets on the British Empire

INTELLECTUAL TURMOIL

Competing philosophies developed as responses to the industrial capitalist system as it emerged. Europe was in intellectual and artistic turmoil for most of the nineteenth century. Important responses to industrialization included Romanticism, Classical Economics, Socialism, Anarchism, and Marxism (and also, eventually, Fascism).

ROMANTICISM

Revival of Gothic fantasies, nostalgia for traditional verities and irrational feelings began in the early to mid 18th century in response to the prevailing rationalism of the **Enlightenment** and were further stimulated by the horrors of the "rationalist" reforms and terror of the French Revolution and the ugliness and brutality of the **Industrial Revolution**. The peak of the movement lay c. 1780–1830. It was expressed in literature, religion, architecture, music, painting, poetry, and philosophy.

CHARACTERITICS OF ROMANTICISM
- Value sincerity, authenticity, and toleration

- Value emotions, religion

- Mysticism, spirituality

- Revival of the Gothic (medieval) style; even factories were sometimes built to look like castles

- Harmony with not control over nature

- Interest in the past, history

- Sensuality, eroticism

- Nationalism

- Worship of nature

- Interest in folklore, folksongs, folktales

- Reaction against materialism

IMPORTANT ROMANTICS

- **Rousseau**—(d. 1778) the *philosophe* never entirely comfortable as an Enlightenment figure. Saw society as corrupt in nature, gave children more freedom to develop, uniqueness of each person

- **Kant**—(d. 1804) German sought to reconcile enlightened rationalism with human freedom, immortality, and God

- **Goethe**—(d. 1832) German writer and poet, deep spiritual struggles, feelings beyond polite society, improvement of mankind, reason cannot save us

- **Caspar David Friedrich**—(d. 1840) German painter, Gothic scenes of loneliness and abandonment, beauty of nature

- **J. M. W. Turner**—(d. 1851) English painter, moves almost to abstract style to convey emotions, natural beauty

- **Beethoven**—(d. 1827) German composer, powerful, emotional, sweeping music

- **William Blake**—(d. 1827) English poet and artist, materialism and injustice of society cause receding imagination and spirituality

- **Wordsworth**—(d. 1850) English poet, loss of child-like vision

- **Lord Byron**—(d. 1824) English poet, personal liberty, heroic motivation, died fighting for Greek independence

- **Mary Shelley**—(d. 1851) *Frankenstein*

- **Fichte**—glorification of great persons, the world the creation of mankind; German culture superior to others (1808)

- **Herder**—(d. 1803) German, revival of folk culture; national character or *Volkgeist*; cultural nationalism

- **Hegel**—(d. 1831) German, all cultures are equally necessary, each contributes to the dialectic—thesis, antithesis, and synthesis

CLASSICAL ECONOMICS

Classical Economics embraced **Adam Smith's** philosophy of *laissez-faire*. The Liberal Party in Britain embraced Classical Economic theory for much of the nineteenth century, and **Liberals** across Europe advocated free trade and free markets.

MALTHUS

T. R. Malthus (d. 1834), a demographer, argued that food production increased at an arithmetic rate and unchecked population at a geometric rate. Since food production only expanded slowly, its growth rate imposed a check (along with disease, war, etc.) on population growth. Artificially enhancing the food supply only created long-term problems in population expansion. Malthus was wrong in the short term. It did become possible to increase food production much more rapidly than he thought. However, in the 20th century worry began about population again outstripping the food supply.

RICARDO

Another economist, **David Ricardo** (d. 1823) built on this work to argue that raising wages, which would allow workers to buy more food and thus produce more children, would create an over-supply of workers driving down the market rate for wages and eventually unemployment. Fewer workers raised wages. (**Iron Law of Wages**). This gave employers a philosophical basis to keep wages as low as possible as a "kindness" to workers. The English **New Poor Law** (1834), though admirable in the sense that the government did not rely purely on charity to support the helpless, indigent, and old, as many continental countries did, was harsh in its treatment of the poor for Ricardian reasons. The British government's inhumane response to the Irish Famine in the 1840s was also to some degree based on this thinking, although it did abolish the **Corn Laws** (1846—[corn = wheat], tariffs that artificially kept the price of food high to protect agricultural profits as a means of making cheaper food available. Ricardo was wrong about parents producing an increasing number of children as their wages went up. The reverse turned out to be the case.

SOCIALISM

UTOPIAN SOCIALISM

Early in the 19th century "**Utopian**" **socialists** began to espouse the idea that a humane society must emphasize the needs of the community over the selfishness of individuals. The critique began of Classical economic theory and the practical, cruel outcomes of industrial capitalism. **Saint Simon** (d. 1825) urged that private wealth be put under greater administrative control. **Fourier** (d. 1837) popularized the idea of utopian communities and more liberated social mores. **Robert Owen** (d. 1858) also set up separate communities and encouraged paternalistic management. **Louis Blanc** recognized the potential of the state as an employer of labor.

ANARCHISM

An offshoot of the revolutionary spirit engendered by socialism. At first more of a theoretical device to critique government and society, suggesting the reduction of regimentation as possible and emphasizing decentralization of power. Towards the end of the 19th century it inspired terrorist attacks on authority figures including kings, empresses, parliaments, and a president of the USA.

MARXISM

The most influential socialist philosophy that eventually became a doctrine that ruled nearly half of humanity in the 20th century and was responsible for deaths of as many as 100 million people. **Karl Marx** (d. 1883) was a middle-class German writer, who lived most of his adult life in England supported by journalism and subsidies from the profits of a Manchester factory owned by his cohort **Friedrick Engels**. They jointly wrote *The Communist Manifesto* (*1848).

Marxism (or **Communism**) was based on the notion that the basis of life is class struggle (**dialectical materialism**); the dialectic (see Hegel above) drove history. The triumph of bourgeois **capitalism** that Marx incorrectly identified with several historical events in the 17th and 18th centuries (such as the English Civil War and the French Revolution) created industrialization, which for the first time gave mankind the opportunity to have abundance. It was no longer necessary to struggle for scarce wealth because machines could give everybody a good life. At the same time capitalism would inevitably concentrate resources in fewer and fewer hands until the **proletariat** (industrial **working class**) would be able to overthrow the rich and exterminate them in a bloody revolution. The rich would resist, sincerely believing in the system of laws they had been established to protect their property and in the religion they had had taught to the workers (that acted as a kind of drug) which emphasized submission and rewards in the next world. Society could then be reordered to eliminate the spirit of competition. Even the institutions of the state such as the police, would wither away since crime was a product of unequal distribution of material goods. History would cease since class struggle would no longer be necessary. Near the end of his life Marx acknowledged it might be possible to achieve change in advanced societies by peaceful means. War would no longer be necessary.

Marx was wrong about almost everything he wrote except that capitalism is cruel and that economic forces are central to history. Above all, it became a puzzlement to his followers why wealth did not become concentrated solely in a tiny group of people in the advanced societies such as England and Germany. The Russian revolutionary of 1917, **Lenin**, later came along and retrofitted Marxism in a way that made it possible to justify revolutions in less economically advanced societies such as Russia and China.

LATER NINETEENTH-CENTURY SOCIALISM

Eventually most mainstream socialists moved towards the notion that redistribution of wealth through the agency of the state was necessary to create more humane and workable societies. Socialists varied from those who wished to do this by democratically elected legislatures imposing taxation on the rich to radical revolutionaries who wished to kill all rich people and establish a dictatorship of factory laborers. Virtually all were republicans, although some socialists came to tolerate constitutional monarchies. "Christian Socialism" (F. D. Maurice in England) tied the Fatherhood of God with the Brotherhood of Man.

Socialism flourished in the effluence of raw capitalism. **Trade unionism** developed, and was effective in helping alleviate working conditions and pay. The spread of male suffrage gave workers a voice, and parliamentary socialist parties worked within constitutional bounds to help the poor. Conservatives were forced to modify unrestrained capitalism or perish. First and Second Internationals met.

RUSSIA
- The terrible conditions of early Russian industrialization were a breeding ground for radical politics. Troops shooting protestors in front of the Tsar's palace in 1905 seriously weakened the bond between the monarch and the people (**Bloody Sunday**) precipitated by loss in Russo-Japanese War (1905).

- Marxist exiles, split into the more moderate Mensheviks, who argued Russia had to become fully industrialized before a Marxist society could emerge, and the radical **Bolsheviks** led by **Lenin**.

- Lenin attributed the continued success of capitalism in the West to the new imperialism (which provided new sources of investment), and he argued a small band of elite revolutionaries could seize control even of an unindustrialized society and guide it to the Communist utopia (Vanguard of the Proletariat) This plan was implemented in 1917.

GREAT BRITAIN

- Radical socialism never took root here. The **Labour Party**, representing working class interests, operated through constitutional and electoral channels. Many working men voted for the Conservative and Liberal Parties due to the influence of religion, patriotism, and other factors

- Socialist intellectuals formed the Fabian Society, which advocated a non-revolutionary path to change

- The governing elite began to move away from *laissez-faire* policies, imposed regulations to protect workers, and implemented welfare reforms

FRANCE

- Socialism was fragmented in France. The Anarchists refused to enter the political system

- **Jean Jaurès** led the socialist revisionists

- **Georges Sorel** led the **Syndicalists** (trade unionists)

GERMANY

- Although banned from political activity under Bismarck, the socialists were brought into the parliamentary (**Reichstag**) system under **Wilhelm II**.

- The leading Marxist leader **Eduard Bernstein** advocated "**Revisionism**", a gradualist and peaceful approach to the long-term victory of the proletariat using the existing structure of the state

- **Bismarck** instituted welfare reforms although working conditions remained harsh in Germany

FEMINISM

Feminism emerged in the early 19th century and intertwined at points with socialism and liberalism. **John Stuart Mill** wrote on the subject. Feminists carried on the ideas of **Wollstonecraft** and **de Gouges**. The fight for political rights was more characteristic of England while the French focused on social, cultural, and legal rights. Feminists agitated with increasing force. Progress was made on issues such as parental rights in divorce cases, divorce, and ownership of property but not the vote. The **Pankhursts** in Britain focused on the later issue with great energy. Contraceptive techniques were improved and knowledge about them disseminated more widely.

CULTURAL CONFUSION

The second half of the nineteenth century produced some of the supreme intellectual achievements in human history. It was also a time of darkening visions. One historian described the feeling in early twentieth century Vienna as "Thunder at Twilight". Humans achieved a greatly enhanced understanding of themselves, but the price was an increasing fear that the world was irrational, morality all relative, and that we exist in a state of uncertainty. The idea of "progress" still held the field, but doubt crept in. There was a more healthy and open attitude towards sex, and an unhealthy appetite for war.

INFLUENTIAL INTELLECTUALS
Charles Lyell
Principles of Geology (1832)

Charles Darwin
published *On the Origin of Species* in 1859. His **theory of evolution** changed the way humans looked at themselves. He met fierce resistance from religious critics. His ideas later spawned the racist theory called **Social Darwinism**.

August Comte (d. 1857)
positivism—social improvement to be based on collection of facts—growth of social sciences to be helpful to society

Herbert Spencer (d. 1903)
evolutionary ethics, Social Darwinism

Theodor Herzel (d. 1904)
Zionism

Pius IX (d. 1878)
the ostrich approach to modern science—ignore it—*Syllabus of Errors*; Vatican I—Pope is infallible when speaking *ex cathedra* (1870)

Leo XIII (d. 1903)
reconciled science with faith and Scripture—***Rerum Novarum***

Gregor Mendel (d. 1884)
genetics

Sir James Frazer (d. 1941)
anthropology

Louis Pasteur (d. 1895)
Pasteurization, vaccinations

Marie Curie (d. 1934)
isolated radium

Pavlov (d. 1936)
behavioralism, "conditioning"

Max Planck (d. 1947)
quantum theory of energy

Albert Einstein (d. 1955)
theory of **relativity**

Lord Rutherford (d. 1937)
nuclear physics

Walter Heisenberg (d. 1976)
uncertainty principle

Sigmund Freud (d. 1939)
psychoanalysis. Human sexual impulses form personality—id, ego, superego. Dreams are the fulfillment of suppressed wishes

Friedrich Nietzsche (d. 1900)
challenged existing morality and values; God is dead; will to power; Christianity the religion of the weak

Schliemann
modern Archeology

Picasso (d. 1973)
pre 1914 period develops **Cubism**, portrays people in inhuman forms

The response to these intellectual developments and world events was increasingly inchoate and pessimistic. The British novelist, **Charles Dickens**, depicted grim realities. The Russian **Count Tolstoy** in his great novels, especially *War and Peace*, saw mankind as victims of fate. Flaubert and Zola rejected Romanticism in a spirit of harsh realism. Ibsen and Shaw were also not optimistic about the human condition and drew searing portraits of inhumanity. Munch's famous painting of an alienated man holding his head, "The Scream" (1908), symbolized profound despair. More romantic impulses fueled Wagner's operas and the beauty of French **Impressionist** paintings.

IMPORTANT DEFINITIONS AND IDENTIFICATIONS

- Alexander II of Russia
- Alexander III of Russia
- Alsace Loraine
- Anarchism
- *Ausgleich*
- Beethoven
- Eduard Bernstein
- Otto von Bismarck
- William Blake
- Louis Blanc
- Bloody June Days
- Bloody Sunday
- Bolsheviks
- Lord Byron
- Capitalism
- Chartists
- Classical Economics
- Communism
- *Communist Manifesto*
- August Comte
- Corn Laws
- Count von Bismarck
- Count Cavour
- Cubism
- Marie Curie
- Dardanelles
- Charles Darwin
- dialectical materialism
- Charles Dickens
- Disraeli
- Dreyfus Affair
- Dual Monarchy
- Duma
- Einstein
- Ems Telegram
- Friedrich Engels
- The Enlightenment
- The Theory of Evolution
- Feminism
- Fichte
- Fourier
- Frankfurt Parliament
- Franco-Prussian War
- Franz Joseph of Austria-Hungary
- Sir James Frazer
- Frederick Wilhelm IV of Prussia
- Sigmund Freud
- David Caspar Friedrich
- Garibaldi
- German Emperor
- William Gladstone
- Goethe
- Olympe de Gouges
- *Gross Deutsch* plan
- Hegel
- Walter Heisenberg
- Herder
- Hohenzollern dynasty
- Home Rule for Ireland
- Impressionism
- Industrial Revolution
- Iron Law of Wages
- *Irredenta*
- Jean Jaurès
- Junker
- Kant
- *Klein Deutsch* plan
- *Kulturkampf*
- Labour Party (Great Britain)
- *laissez-faire*
- Lenin
- Pope Leo XIII
- Liberalism
- Charles Lyell
- Thomas Robert Malthus
- Karl Marx
- Marxism

- materialism
- Mazzini
- Gregor Mendel
- Mensheviks
- Prince Metternich
- John Stuart Mill
- Count von Moltke
- Napoleon III of France
- New Poor Law
- Nicholas I of Russia
- Nicholas II of Russia
- Friedrich Nietzsche
- Florence Nightingale
- *On the Origin of Species*
- Robert Owen
- Pankhursts
- Paris Commune
- Louis Pasteur
- Pavlov
- Picasso
- Pope Pius IX
- Max Planck
- Positivism

- Proletariat
- psychoanalysis
- *Realpolitik*
- *Reichstag*
- The Theory of Relativity
- *Rerum Novarum*
- Revisionism
- Revolution of 1905 (Russia)
- David Ricardo
- Risorgimento
- Romanticism
- Rousseau
- Russo-Japanese War
- Lord Rutherford
- Battle of Sadowa
- Saint Simon
- Schleswig-Holstein
- Heinrich Schliemann
- Second Empire
- Second Reform Act (Britain)
- Mary Shelley
- Six Weeks War
- Adam Smith

- Social Darwinism
- socialism
- Georges Sorel
- Stolypin
- Syndicalism
- Third Reform Act (Britain)
- Third Republic
- Count Tolstoy
- "Tory Democracy"
- trades unionism
- J.M.W.Turner
- Utopian Socialism
- Victoria of Britain
- Wilhelm I of Germany
- Wilhelm II of Germany
- Count Witte
- Mary Wollstonecraft
- Wordsworth
- Working class
- "Young Italy"
- *Zollverein*

IMPORTANT DATES

*1848 Year of uprisings and revolutions

publication of the *Communist Manifesto*

1853–56 Crimean War

1859 publication of *On the Origin of Species*

*1861 Serf Emancipation in Russia

1867 *Ausgleich* splits Austria and Hungary into Dual Monarchy

*1871 Franco-Prussian War

Proclamation of the German Empire

Paris Commune

Foundation of the Third Republic

1905 Russo-Japanese War

*1914 Outbreak of First World War

1917 Russian Revolution

CHAPTER 8
MULTIPLE-CHOICE QUESTIONS

Questions 1.1–1.3 refer to the creation of the German Empire in 1871 the proclamation of which is depicted in the painting below.

1.1 The figure in this painting wearing the white uniform was Chancellor Otto von Bismarck. Why is he standing at the center rather than Emperor Wilhelm I?

(A) Bismarck was made the Emperor of the new state
(B) Bismarck's statesmanship led to the creation of the empire
(C) Wilhelm I was too mentally unbalanced and aggressive to be allowed to rule
(D) It was clear the monarchy would not last for long

1.2 The proclamation of the German Empire took place in a French palace because?

(A) Bismarck preferred French culture
(B) Wilhelm I was visiting his friend Napoleon III
(C) France had just been defeated in a war that made way for the German Empire to be founded
(D) The Palace of Versailles was the largest building in Europe and so seen as an appropriate setting

1.3 The Hall of Mirrors at Versailles illustrated here would also be the site of what other event in modern German history?

(A) Commemoration celebrations of the founding of the German Empire in 1896
(B) The dissolution of the German Empire in 1919
(C) Hitler's establishment of the Vichy Republic in 1940
(D) The end of the Second World War in Europe in 1945

Questions 2.1–2.3 relate to the following document.

A band of wicked men, chiefly consisting of foreigners, who, although searched for, have succeeded in concealing themselves for more than a week, and have filled the minds of my faithful and beloved Berliners with thoughts of vengeance for supposed bloodshed; and thus have become the fearful authors of bloodshed themselves. My troops, your brothers and fellow country-men, did not make use of their weapons till forced to do so by several shots fired at them.

It is now yours, inhabitants of my beloved native city, to avert a fearful evil. Acknowledge your fatal error; your King, your trusting friend, enjoins you, by all that is most sacred, to acknowledge your fatal error. Return to peace; remove the barricades which are still standing; and send to me men filled with the genuine ancient spirit of Berlin, speaking words which are seemly to your King; and I pledge you my royal truth that all the streets and squares shall be instantaneously cleared of troops…. Listen to the paternal voice of your King.

Your loving Queen, and truly your genuine mother and friend, who is lying on a sick bed, joins her heartfelt and tearful supplications to mine.

Frederick William IV, King of Prussia, address, 1848

2.1 To what degree do you think this statement reflects the true sentiments of the king towards the radical populace of Berlin?

(A) He fully understands the demands of the people and agrees with them
(B) He is delusional and cannot understand anything that is going on
(C) He is trying to appeal to moderates and isolate the radicals
(D) He is optimistic that further bloodshed can be avoided

2.2 The principal demand made by the protesters to which Frederick William IV finally agreed was which of the following?

(A) A new constitution
(B) Religious reforms
(C) His abdication
(D) Unification with the Netherlands

2.3 The Parliament that met in Frankfurt in 1848 did which of the following?

(A) Declared Germany a republic
(B) Ousted Frederick William from the throne of Prussia
(C) Offered Frederick William IV the imperial crown of a united Germany
(D) Declared the unification of Germany excluding Prussia

Questions 3.1–3.3 relate to the following passage.

The 1871 Paris Commune's socialist origins were vague and its socialist intentions, dubious. It disappeared, leaving scarcely a trace on the institutional life or development of France.

It has been rescued, however, from its somewhat insignificant position as an incident in the history of France, by the activity of the socialists and communists. In their hands it has become an event of world-shaking importance, a proletarian and socialist revolution par excellence, and the first real government of the working class. The Commune of Paris is, in the opinion of the communists, the immediate forbear of the Russian Soviet.

Was it proletarian and was it socialist? Was it a revolutionary class struggle or something quite other than this? The Marxian version has it that the Commune was socialist because it was proletarian, "for the proletariat can fight for no other cause than socialism." But this is a complete non sequitur to any other than a believer in Marxian theory of an economically determined class struggle in which the participants are a class-conscious proletariat and class-conscious bourgeoisie.

The Commune of Paris, as a matter of fact, sprang from an exceedingly complicated historical situation. Irritation and disgust at the loss of the [Franco-Prussian] war, the misery of the four-month siege of Paris, the struggle of republicanism against monarchy, socialist desires and aspirations clothed in the ideas of Proudhon and Blanqui, all mingled inextricably in the causes of the revolution. No simple explanation such as that implied in the socialist theory of the class struggle can be accepted.

Edward S. Mason, historian, *The Paris Commune*, 1930

3.1 The author of this passage argues that the true history of the Commune has been distorted for which of the following reasons?

(A) Because it was too complicated to be explained easily
(B) Proudhon and Blanqui wrote the early accounts
(C) To serve a political cause
(D) Because not all the facts were available

3.2 Which great event did the Paris Commune happen in the midst of?

(A) The rise of Emperor Napoleon III
(B) The struggle for German unification
(C) The restoration of the Bourbon dynasty
(D) The disintegration of the French empire overseas

3.3 Karl Marx regarded the revolutions in Paris in 1848 and 1871 as

(A) The path to socialism in Russia
(B) A huge setback for communism
(C) Spoiled by the intervention of the Pope
(D) The seeds of the destruction of capitalism

Questions 4.1–4.3 relate to the following passage.

Are we then to conclude, that the only effect of the Reform Act of 1832 has been to create in this country another of those class interests which we now so loudly accuse as the obstacles to general amelioration? Not exactly that. The indirect influence of the Reform Act has been not inconsiderable, and may eventually lead to vast consequences. It set men a-thinking; it enlarged the horizon of political experience; it led the public mind to ponder somewhat on the circumstance of our national history; to pry into the beginnings of some social anomalies, which they found, were not so ancient as they had been led to believe, and which had their origin in causes very different from what they had been educated to credit; and insensibly it created and prepared a popular intelligence to which one can appeal, no longer hopelessly, in an attempt to dispel the mysteries with which for nearly three centuries it has been the labour of party writers to involve a national history, and without the dispersion of which no political position can be understood and no social evil remedied.

Benjamin Disraeli, *Sybil or the Two Nations*, 1845

4.1 What was Disraeli's view of the impact of the First Reform Act of 1832?

(A) It had positive outcomes
(B) He was indifferent to it
(C) It had negative outcomes
(D) He wants it reversed

4.2 Disraeli, a leader of the Conservative party, believed it was possible to do which of the following?

(A) Create a complete democracy in Britain
(B) Have the Conservatives make an alliance with the mass of voters
(C) Crush the Communist Party
(D) Hoodwink the ignorant masses into acting against their own self-interest

4.3 Disraeli was later the author of the Second Reform Act (1867) that enfranchised which group?

(A) Universal suffrage
(B) Women
(C) The peerage
(D) Property owners

Questions 5.1–5.3 refer to the work of Florence Nightingale during the Crimean War illustrated below.

5.1 Florence Nightingale and over 30 nurses arrived in 1854 to tend soldiers wounded in the Crimean War. This conflict involved which nations?

(A) Britain, France, and the Ottoman Empire against Russia
(B) France, Italy, and Germany against Russia
(C) Spain and England against the United States
(D) Germany against Austria and France

5.2 Nightingale's pursuit of nursing in a theater of war was

(A) Derided by the press
(B) Rejected by the wounded
(C) Transformed views about women
(D) Blocked by physicians jealous of her publicity

5.3 Thanks to Nightingale nursing

(A) Began to be regarded as of higher status than being a physician
(B) Became the first professional career open to women
(C) Was banned as a profession open to women
(D) Led to a large intake of women into the legal and military professions

Questions 6.1–6.3 relate to the 1913 cartoon entitled "Mr. McKenna, Forcible-Feeder-in-Chief to the Cabinet, has described with moving candour the loving and chivalrous care, the almost pious delicacy, with which the Government treats those of its Suffragist enemies who fall into their tender hands" reproduced below

6.1 The message of this cartoon is which of the following?

   (A) Support for the treatment of Suffragette prisoners by the Government

   (B) Critical of the brutality of the Government in the treatment of Suffragette prisoners

   (C) Indifferent amusement to the fate of Suffragette prisoners

   (D) Critical of the passivity of Suffragette prisoners

6.2 This cartoon contrasts the

   (A) Insensitivity of men to the innocence of women

   (B) Criminality of violent Suffragettes to the peaceful response of the Government

   (C) Guilt on both sides of the issue

   (D) Gentleness of Government treatment to the violent resistance of the Suffragettes

6.3 The campaign for women's suffrage can be characterized in which of the following ways?

   (A) Just began to emerge as significant in 1913

   (B) Built up over the course of the second half of the 19th century

   (C) Had become a minor issue by 1913

   (D) Was counterproductive the longer it went on

SHORT-ANSWER QUESTION

Question 1

Who are these old men and women? They are the veterans of industry, people of almost endless toil, who have fought for and won the industrial supremacy of Great Britain. Is their lot and end to be the Bastille of everlasting pauperism? The laborer has a right to some consideration from the State. Here in a country rich beyond description there are people poverty-stricken beyond description. There can be no earthly excuse for the condition of things which exists in this country today. If it is necessary to have a strong Army and Navy to protect the wealth of the nation, do not let us forget that it is the veterans of industry who have created that wealth; let us accept this proposed state pension scheme as an installment to bring decency and comfort to our aged men and women.

Henry Herbert Asquith, speech in the House of Commons, July 9, 1908

H. H. Asquith became leader of the Liberal Party and Prime Minister of Great Britain in 1908. The Liberals proposed a state-funded pension and other welfare measures followed. Based on this quotation and your knowledge of European history answer the questions below (A and B).

A) Identify and explain ONE argument Liberals made to justify giving pensions to workers funded by taxes paid by the middle and upper classes.
B) Identify and explain TWO ways in which Asquith's Liberalism had changed from earlier, nineteenth-century Liberalism.

CHAPTER 9

WORLD SUPREMACY

Spain and Portugal had established large empires in the 16th century followed by the Dutch, French, and British. By the 1820s, however, much territory had been lost or influence shifted among the imperial powers. For example, the British lost the Thirteen Colonies in North America in 1783 and the Spanish empire in South America evaporated in the 1820s. However, Britain established an "informal" empire in places such as Argentina and Brazil in which they came largely to dominate the financial and commercial operations of those countries. Although the British lost territory in North America its grip tightened over the immense population of the subcontinent of India, where the French, Portuguese and Dutch were mostly expelled. The latter country continued to hold a vast empire in the East Indies (today Indonesia), but it lost the chance to assert control over Australia and Malaya which were acquired by the British. During the nineteenth century many countries competed over the prostrate body of China in decline, but the British crushed Qing military forces in two wars and established key trading centers in **Hong Kong** and Shanghai. They even took over the revenue administration of the country, doling out money to the government like a parent giving a teenager an allowance.

Two explosive surges of European influence across the globe took place in the nineteenth century, emigration and the colonization of Africa, although the rush by Russia and the United States and Britain to explore and conquer Central Asia, Siberia, and the western half of North America were also massive extensions the European global reach.

EMIGRATION

Emigration from Europe reached a peak in the late nineteenth and early twentieth centuries. Cheap steamboat transportation made it possible for even poor families to travel, often with a father going first, and then earning the money to allow his wife and children to follow. People fled political oppression, religious persecution, famine, and poverty. Ireland, southern Italy, and Russia produced the greatest number, but people also sought a new life in proportionally high numbers from Scandinavia, Spain, and Germany. Destinations included North and South America, Asiatic Russia, and Australia.

MAP OF EUROPEAN COLONIES IN 1900

THE NEW WAVE OF IMPERIALISM

During the second half of the 19th century, especially between 1880 and 1900, European powers used their military and economic might to impose control on vast new portions of the globe, notably in Africa and the Pacific. As most colonies won independence in the 1940s–70s, views on imperialism both among the colonized and the European intelligentsia were almost wholly negative and condemnatory. Most historians also concluded that only in certain instances did Europeans actually net a profit from imperial control. Often they ruled at a loss. In recent years African, Asian, and European historians have begun to see the process in a less ideological way and noted the benefits as well as the losses and humiliations inherent in the process.

CAUSES OF THE "SCRAMBLE FOR AFRICA" AND ELSEWHERE

- Search for more markets from European manufactured goods

- Search for raw materials: rubber, coco, gold, diamonds, oil, and minerals

- **Missionaries** sought to convert non-Christian peoples

- "Keeping up with the Joneses"—search for status and desire not to "fall behind"

- **Explorers** and adventurers desiring to visit uncharted regions

- Need for supply and **coaling stations** for ships

- Need to secure strategic points in order to protect existing empires(e.g. **Suez Canal**, Malta, Cape Town, Singapore)

- Search for places to invest capital

- **Social Darwinism**—sense of racial superiority, paternalism, "White Man's Burden"

- Discovery of quinine made penetration of malarial areas, especially in Africa, possible for the first time

- Railways, telegraph, the machine gun, steamboats, etc. used to control vast areas cheaply

THE OUTCOMES OF NEW IMPERIALISM

GREAT BRITAIN

- Britain secured a dominant global position not seriously challenged until 1914, and not wholly lost until after World War II

- control of the **Suez Canal**, Malta, and Gibraltar made the Mediterranean a British lake until 1945

- fought to suppress **Boer** control of mineral rich South Africa (1899–1902)—gold, diamonds

- Huge empire in Africa

- Asserted control over Australia, New Zealand and many islands in the Pacific

- A dominant commercial force in China and South America

- Vast empire in South Asia: India, Ceylon, Burma, Malaya, Singapore, Borneo, New Guinea

- Lays undersea telegraph cables that connect all populated areas of the planet in real time

- Refrigerated ships open global trade in meat and fruit. Britain controls a large proportion of all commercial shipping and most maritime insurance

FRANCE

- French empire smaller but important to trade and national pride and identity

- Came into conflict with Britain (**Fashoda**) and Germany (Morocco)

HOLLAND

- Dutch empire did not expand, but discovery of oil in the East Indies sustained power at a higher level than Holland's size would otherwise have justified

GERMANY

- The Germans got the booby prizes, the pickings left over after the British and French had finished. Heightened German paranoia and tension with Britain and France

ITALY

- Like the Germans, Italy came late to the final upsurge of imperialism. It gained Libya but lost in a war to take over Ethiopia, injuring national pride

JAPAN

- Japan industrialized rapidly in the later nineteenth century and became an imperial power in its own right. It defeated China and Russia in the 1890s and 1905. Made an alliance with Britain to allow the latter to concentrate its fleet in home waters to defend against Germany

UNITED STATES

- The USA became a major imperial power in China and the Pacific. Purchased Alaska from Russia. Defeated Spain in 1898 and took the Philippines and Puerto Rico. Builds **Panama Canal**

PROS AND CONS OF THE NEW IMPERIALISM	
PROS	CONS
• The standard of living in Western Europe rose and the range of consumer products was greatly diversified. • Huge improvements in infrastructure were made in the colonies: roads, railways, ports, bridges, etc. built. The gigantic British railway system in India remains one of the country's most prized possessions. • Hospitals, schools opened. • Children of native elites were educated in Britain and France. • New agricultural techniques and crops were introduced, and famines relieved or eliminated. • Cruel and inhumane native practices abolished (Sati, head-hunting, etc.) and slavery largely ended • Some conquered people had long been ruled by invaders (India, for example, with its Persian emperors), and the replacement by European rulers was often a matter of indifference or even an improvement	• Lower class workers in Europe were persuaded by their governments that they were racially superior masters over the colonized and "inferior" peoples of Asia and Africa. This lessened social tension at home and created a cross-class shared sense of national mission and solidarity based on **Social Darwinist** ideologies • Cruel and inhumane treatment of some native peoples by Europeans, especially in **Leopold II** of Belgium's Congo and the Germans in South West Africa • **"One crop" agriculture** introduced in many British and French possessions. Native peoples who were previously protected from poor weather and war by being able to fall back on alternative crops were now vulnerable to the rise and fall of world markets and a cash economy • Terrible famines continued in India and China, sometimes exacerbated by imperialist policies (although also simply tied to weather events) • Many peoples were humiliated, degraded and infantilized by "superior" European rulers who pursued the home country's advantage at the expense of aboriginal peoples • The ruthlessness of colonial rule spilled over back into political and social systems in the home countries

SECOND INDUSTRIAL REVOLUTION

After 1850 industrialization was stimulated by a number of innovations that constituted a new technological era.

- **Bessemer process** of steel making, which made it possible to build much stronger ships, bridges, buildings, and other large structures.

- The decline of the whaling industry put pressure on explorers and scientists to find alternative sources of oil. The invention of the **turbine** (1884) and gasoline fueled **internal combustion engine** (1884) created a huge demand for petroleum, first exploited in Pennsylvania, the Caspian region, Persia, and the East Indies. **Petroleum** was a much more efficient fuel to power ships and vital for the operation of automobiles.

- The **vulcanization** process (1844) for rubber made it possible to use the product for clothing and in machinery, making it a vital commodity in the second half of the century. Automobiles (Daimler 1887) would not have been possible without rubber for tires. Until the development of synthetics in the mid-twentieth century rubber helped ensure the continuation of European and American global dominance.

- Discovery of large quantities of diamonds made it possible to develop cutting instruments for metal using industrial stones. This allowed for much more accuracy in machining manufactured products.

- Discoveries of new chemical dyes allowed whole new industries to emerge and provided high quality products traded around the world. Advancements in chemical research improved manufacturing processes and the creation of new products such as **dynamite**. The latter made construction of tunnels and canals much easier and made war much deadlier.

- Understanding and mastering **electricity** made it possible to create electric light and small machines that operated everything from pumps to elevators radically reducing the amount of human and animal labor necessary to operate farms, factories, and cities.

- The **telegraph** and **telephone** radically transformed communication and made colonies easier to rule. Commerce expanded exponentially.

MATURE INDUSTRIALIZATION

Turbines and electric motors made it possible to cross the Atlantic in less than a week and unclog urban traffic with underground railway systems. Refrigeration transformed the commerce in fresh vegetables, fish, fruit, and meat.

Research into "flight" was advanced enough so that by 1914 war could be conducted in the air, while submersible vessels made **submarines** a new menace that threatened Britain's naval superiority.

Industrial organization moved to a larger and larger scale, particularly in the coal and steel industries and armaments. This was made possible by the legal reforms establishing protection for shareholders from indebtedness (**Limited Liability**—Ltd.), and the creation of cartels (Krupp in Germany, Vickers Armstrong in England, Schneider-Creusot in France).

A **consumer economy** developed characterized by sophisticated advertising, department stores, inexpensive luxuries. Mass circulation newspapers and magazines appeared.

Child labor and working hours for adults declined. **Welfare legislation** was introduced in many countries to provide for sickness and injury, pensions, and education.

The draft was introduced or reformed in many countries both to provide the number of troops required for modern mass armies and to bind young people from diverse regions into a single patriotic mass.

The rise of a very large middle class in the developed countries created dramatic demand for schools and eventually more universities. The **professions** expanded rapidly and set standards for admission—teachers, physicians, engineers, etc. The officer corps grew large as armies expanded into multi-million man organizations. Many new occupations of a "white collar" nature such as secretaries, typists, telephonists, clerks, while they did not pay very well, created a "**lower middle class**" separate from factory workers.

Jews were gradually emancipated in most countries, although anti-Semitism was serious in France and Austria, and horrific in Russia.

Aristocrats were challenged in more and more ways, by democracy, promotion by merit, industrial wealth, and a popular press. However, many retained considerable riches and power.

Urbanization continued to progress as more and more people moved from rural areas into cities. Poor housing and sanitation remained, but improvements were made and fewer outbreaks of disease occurred. The centers of many major cities were redesigned and public parks built (Paris under **Baron Haussmann** saw the most radical transformation). Large broad boulevards, museums, subways systems, parks, zoos, and new monuments such as the Eiffel Tower were built. Suburbs expanded.

Women remained dependent on and legally inferior to men. Middle class women did not work and those in the lower classes suffered inferior pay. Most now withdrew from the labor force upon marriage. However, feminism was gathering support, focused largely on gaining the vote and legal equality for women. New technologies such as electricity and vacuum cleaners created an easier work environment at home.

Compared with other areas of the world, Europeans in the developed regions married late, had smaller families, lived longer, and accumulated more wealth. Many families practiced contraception.

IMPORTANT DEFINITIONS AND IDENTIFICATIONS

- Bessemer process
- Boer War
- cartels
- coaling stations
- consumer economy
- dynamite
- electricity
- emigration
- Fashoda
- Baron Haussmann

- Hong Kong
- internal combustion engine
- Leopold II of Belgium
- Limited Liability
- lower middle class
- missionaries
- "one crop" agriculture
- Panama Canal
- petroleum
- professions

- "scramble for Africa"
- Social Darwinism
- submarines
- Suez Canal
- telegraph
- telephone
- turbine
- urbanization
- vulcanization
- welfare legislation

IMPORTANT DATES

1880–1900   "Scramble for Africa"

*1914   First World War

CHAPTER 9
MULTIPLE-CHOICE QUESTIONS

Questions 1.1–1.3 relate to the following passage.

It is well known that Indian widows sometimes sacrifice themselves on the funeral pile of their husbands, and such victims are called *suttees* (the practice of *sati*). The practice is ascribed by our missionaries to the degraded condition to which a women who outlives her husband is condemned. It is more probable that the hopes of immediately entering on the enjoyment of heaven and of entitling the husband to the same felicity, as well as the glory attending such a voluntary sacrifice, are sufficient to excite the few enthusiastic spirits who go through this awful trial.

The sight of a widow burning is a most painful one; but it is hard to say whether the spectator is most affected by pity or admiration. The more than human serenity of the victim, and the respect which she receives from those around her, are heightened by her gentle demeanor. One is humiliated to think that so feeble a being can be elevated by superstition to a self-devotion not surpassed by the noblest examples of patriots and martyrs.

On the other hand, frightful instances have occurred of women bursting from amidst the flames, and being thrust back by the assistants.

As the Hindus insisted that the rite was a part of their religion, the English did not for many years venture to oppose it by the making of any law. At length, Lord William Bentinck, Governor General, proposed in 1829 a regulation in Council declaring all who abetted the *suttee* to be guilty of "culpable homicide." There was opposition on the part of Europeans as well as natives, but the regulation was carried.

Mountstuart Elphinstone, Indian Customs and Manners, 1840.

1.1 How would you characterize Elphinstone's attitude towards Indians who participated in *sati*?

(A) Horror and disgust at a barbaric ritual
(B) Whole-hearted approval of courage and devotion
(C) Mixed feelings of revulsion and admiration
(D) Disdain prompted by European sense of superiority

1.2 Why might British officials have been reluctant to end the practice of *sati* before 1829?

(A) Admiration for Indian religion
(B) Fear of allowing the practice to become a focus of political protest
(C) Desire to separate commercial and religious relationships with Indians
(D) Keeping down the rapid rate of population growth

1.3 The Indian "Mutiny" of 1857 (First War of Independence) led to which of the following outcomes?

(A) The British take-over of China
(B) Ending of direct British rule over India
(C) Prompted Russian attempts to invade India through Afghanistan
(D) Confirmed fears religion could ignite rebellion

Questions 2.1–2.3 relate to the following passage.

Egypt may now almost be said to form part of Europe. It is the high road to the Far East. It can never cease to be an object of interest to all powers of Europe, and especially to England. European capital to a large extent has been sunk in the country. The rights and privileges of Europeans are jealously guarded.

It has to be borne in mind that in 1882 the [Egyptian] army was in a state of mutiny; the treasury was bankrupt; every branch of the administration had been dislocated.

It may be doubted whether any instance can be quoted of a sudden transfer of power in any civilized or semi-civilized community to a class so ignorant as the pure Egyptians, such as they were in the year 1882.

By the process of exhausting all other expedients, we arrive at the conclusion that armed British intervention was, under the special circumstances of the case, the only possible solution of the difficulties which existed in 1882.

Earl of Cromer, *Modern Egypt*, 1908

2.1 What vital concern does Lord Cromer, the senior British official in Egypt 1883–1907, leave undiscussed in making his case for the imperial take-over of Egypt in 1882?

(A) Fear of a military rival such as Russia or France pushing Britain out of Egypt
(B) Desire to improve medical care for Egyptians
(C) Concern about the state of ancient monuments in Egypt
(D) The chaotic state of the Egyptian army and government

2.2 Egypt became particularly important to Great Britain in 1869 after what event took place?

(A) The conquest of the Island of Cyprus
(B) The Italian invasion of Ethiopia
(C) The Independence of Greece
(D) The opening of the Suez Canal

2.3 Why might the British have decided to leave the native ruler of Egypt in office after taking control of the country in 1882?

(A) He provided a public front behind which the British could rule without antagonizing nationalist feelings
(B) Because of the Muslim respect for Queen Victoria, the British feared a backlash if they overthrew the monarchy
(C) He was also the ruler of other African territories that the British did not control
(D) He was too powerful to remove

Questions 3.1–3.3 refer to the statistical table below.

HEALTHY AND UNHEALTHY LOCATIONS AS EVIDENCED BY TROOP MORTALITY

Location	Troop nationality	Period	Death rate per thousand
New Zealand	British	1846–55	9
Cape Colony (S. Africa)	British	1845–49	10
Canada	British	1818–36	6
Gibraltar	British	1817–36	21
Bombay	British	1830–38	37
Bengal (India)	British	1830–38	71
Martinique, WI	French	1819–36	112
Jamaica, WI	British	1817–36	130
Senegal (W. Africa)	French	1819–28	165
East Indies	Dutch	1819–28	170
Sierra Leone (W. Africa)	British	1819–36	483

3.1 Why was Sierra Leone in Africa so much more deadly than New Zealand?

(A) Hostile native population in Sierra Leone
(B) Endemic malaria in West Africa
(C) Absence of hostile indigenous population in New Zealand
(D) War with France in Sierra Leone

3.2 According to these statistics mortality was lowest

(A) The further the troops were stationed from the equator
(B) In the Americas
(C) In Africa
(D) In India

3.3 The European powers imposed imperialism later in which region?

(A) India
(B) North America
(C) The West Indies
(D) Equatorial Africa

Questions 4.1–4.3 refers to Queen Victoria of Great Britain, Empress of India pictured in 1893 with an Indian servant in the photograph below.

4.1 Queen Victoria allowed herself to be photographed intending viewers to believe all of the following EXCEPT?

(A) She was hardworking
(B) She supported the Suffragettes
(C) She was mistress of an empire
(D) She was a responsible monarch

4.2 How is the relationship between the Queen and the Indian man portrayed?

(A) A European woman friends with an Asian man
(B) An Asian man serving a European woman
(C) The Indian is a superior being looking down on the Queen
(D) The Queen despises Asians

4.3 India was valuable to Great Britain in the 19th century for which of the following reasons?

(A) It supplied fish and coal
(B) It provide a market for British goods
(C) The shipbuilding industry was very large
(D) A source of immigrant factory workers

SHORT-ANSWER QUESTION

Question 1

The only healthy alternative to the European living alongside an inferior race is he should go and completely drive out the inferior race. That is practically what the white man has done in North America. I venture to assert, then, that the struggle for existence between white and red man, painful and even terrible as it was in its details, has given us a good far outbalancing its immediate evil. In place of the red man, contributing practically nothing to the work and thought of the world, we have a great nation, mistress of many arts, and able, with its youthful imagination and fresh, untrammeled impulses, to contribute much to the common stock of civilized man.

Karl Pearson, *National Life from the Standpoint of Science*, 1900

The passage above was written by a mathematician and statistician who embraced imperialism as an expression of natural selection and asserted that his was a "scientific" view. Based on the quotation and your knowledge of European history answer the questions below (A and B).

A) Identify and explain ONE argument made by Social Darwinists to justify their argument that Europeans had the right to establish colonies elsewhere in the world.
B) Identify and explain TWO arguments besides the Social Darwinist one used by Europeans to justify the expense and cost in lives of creating a colonial empire.

CHAPTER 10

WAR, REVOLUTION AND DICTATORSHIP

WORLD WAR I (*1914–*1918)

The Great War, as it was known until *1939, was the most important formative event of the 20th century. It also killed more people that any other human activity in history up until that time. Its horror was only exceeded by the Second World War, and in the case of France and Britain far fewer soldiers were killed 1939–45 than 1914–18. It is hard to assign blame to any single country or person for the outbreak of this war, although Serbia stands as perhaps the guiltiest, with Germany not far behind. However, even the English concealment of a military agreement with France, which led to German miscalculation, was also a factor.

CAUSES OF THE FIRST WORLD WAR

DIPLOMATIC

- The **alliance systems** (see listing below) that developed after 1871 to provide security eventually became seen as threats and dragged countries uninvolved in the immediate dispute that led to war into the maelstrom. While Bismarck was in office, he was able to structure alliances that retained the balance of power in a way his successors could not

- Austria sought promises of support from Germany. Germany issued a "**blank check**", essentially giving Austria total control over the diplomatic situation and urged Austria to solve the Serbian threat once and for all. Austrians issued an ultimatum demanding a major surrender of Serbian national integrity

- Serbia sought support from Russia. Russia threatened to "mobilize" against Austria but the **mobilization plan** could only be implemented against Austria and Germany together, as it was always assumed any war fought against one would be fought against both

- Russia sought support from France. France issued a "blank check" to Russia

141

- On the German invasion of France through Belgium (part of the **Schlieffen Plan**) Britain demanded German withdrawal due to an 1830 treaty protecting Belgium, but in reality because a secret diplomatic agreement with France required it to lend aid to Paris (part of the **Entente Cordiale**)

IMPERIALISM
- Imperial rivalries created tensions and distrust

- First and second Moroccan Crises—German threats and aggression against French interests in Africa (1905, 1911)

POLITICAL
- Gradual collapse of the Ottoman Empire created instability and tempted the greedy—"Sick Man of Europe"

- The character of Kaiser **Wilhelm II**—unstable, paranoid, politically insensitive, aggressive. He created alarm and fear even when no harm was meant

- The character of Tsar **Nicholas II**, weak, prevaricating, and inept

- Russian bitterness towards Austria both for its failure to help in the Crimean War and annexation of **Bosnia** without giving promised support to Russia to open the Dardanelles to Russian ships

MILITARY SECURITY
- German fears that Russia, when fully industrialized, would overpower all other continental powers, and dictate to Europe—Germany had no natural frontier to protect her on the East

- The "Tirpitz" naval build up in Germany, for which the British could see no purpose except an attack on them

- The invention of the "**Dreadnought**" (1906) type of battleship by the British, a new technology that was easy to copy and destroyed Britain's historic vast superiority in numbers over other navies; **naval race**

- Failure of political and military leaders to have adequate options available for military **mobilization**

- Germany demanded a halt to Russian mobilization. It had only one (**Schlieffen**) plan, which had to be launched immediately if Russia began to mobilize. This plan was built on the assumption that any war against Russia would be fought against its ally France as well. To cope with the threat of a "two front" war the Germans intended to defeat France first, swiftly, and then turn on the slower Russia. Only immediate mobilization could make this successful

- First and Second Balkan Wars—threats to Ottoman Empire (1911, 1912)

NATIONALISM
- Rivalries in the Balkans exacerbated other problems

- Fragility of the Austro-Hungarian empire made leaders overly aggressive to nationalist threats, especially among the southern slavs

- Slavophile pressure on Russian Tsar to intervene to protect Serbia from Austria

- French desire for revenge against Germany and to regain **Alsace Lorraine** lost in 1871

- Italian bitterness about failing to reclaim the *irredenta* controlled by Austria. Italy offered to aid Germany and Austria if the *irredenta* was returned. They refused, so Italy turned to France and Britain (Treaty of London 1915)

- Serbian desire to create a "Greater Serbia" that included Serbs living under Habsburg rule and gaining access to a seaport on the Adriatic

- Assassination of the Archduke **Franz Ferdinand**, heir to the Austrian throne, June *1914 at Sarajevo in Bosnia. The Serbian government had knowledge of the terrorist threat, encouraged it, and wanted Franz Ferdinand dead because it was feared that his plan for a "Triple Monarchy" giving Slavs autonomy comparable to the Hungarians might succeed in blocking the creation of a Greater Serbia

CULTURAL
- **Social Darwinism** encouraged the notion that war was healthy and good

ECONOMIC
- The rapid creation of a giant Germany and even more speedy industrialization created tensions and anxieties that made for oversensitive responses to perceived threats

- British fears that Germany was rapidly overtaking her in industrial production and world trade. Britain's large population packed into a small island could only survive by industry and trade

ALLIANCE SYSTEMS 1914	
TRIPLE ALLIANCE	TRIPLE ENTENTE
Germany Austria-Hungary Italy	France Great Britain Russia
ALLIANCE SYSTEMS 1915–18	
CENTRAL POWERS	ALLIES
Germany Austria-Hungary Ottoman Empire Bulgaria (from 1915)	France Great Britain Russia (until 1917) Serbia Japan Portugal Italy (from 1916) Romania (from 1916) USA (from 1917)

In 1917 the USA entered the war due to

- German pursuit of unrestricted submarine warfare

- Sinking of the "**Lusitania**" (1915)

- the **Zimmermann Telegram** (1917)

- overthrow of the Tsar in Russia removed an odious impediment to joining the Allies

MILITARY ENGAGEMENTS

- **Battle of the Marne** (1914)—French and British barely halt the German advance near Paris

- Dardanelles (**Gallipoli**) assault to defeat the Ottomans and render aid to Russia failed

- **Battle of Verdun**—horrific defense by the French 1916

- **Battle of the Somme**—British/German stalemate 1916

- **Battle of Jutland** (1916)—only major naval engagement of the War. British suffered greater losses, but retained overwhelming naval superiority. The German fleet was successfully confined to port thereafter

MILITARY TACTICS

"The Trenches"—many people thought the war would be over quickly. They had not realized that defensive tactics had overtaken offensive ones. A defensive line of trenches was built from the North Sea to Switzerland that remained relatively fixed for five years. Machine guns and barbed wire had made cavalry obsolete and infantry charges ineffective.

The war became one of attrition and stalemate in which all of the following weapons proved ineffective

- Mustard gas

- airplanes

- tanks

- flame-throwers

- Massive artillery barrages

- Airships (Zepplins)

- Submarines (convoy system rendered moot)

Total War, a concept of organizing all facets of the state and the economy to win what became a war of **attrition** was developed by Walter Rathenau of Germany but most effectively implemented in Great Britain involved unprecedented central planning and invasion of private business and life

Germany tried to break the stalemate by encouraging the collapse of Tsardom and then the Provisional Government, especially by sending the Bolshevik **Lenin** from Switzerland to Petrograd in a "sealed train". Eventually signed the **Treaty of Brest-Litovsk** (1918) with the Bolsheviks taking Russia out of the War, but this victory came too late to save the German Empire.

The prospect of fighting against millions of freshly trained, well fed, and well armed Americans finally led to the collapse of German morale. In order to avoid the disintegration of the army, which was the only defense the elites had for their property against socialist revolution at home and Communist invasion from Russia, the top generals forced the Kaiser to abdicate and flee to Holland, and surrendered to the Allies on November 11, 1918*.

THE RUSSIAN REVOLUTION—*1917

CAUSES OF THE COLLAPSE OF IMPERIAL RUSSIA

- Defeats and suffering due to the war

- War with Germany and Austria placed too heavy a burden on Russian resources, and it could not be adequately supplied by the Allies because no railway line existed to the ice-free White Sea, and the Black Sea was blocked by the Ottomans

- Tsar **Nicholas II** inept, incompetent, and unworthy of his position.

- **"Bloody Sunday"** and the loss of the Russo-Japanese War in 1905 had undermined his authority.

- Tsar's departure from the capital in 1915 to take personal command of the army meant he
  a) then had to accept personal responsibility for defeats
  b) left his wife in charge of the government
  Tsaritsa **Alexandra** a neurotic, unpopular German (seen as a traitor) influenced by a corrupt charlatan, **Rasputin**, who gained ascendancy due to the illness of the heir to the throne, a hemophiliac. Under the monk's influence government ministries went to crooks and incompetents

- Middle class democratic politicians (Kadets) were alienated and distrustful

- Workers in the factories supported radical change

- Food crisis in St. Petersburg precipitated revolt. Troops and **Duma** failed to support the Tsar, and he was forced to abdicate in March

- New **Provisional Government** established by Prince Lvov and **Kerensky** tried to negotiate with Germany, but found Berlin's demands excessive. Decision to continue the war and subsequent defeats further weakened morale. Soldiers ceased to fight and deserted in large numbers

- Lenin and the **Bolsheviks** organized a coup that overthrew Kerensky in November *1917. Lenin's leadership was crucial; he was a political genius and utterly ruthless; he promised "Peace, Land, and Bread"

When the Bolsheviks failed to win the first true democratic elections in Russian history, the legislature was closed and a Communist dictatorship was imposed by force. The Tsar and his wife and five children were murdered. Opposition from monarchists, democrats, Orthodox Christians, and aristocrats was eventually crushed in a civil war. The **Red Army** was successfully led by **Leon Trotsky**.

OUTCOMES OF THE RUSSIA REVOLUTION
- Romanov monarchy and democratic Provisional Government overthrown

- Bolsheviks gain power and gradually destroy all opposition

- Trotsky negotiated peace with Germany at **Brest-Litovsk**. Russia suffered huge territorial losses, but regained much of the land after German defeat

- **Communism** became a frightening threat to both conservative dictatorships in central Europe and capitalist democracies in the West

- **Stalin** took power after Lenin's death in 1924 and established the most brutal dictatorship known to history causing massive numbers of deaths due to famine, murder, and inhuman conditions in concentration camps (the gulags)

THE TREATY OF VERSAILLES

A peace conference in Paris took place in *1919 without the presence of the Germans or Austrians. The "Big Four," **David Lloyd George** of Britain, **Georges Clemenceau** of France, **Woodrow Wilson** of the USA, and Orlando of Italy met to impose terms on the defeated. This became the "Big Three" after Orlando departed incensed when denied the entire *irredenta*. This was due to one of Wilson's "**Fourteen Points**," which promised self-determination to oppressed peoples. Lloyd George and Clemenceau were ready to abandon their promises to Italy in order to win Wilson's agreement to their own agendas. Indeed, they conceded Wilson the **League of Nations** (which they did not value highly) in exchange for his concessions on reparations and territorial adjustments that favored France and Britain.

PROVISIONS OF THE TREATY

Most important clause
- **War Guilt Clause**—Germany forced to accept total responsibility for the outbreak of the war

Economic provisions
- **Reparations**—Germany forced to pay most of the costs for war damage and for the loans, pensions, education of orphans, etc.—a gigantic sum in gold. In addition much of its merchant fleet was confiscated by the British, and railway freight cars and factory machinery by the French. This was the equivalent of asking a man to run a 100-yard dash and then cutting off his legs.

Territorial changes
- The Saar border region was temporarily annexed by France to compensate for loss of coal production in occupied territories during the war

- Alsace and Lorraine were returned to France

- Poland was recreated and given territory taken from Germany, Austria, and Russia. A "**Polish corridor**" was cut through Prussia to give the new state access to the port of Danzig, and hence a million Germans were denied self-determination and the German state was in two pieces

- An entirely new state of Czechoslovakia was created out of Bohemia and Moravia, formerly part of Austria. In order to give it a defensible natural frontier, the mountainous **Sudetenland** along the German border was given to the new country, and thus two million Germans were denied self-determination

- Austria was reduced to a pygmy state too small to support its huge capital at Vienna

- Hungary was established as an independent state, largely shorn of its non-Magyar subject peoples, but also with Hungarians placed under the rule of Yugoslavia, Czechoslovakia, and Romania.

- **Plebiscites** were held to achieve **self-determination**, but the checkerboard nature of ethnic distribution did not yield clear borders in many instances

- **Yugoslavia** was established as an independent state. This made Serbia the biggest winner of the war and gave them more territory than they had ever anticipated gaining. Many smaller ethnic groups—Albanians, Croatians, Slovenians, Hungarians, Romanians, Italians, Montenegrins, Macedonians, etc. were placed under their rule without regard for self-determination

- Romania was almost doubled in size with additions coming mainly from Hungary

- Bulgaria was reduced in size

- Greece gained territory

- The Ottoman Empire was liquidated. The core became the Republic of Turkey when the Sultan was overthrown soon after the war.

- **Mandates** (protectorates) under the League were established in Palestine, Jordan, and Iraq (Britain) and the Lebanon and Syria (France). Britain had promised an Arab throne to the ruler of Mecca for help during the war against the Ottomans (British officer, Lawrence of Arabia, helps lead Arab revolt), but the rising Saudi dynasty drove them out and established an independent Arabia. Hence the Hashemite family were made kings of Iraq and Jordan instead

- Japan was given German territory in the Pacific and China

- Britain gained German territories in Africa

- Finland, Estonia, Latvia, and Lithuania were given independence from Russia

Other provisions
- The **League of Nations** was established to settle international disputes—a total failure as an institution

- The Rhineland was demilitarized

- The size of the German military was radically reduced

OUTCOMES OF THE TREATY

Germany, Poland, Czechoslovakia, and Austria became republics. Hungary was ruled by a Regent who denied the Habsburg pretender the right of return. The Kings of Serbia became rulers of Yugoslavia, and the reigning dynasties survived in Romania, Bulgaria, and Greece.

Wilson's "**Fourteen Points**" were more honored in the breach than in the letter. The British succeeded in blocking "freedom of the seas", and although the League was established, it failed to have much impact, in part because Russia, Germany, and even the USA were not members.

Russia and Germany were the ghosts at the feast. Neither was represented in the negotiations. Indeed, France, Britain, Japan, and the USA invaded Russia and tried to put down the Communist revolution. Her western borders, though better than those imposed by Germany at Brest-Litovsk, were imposed without consultation and included loss of territory and population.

Germany initially refused to sign the treaty, and only did so when faced with a blockade and starvation. The English economist, **John Maynard Keynes** called Versailles a "Carthaginian Peace" (excessively harsh) and predicted that German economic weakness would make it impossible for them to pay the ridiculously high reparations. He called this situation very dangerous. He was right. However, it is hard to see how **Lloyd George** and **Clemenceau** could have done anything else as the democratically elected leaders of nations that had suffered unprecedented numbers of casualties (one in two Frenchmen between the ages of 18 and 40 was killed or wounded). Only **Wilson** might have salvaged something, but he was out-maneuvered and placed excessive faith in the League, which he believed could rectify mistakes made in Paris.

The United States Senate refused to ratify the Versailles treaty and the USA withdrew into reckless isolationism.

OUTCOMES OF THE FIRST WORLD WAR

POLITICAL

- The Versailles settlement did not destroy Germany, but left it bitter and revengeful and able to rise again

- The Russian Revolution and rise of the USSR

- Use of propaganda greatly developed and refined as a political and military weapon; hatreds encouraged by governments to help win the war make it hard to build peace; "disinformation"

- Collapse of the ancient dynasties

- Especially disastrous was the disappearance of the Habsburg monarchy, which with all its failings had created an center of stability and peace in central Europe. Now a vacuum existed that great powers would vie to fill

- The overthrow of the Ottoman Empire also left a cauldron of troubles in the Middle East

SOCIAL

- Collapse of the old landed elites—liquidated physically in Russia, discredited in Germany, and put under severe economic stress in Britain. Heavy taxation, loss of sons in the war, a new democratic spirit in the West, lack of servants, and other factors largely eliminated aristocrats from the center of affairs and the top of society, although individual figures such as Churchill remained important

- Women got the vote in many countries, and their work in jobs replacing male soldiers earned them new respect, and the change in skirt lengths was physically liberating. However, many women had to leave the work force and lost their financial independence on the return of the men from the front

- Victorian morality was largely abandoned and sexual mores loosened

- Old-fashioned values of "honor" and deference seemed outdated or were associated with a discredited social and political system enabling men previously unacceptable as leaders of great states such as Hitler, Mussolini, and Stalin to emerge

ECONOMIC

- **"Total War"** had led to large-scale interventions into economies that did not fully disappear after the war

- Heavy taxation was instituted during the war and remained a means of government management thereafter

- Serious economic dislocations changed the structure of nations and the world. Britain and Germany lost markets to the USA and Japan. Huge war loans burdened recovery; supporting millions of widows, orphans and the disabled imposed serious financial burdens

- Labor unions strengthened and socialists gained mass support and moved towards gaining control of governments

- Tariffs were increasingly put up to protect home economies

GLOBAL

- The USA became a world power

- Japan became the first Asian power in modern times to be accepted as an equal in treaty negotiations

- The Colonial empires of France and Britain survived, though increasingly native peoples challenged European rule. Native soldiers also felt their service in the war ought to be rewarded, and the ideals of freedom for which the Allies claimed to be fighting ought to apply to them also.

- Canada, Australia, New Zealand "came of age" as nations, but they also remained tightly tied to Great Britain by culture and sentiment until after 1945, following the UK into the Second World War, which was critical for the British victory against Hitler

CULTURAL

- World War I weakened human regard for the value of life. The deaths and maiming of millions of young men under the most inhumane conditions was unprecedented and shattered all previous conceptions of decency and what was allowable. The devaluing of life undermined limits that would help condone even more terrible killing twenty years later

- Disillusion and denial of rationality; Wilfrid Owen and other war poets; Remarque, *All Quiet on the Western Front*

THE POST WAR WORLD

The 1920s witnessed a return to prosperity and peace, but the 1930s were dark years both in economic terms and politically. The **Locarno Treaty** 1925 and the **Kellogg-Briand Pact** 1928 created the illusion that peace might be permanent.

FRANCE

- Obsessed by a search for security against Germany.

a) Created an Eastern Alliance system of useless allies.

b) Spent huge sums on defenses along the German border (the **Maginot Line**) that proved equally worthless.

c) **Occupied the Ruhr** industrial area in Germany to force payments of reparations (1923), a policy that precipitated **hyperinflation** and even more bitterness in Germany.

- Unstable political system

GREAT BRITAIN

- Full democracy established. All men and women get vote in 1918 and 1928

- **Labour Party** enters government in a coalition

- Depressed economy, unemployment and a general strike in 1926

- Aspects of the welfare state expanded

- Southern Ireland given independence

- Military weakness, although government sponsored research produces RADAR and superb fighter aircraft designs and Royal Navy remains the most powerful in the world

GERMANY

- Democratic **Weimar Republic** established, but with a vulnerable constitution

- The most formidable democratic statesman, Gustav Stresemann died in 1929

- **President Field Marshal von Hindenburg** inept and in ill health

- Occupation of the Ruhr by France leads to hyperinflation that nearly destroyed the middle class. Economy staggered under many burdens

- Powerful elements on the right and left do not accept a democratic republic

RUSSIA
- Lenin instituted modified capitalism (New Economic Program—**NEP**) to restore strength to the economy

- **KGB** (Cheka) set up

- **Trotsky** (who believed the Russian experiment could only succeed if the revolution spread around the world) and Stalin (who argued for "socialism in one country", that is building up the strength of Communism in Russia first) struggled for power. Stalin won

- Stalin **collectivized** agriculture and instituted **Five Year Plans** to build up heavy industry first before military and consumer production could begin

- Millions were killed, imprisoned or died in famines during the seizure of agricultural land. Prosperous peasants (**kulaks**) were targeted

- Slave labor and terror were used to implement the Five Year Plans, millions more died in the labor camps (**gulags**)

ITALY
- Humiliation at Versailles and political instability led to the success of **Benito Mussolini**, founder of an anti-capitalist, anti-communist, extreme nationalist party, the **Fascists**. He used street violence, murder of opposing leaders, and a March on Rome to force conventional politicians and the King to give him power. He ruled 1922 to 1943

POLAND
- political instability led to the take over in 1926 by a dictator, Marshall Pilsudski

CZECHOSLOVAKIA
- a good industrial base helped create prosperity, and sustained democracy under the leadership of Thomas Masyrak

HUNGARY
- authoritarian rule under Admiral Horthy

AUSTRIA
- one-party rule under Dolfuss and then Schuschnigg

YUGOSLAVIA
- ruled by King Alexander I until his assassination in France and then the Regent Paul, who sympathized with fascism and was incapable of securing effective security alliances

TURKEY

- Ruled by the military dictator **Kemal Ataturk**, who imposed radical secularization and Westernization on the remnants of the old Ottoman state shorn of its empire

THE GREAT DEPRESSION *1929–1939

CAUSES OF THE GREAT CRISIS OF CAPITALISM

- The financial disruption and burdens produced by the war

- Inflated currencies

- Tariff barriers

- Lack of strong economic leadership and Hoover's failures as a President of USA

- Flood of cheap wheat from the Americas to Europe undermined agricultural prices. Farmers had to pay more for goods due to rising industrial wages

- Unemployment reduced consumption

- Crisis of production and distribution of goods in the world market, outstripped demand, which led to stagnation

- Crash of the stock market in New York 1929 due to excessive speculation

- Credit crises in European banks 1931

Not everything went wrong during the depression and each country experienced it differently. By and large the worst sufferers were older chronically unemployed men in the most vulnerable industries such as agriculture and coal mining. Many middle class families were relatively unaffected or prospered.

Technological advancements continued.

- **Radio** for wireless communication was followed by general broadcasting for the public. This created a new world of entertainment, information, propaganda, and education

- Television was born in Britain just before the Second World War

- Electricity continued to be spread to rural areas and lightened the lives of millions of farm families

- **Synthetics** had been introduced during the war to replace unavailable products. These were improved and expanded. More cheap and attractive goods became available to ordinary people

- Automobiles were greatly improved technologically and became less expensive. This promoted the growth of many industries and the building of highways

- Air travel increased. Lindbergh flew the Atlantic, and long distance services became available just before the next war. Trans-Atlantic telephone cables were laid, and telephones became more common

Britain went off the gold standard, erected tariff barriers, cut benefits, and raised taxes. A **National Government** helped lead the recovery, but permanent unemployment arose in some industries. France followed a similar path, although a Popular Front of left wing parties under **Leon Blum** tried to extend social benefits. Unemployment was never as serious as in Britain.

Germany suffered seriously during the depression, and the untimely death of a leading statesman, Gustav **Stresemann**, left a vacuum of political leadership.

John Maynard Keynes, the economist advocated (1936) "pump priming" as a solution to the depression— government spending to provide employment and inject money into the economy.

TOTALITARIANISM

The rise of fascism and communism, both responses to the weaknesses of capitalism, changed the face of political and social organization, to say nothing of culture, between 1919 and 1939. In many ways they were similar and in many different. It is perhaps more useful to think of them as opposite ends of an almost closed circle than as on the right and left of a continuum.

SIMILARTIES—DIFFERENCES BETWEEN COMMUNISM (C) AND FASCISM (F)	
SIMILARITIES	DIFFERENCES
state over the individual	C—goal was no government
totalitarian	F—state is everything
militaristic	
secret police/censorship	
concentration camps	C—goal is internationalist
individual counts for nothing	F—intensely nationalistic
One party	
tolerate no opposition	
one leader	C—goal is to promote equality
cult of personality	F—inequality is seen as natural
ambitions of world conquest	
mutual antagonism	C—goal—peace and prosperity
anti-capitalist	F—war is good and slavery or death for the losers
anti-religious	
propaganda over truth	
messianic, provide a whole belief system	
use of modern technology to lie and murder	
millions of people	
utopian	
based on hate	
European in origin	
planned economies	
provide full employment	
attempt to solve class conflict engendered by industrialization	
revolutionary	

TOTALITARIAN LEADERS
- Mussolini, the founder of fascism, was a gifted speaker and propagandist, but unlike Hitler he was not driven by racism. He worked out a **concordat** with the Church and tolerated the constitution, including his

own official subordination to the monarchy (he was legally appointed to office by the King in 1922, though the "March on Rome" was a kind of blackmail), which meant he was never really supreme leader of the state. Italy remained economically and military weak. He called himself the Leader, **_Duce_**.

- Hitler attempted a coup in the early 1920s (was jailed and wrote **_Mein Kampf_**), but eventually came to power in *1933 by constitutional means. Although his fascist party, the National Socialist Party (Nazi), never won a majority of the votes, in coalition with other right wing groups, he did control a majority of seats in a democratically elected legislature. The President, the old junker **von Hindenburg**, despised him (Hitler had never been more than a corporal in the army and came from a lower middle class family, the first truly common man to dominate Europe's stage), but really had no option but to appoint him Chancellor. Hitler suspended the constitution quite legally after the Reichstag fire, and when the old aristocrat died, he never held another election. His will became the law of the land. He called himself, The Leader, **_Führer_**.

- Stalin was a human monster, utterly indifferent to human life and deeply paranoid. He gained power by skilful manipulation of the machinery of the Communist Party and held it by slaughtering both active and potential enemies. His murder of the top generals in the late 1930s could have backfired, but he was lucky to find enough replacements to survive the German invasion in 1941.

- Fascism also came to Spain in the aftermath of a bloody civil war 1936–39 between the left (aided by Stalin) and the right (aided by Mussolini and Hitler). The conservative general, Francisco Franco, established a Falange Party, and called himself the Leader, _Caudillo_.

- Various dictators in Eastern Europe also adopted fascism.

RESULTS OF TOTALITARIANISM

DEATH

Stalin was the greatest murderer among the three totalitarian leaders. At least 10 million people died as a direct result of his rule, although if Hitler's responsibility for the Second World War is added to the killing of civilians, then his total could be counted as high as 40 million. Mussolini used murder infrequently, and most of the deaths for which he was responsible were due to greed and incompetence. The killings of opponents and the use of terror to build political and economic power were rational, if inhuman in their scale. Franco was a ruthless killer, but stopped mass murder once he was secure in power. Much of the killing, the **Great Purges** in Russia or the **Holocaust** of the Jews ordered by Hitler, was irrational, counter-productive, the product of madness, paranoia, and immoral, unlimited power.

CONQUEST

Mussolini developed the fascist ideology (1919–22). He was outraged by the **_irredenta_** crisis and feared that socialism would sap the national character. He dreamed of reviving the Roman Empire and resolving the class conflicts aroused by capitalism. He established state control over the economy. Hitler was driven by ambition comparable to that of Napoleon, and possessed political skills of a high order. However, his vision was warped by malignant racism and a fantastic vision of the world that led him to prolong the war so that he could punish his own people for failing him. Franco turned out to be a better survivor than his mentors. He wisely escaped a military alliance with the Axis. Unlike Hitler and Mussolini he even made preparations for a successor after his death. In the end all the fascists failed except Franco, who knew when to stop and actually possessed some skill as a general. Stalin hoped to conquer the world but was content to take Eastern Europe.

HITLER'S DRIVE TO WORLD CONQUEST

Hitler planned to establish a great German Empire stretching across much of Europe dominated by the "Aryan" race. The Scandinavians, British, French, Spanish, and Italians would be his allies or neutral. The Slavic peoples would be slaves. Communism and capitalism would be eliminated. The German people, packed tightly into a small place would gain *lebensraum* (space to expand) in a gigantic, largely agricultural "utopia". He planned to rectify all the mistakes made at Versailles.

    *1933   Germany withdrew from the League of Nations

    1935   Germany renounces restrictions on rearmament

    1936   Rome/Berlin **Axis**
            Germany reoccupies the Rhineland with military forces

    1938   *Anschluss* (union) with Austria
            Munich Crisis over reoccupation of the **Sudentenland**

    *1939   Germans occupy Prague
            Nazi-Soviet Pact
            Germany invades Poland
            Britain and France declare war

APPEASEMENT

Britain, France, and the USA kept giving in to German, Italian, and Japanese demands or failed to prevent or punish their aggression until 1939 in the case of the France and the UK and 1941 for the USA. The leading "Appeaser" was Prime Minister **Neville Chamberlain** of Britain. **Winston Churchill** was the leading opponent of **Appeasement**.

RATIONALE FOR APPEASEMENT

- Fear of another war with massive loss of life

- Desire to spend money on social programs rather than rearmament

- Guilt about the mistakes made at Versailles

- Fear of Communism greater than fear of fascism, and Hitler was seen as a force to be used against the USSR. Indeed, the ideal scenario was for the fascists and communists to kill each other off

- Hitler's **anti-Semitism** accorded with the feelings of many leaders in the West (he had made no explicit statement threatening mass murder)

- USA **isolationism**. France and Britain did not want to go to war without American support

- Chamberlain's naiveté and failure to grasp that he was not dealing with statesmen but moral gangsters; he "gave away" Czechoslovakia

IMPORTANT DEFINITIONS AND IDENTIFICATIONS

- Alexandra of Russia
- alliance systems
- Allies
- Alsace Lorraine
- *Anschluss*
- Anti-Semitism
- Appeasement
- Kemal Attaturk
- Attrition
- Axis
- blank check
- Leon Blum
- Bolsheviks
- Bosnia
- Bloody Sunday
- Treaty of Brest-Litovsk
- Central Powers
- Neville Chamberlain
- Winston Churchill
- Georges Clemenceau
- Collectivization of agriculture
- Communism
- concentration camps
- concordat
- cult of personality
- "Dreadnought"
- *Duce*
- Duma
- Entente Cordiale
- Fascism
- Five Year Plans
- Fourteen Points
- Francisco Franco

- Franz Ferdinand of Austria
- *Führer*
- Gallipoli
- The Great Purges
- Gulags
- von Hindenburg
- Adolf Hitler
- The Holocaust
- hyperinflation
- *Irredenta*
- isolationism
- Battle of Jutland
- Kellogg-Briand Pact
- John Maynard Keynes
- Alexander Kerensky
- KGB
- Kulaks
- Labour Party (Great Britain)
- League of Nations
- *lebensraum*
- Lenin
- David Lloyd George
- Treaty of Locarno
- "Lusitainia"
- Maginot Line
- mandates
- Battle of the Marne
- *Mein Kampf*
- mobilization plans
- Benito Mussolini
- National Government
- naval race
- Nazi-Soviet Pact

- New Economic Policy (NEP)
- Nicholas II of Russia
- plebicites
- Polish Corridor
- Popular Front
- propaganda
- Provisional Government
- radio
- Rasputin
- Red Army
- Reparations
- Occupation of the Ruhr
- Schlieffen Plan
- Self-determination
- Social Darwinism
- Battle of the Somme
- Stalin
- Gustav Stresemann
- Sudetenland
- synthetics
- Total War
- Triple Alliance
- Triple Entente
- Leon Trotsky
- Battle of Verdun
- Treaty of Versailles
- War Guilt Clause
- Weimar Republic
- Wilhelm II of Germany
- Woodrow Wilson
- Yugoslavia
- Zimmermann Telegram

IMPORTANT DATES

*1914 Outbreak of the First World War
Assassination of Archduke Franz Ferdinand
German invasion of France
Battle of the Marne

1916 Battle of Jutland

*1917 Russian Revolution
US entry into the War

*1918 End of the war

*1919 Treaty of Versailles

1922 Mussolini gains power

1923 Occupation of the Ruhr

1929 The Great Depression begins

*1933 Hitler gains power

*1939 Outbreak of the Second World War

CHAPTER 10
MULTIPLE-CHOICE QUESTIONS

Questions 1.1–1.3 refer to the statistical table below.

WAR EXPENDITURES 1914–19 (in 1913 billions of dollars)	
British Empire	23.0
France	9.3
Russia	5.4
Italy	3.2
USA	7.1
Germany	19.9
Austria-Hungary	4.7
Bulgaria and Turkey	0.1

1.1 Which of the following statements is accurate with relations to this data?

(A) The Central Powers outspent the Allies
(B) Britain spent the most per year
(C) Allied resources were much greater than those of the Central Powers
(D) Russia could have matched France had it been able to stay in the war longer

1.2 From whom could the British and French borrow to an almost unlimited extent to pay for war supplies?

(A) Russia
(B) China
(C) USA
(D) Spain

1.3 Which of the following was also a critical factor in helping the Allies win the War?

(A) Access to raw materials, food, and munitions from Canada, Australia, New Zealand, and South Africa
(B) Submarine warfare against the German merchant marine
(C) Support from the Ottoman Empire
(D) Military recruitment in South America

157

Questions 2.1–2.3 refers to the document below.

Article 231. The Allied and associated Governments affirm and Germany accepts the responsibility of Germany and her allies for causing the loss and damage to which the Allied and Associated Governments and their nationals have been subjected as a consequence of the war imposed upon them by the aggression of Germany and her allies.

Article 232. The Allied and Associated Governments require, and Germany undertakes, that she will make compensation for all damage done to the civilian population of the Allied and Associated Powers and to their property during the period of belligerency of each as an Allied or Associated Power against Germany by such aggression by land, sea, and from the air, and in general….

Article 233. The amount of the above damage for which compensation is to be made by Germany shall be determined by an Inter-Allied Commission, to be called the Reparations Commission.

The Treaty of Versailles, 1919

2.1 On what assumption did the Reparation demands made by the Allies rest?

(A) Germany was the richest country in Europe
(B) Germany looted Austria
(C) The Ottomans would help pay
(D) Germany started the war

2.2 Which of the following statements is true of the Reparation demands?

(A) An impossible burden that Germany could not pay
(B) Could be paid off easily by Germany
(C) Returned Europe to economic health
(D) Left no lasting legacy

2.3 The most important outcome of the Versailles Treaty was which of the following?

(A) The French feeling that Germany should have been punished more harshly
(B) The German feeling that they were treated unjustly
(C) Britain's refusal to sign the Treaty
(D) The establishment of the League of Nations

Questions 3.1–3.3 refer to the following passage.

First of all, as regards the future development of mankind,—and quite apart from all present political considerations—Fascism does not, generally speaking, believe in the possibility or utility of perpetual peace. It therefore discards pacifism as a cloak for cowardly supine renunciation in contradistinction to self-sacrifice. War lone keys up all human energies to their maximum tension and sets the seal of nobility on those peoples who have the courage to face it.

Such a conception of life makes Fascism the resolute negation of the doctrine underlying so-called scientific and Marxian socialism, the doctrine of historic materialism which would explain the history of mankind in terms of the class-struggle and by the changes in the processes and instruments of production, to the exclusion of all else.

After socialism, Fascism trains its guns on the whole block of democratic ideologies, and rejects both their premises and their practical applications and implements. Fascism denies that numbers, as such, can be the determining factor in human society; it denies the right of numbers to govern by means of periodic consultations; it asserts the irremediable and fertile and beneficent inequality of men who cannot be leveled by any such mechanical and extrinsic device as universal suffrage.

Benito Mussolini, *Fascism: Doctrine and Institutions*, 1935

3.1 Which of the following probably influenced Mussolini most directly in developing his political ideology?

(A) The ideas of Adolf Hitler
(B) Josef Stalin's modifications of Marxism
(C) The Enlightenment
(D) Italy's failures to achieve its war aims

3.2 Fascism and Communism both set out to respond to the problems engendered by which of the following?

(A) The Renaissance
(B) The Reformation
(C) The French Revolution
(D) The Industrial Revolution

3.3 Mussolini aspired to revive the glories of which of the following?

(A) The Roman Empire
(B) The Holy Roman Empire
(C) The Empire of Philip II
(D) The Ottoman Empire

Questions 4.1–4.3 refer to the document below.

1. The contradiction between the national idea, exemplified by National Socialist Germany, and the idea of world revolution, exemplified by the U.S.S.R., has in past years been the sole cause for the alignment of Germany and Russia in ideologically separate and hostile camps. The developments of the recent period seem to show that differing philosophies do not prohibit a reasonable relationship between the two States, and the restoration of new, friendly cooperation. The period of opposition in foreign policy could therefore be brought to an end once and for all….

2. There exist no real conflicts of interest between Germany and Russia. … The Reich Government are of the opinion that there is no question between the Baltic Sea and the Black Sea which cannot be settled to the complete satisfaction of both countries.

3. The Reich Government and the Soviet Government must, judging from past experience, take into account that the capitalist Western democracies are implacable enemies of both National Socialist Germany and Soviet Russia. They are today trying again, by the conclusion of a military alliance, to drive Russia into war against Germany.

Joachim von Ribbentrop, German Foreign Minister, message to the Soviet Government,
August 14, 1939

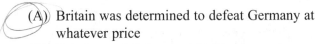

4.1 What underlying factor made it possible for Stain and Hitler to come to an agreement on non-aggression in August 1939?

   (A) Both felt threatened by the rising power of Poland
   (B) Both sought the peace and brotherhood of mankind
   (C) Both trusted the other to abide by their agreements
   (D) Both found it momentarily convenient to avoid war

4.2 What other powers had appeared in Moscow in the summer of 1939 and tried to reach an agreement with Stalin?

   (A) The United States and Spain
   (B) Turkey and Great Britain
   (C) France and Great Britain
   (D) France and Italy

4.3 After Hitler invaded Russia in June 1941 why was Britain willing to ignore the Nazi-Soviet pact and offer Stalin assistance?

   (A) Britain was determined to defeat Germany at whatever price
   (B) Britain needed desperately Russian war materials and munitions to survive
   (C) The United States urged the British to make an alliance with Russia
   (D) Churchill hoped Stalin would turn over a new leaf

Questions 5.1–5.3 relates to the 1938 cartoon "Which Backbone" reproduced below.

5.1 This cartoon portraying the British Foreign Secretary, Lord Halifax, in 1938 (FO = Foreign Office)

  (A) Is critical of the policy of Appeasement
  (B) Supports Halifax for Prime Minister
  (C) Is critical of Halifax's love of luxury
  (D) Assumes Halifax wants war

5.2 The fact that Halifax and Winston Churchill were the only serious contenders for Prime Minister when Chamberlain resigned in 1940 suggests what about Great Britain?

  (A) It had no adequate leaders
  (B) The aristocracy was still a dominant force in politics
  (C) Hitler had scared away most of the other candidates
  (D) Democracy did not work in Britain

5.3 What led Britain to declare war on Germany in 1939?

  (A) An oil embargo
  (B) The attack at Pearl Harbor
  (C) Realization that Hitler could not be trusted
  (D) Fear of losing control of India

SHORT-ANSWER QUESTION

Question 1

Hundreds of British soldiers were running forward through a flat communication trench, little troubled by the weak gunfire we were able to direct at them. The scene was indicative of the inequality of resources with which we had to fight. Had we essayed the same thing, our units would have been shot to pieces in a matter of minutes. While on our side there was wasn't a single captive balloon to be seen anywhere, the British had about thirty clustered into one vast luminous-yellow bunch, watching with Argus eyes for the least movement to show itself anywhere in the crumpled landscape, to have a hail of steel directed against it.

Ernst Jünger, *Storm of Steel*, 1920

This account of trench warfare in 1916 written by a young German officer portrays battle on the Western Front in the First World War. Using the quotation and your knowledge of European history answer the following questions (A and B).

A) Identify and explain ONE factor that made it impossible for either side to make much progress against the other in trench warfare.

B) Identify and explain TWO reasons why the Allies were ultimately able to defeat the Germans in 1918.

CHAPTER 11

WARS—HOT AND COLD

WORLD WAR II 1939*–1945*

PRINCIPAL ACTIVE COMBATANTS IN THE SECOND WORLD WAR	
ALLIES	AXIS
Great Britain	Germany
British Empire	Italy
France (until 1940)	Japan
United States	Romania
USSR	Bulgaria
Poland	Hungary
Canada	
Australia	
South Africa	
New Zealand	
India	
China	
Yugoslavia	
The Netherlands	
Belgium	
Denmark	
Norway	
Greece	

THE CONDUCT OF WAR

THE PHONEY WAR

Initially, Germany and the USSR split Poland and fighting stopped. The Phoney War (1939–40) was a period when Hitler hoped France and Britain would negotiate a peace.

THE INVASION OF FRANCE

In April Germany invaded France, as in the First World War, sweeping around French defenses by going through Belgium. France collapsed quickly: the heart of its people was not ready for another long and bloody war, many of the French were sympathetic to anti-Semitism and fascism, and the leadership of the army was both incompetent and traitorous. A quasi-fascist regime was set up under Marshal Pétain at **Vichy**. Among the military leaders, only **Charles de Gaulle** escaped to England to establish a Free French government. The small British army was pushed aside, lost all of its equipment, and barely managed to escape at the last minute by sea at **Dunkirk**.

THE BATTLE OF BRITAIN

Winston Churchill replaced Chamberlain as Prime Minister of Britain, rallied his nation and saved freedom for the world. President **Franklin Roosevelt** grasped the nature of the emergency and established a **Lend-Lease** program circumventing neutrality to help supply the British with war materials. The Germans sought to achieve air and sea superiority in the English Channel in order to invade Britain. However, the Royal Navy was much stronger than the German fleet and in August and September of 1940 the RAF defeated the *Luftwaffe* and blocked the invasion. The invention of **RADAR** and the superb quality of British airplanes and pilots saved the day.

THE DESERT WAR

When it seemed safe, Italy entered the war on the side of Germany (Axis powers) and engaged the British in North Africa and attempted to invade Greece. Both campaigns failed, and Hitler had to deploy troops unexpectedly to salvage the situation. In the end the Axis failed to take Cairo and the Suez Canal and were driven out of Africa. Yugoslavia and Greece were captured.

THE INVASION OF RUSSIA

The price of delaying the invasion of Russia, which came in June 1941, to help **Mussolini**, was failure on the Eastern Front. Although the Germans reached the suburbs of Moscow, they had too little time before a terrible winter of 1941–42 set in to achieve victory. Stalin was also saved by British supplies, US entry into the war, and the valor of his people aroused by a patriotic fervor inspired by the brutality and racism of the Nazis. Somewhere between 20 and 30 million Russians died.

THE UNITED STATES ENTERS THE WAR

The Japanese attack on **Pearl Harbor, Singapore**, the Philippines, and Dutch East Indies in December 1941, provoked by Roosevelt's embargo on oil, which would have forced Tokyo to withdraw from its empire in China, allowed the Japanese to get fuel from the Dutch East Indies. Roosevelt was able to carry the USA into the conflict in Europe (thanks to a declaration of war by **Hitler**—one of the great puzzles of modern history, probably attributable to his gross ignorance of the world outside Europe and his racism, which led him to believe the USA was a "mongrel" nation incapable of success in war). The USA and Britain agreed to fight a defensive war in Asia and an offensive one in Europe ("**Germany First**"), where most of their resources would be invested. Japan was an economic pygmy compared to the Third Reich.

THE TURNING POINTS

Russia halted the German advance at the bloodiest battle in human history at Stalingrad in 1942. Mussolini was overthrown in 1943. North Africa and Italy were invaded by the US and British in 1943, and the **D-Day** invasion of **Normandy** took place in June 1944. Germany was defeated in May 1945*. Hitler committed suicide and his officials were imprisoned and some executed after the **Nuremburg Trials**. Atomic bombs were dropped on **Hiroshima** and Nagasaki in August 1945, and Japan also surrendered. The top leadership of Japan, with the exception of the emperor were also tried and executed.

THE HOLOCAUST

It was revealed that Germany had organized a massive campaign to murder millions of Jews, men, women, and children, and also gypsies, homosexuals, clergymen, the mentally retarded, the aged, liberals and communists in what became known as the **Holocaust**.

MAKING PEACE

Churchill, Roosevelt, and Stalin worked closely together (if not always amicably) to coordinate the conduct of the war and the settlement afterwards. At a series of conferences at Washington, Quebec, Casablanca, Tehran, **Yalta**, and **Potsdam** strategy was hammered out and the peace arranged. No formal treaty like Versailles was ever signed to end the Second World War. Roosevelt's failing health perhaps weakened his judgment in making concessions to Russia that Churchill did not want to make. However, in Eastern Europe the reality was that Britain and the USA could do little to restrain Stalin unless they wished to fight a Third World War. At Potsdam the dead Roosevelt was replaced by **Harry Truman**, and Churchill lost an election to **Clement Atlee**.

Unconditional surrender was demanded by the USA and Britain, as a way of reassuring Stalin they would not make a separate peace. Russia also accepted no conditions.

CAUSES OF THE AXIS DEFEAT

ECONOMIC

- The vast economic and material superiority of the capitalist democracies over Germany and Japan. The Allies also made more efficient use of their resources, including the female workforce

- The steadfast support of Great Britain, when fighting alone, given by Canada, Australia, South Africa, and New Zealand. Even the masses in India remained loyal or neutral, which relieved pressure on security and provided invaluable supplies and personnel

- The Japanese economy was weak and over extended. Once oil was cut off from the East Indies, they were doomed

- The Italian economy was very weak and proved a drag on German resources

POOR LEADERSHIP

- The fear and loathing provoked by the Germans in Russia, which outweighed people's dislike of the Communist regime

- The fear and loathing of Japan in China and elsewhere in Asia provoked by racism and bad treatment of conquered peoples

- Italy was unprepared for the war and the population did not give the conflict full support

- Hitler not only made serious strategic and tactical errors from Dunkirk to Stalingrad but also devoted resources to projects such as the Holocaust that were needed elsewhere to fight the war. Racist ideology distorted reality

TECHNOLOGY

- The technological superiority (except in rocketry) of the British and Americans ranging from the invention of **RADAR** to the **Atomic Bomb**. Decryption of German and Japanese intercepts gave the Allies the advantage in intelligence

- Superiority in airpower both the Atlantic and Pacific of the Allies, especially in aircraft carriers

IDEOLOGY

- The Allies offered a more optimistic and humane vision of the future for the world

SUPERIOR ALLIED LEADERSHIP

- Superior leadership of **Winston Churchill** and **Franklin Roosevelt**, and the top generals Alan Brooke and **George Marshall**.

OUTCOMES OF THE SECOND WORLD WAR

- Germany was divided into four zones (the French were included) and ruled by military force until "denazification" could be completed and a new constitution written.

- Berlin lay within the Soviet Zone and was itself divided into four zones.

- The Allied sectors eventually emerged as the democratic Federal Republic (West Germany) while the East became a Soviet satellite state until it merged with the West in 1990. West Germany made a remarkable and rapid economic recovery

- Poland was reconstituted, and absorbed East Prussia. It quickly fell under Soviet domination

- Finland and Austria retained their independence, but the Soviets held a kind of veto on their foreign policies—"Finlandization"—until 1989

- Estonia, Latvia, and Lithuania were absorbed directly into the Soviet Union

- Hungary, Czechoslovakia, Romania, and Bulgaria fell under Soviet rule in the years immediately after the war

- Yugoslavia and Albania went communist but were led by resistance figures (**Tito** and Hoxha) unfriendly to Russia

- Italy abolished the monarchy and established an unstable but ultimately successful democracy

- Greece fought a bloody civil war in which the communists were defeated with British and then American (the **Truman Doctrine**) aid

- France established the 4th Republic that proved hopelessly unstable

- Britain survived but was economically weak and spiritually exhausted. It ceased to be a superpower and the empire evaporated soon after the war

- The USA and the USSR emerged as superpowers in a new bi-polar world

- China was liberated from Japanese rule but plunged into a civil war in which the Communist **Mao Zedong** triumphed in 1949

- Japan retained its emperor but had an American devised democratic constitution imposed on it. Japan managed an extraordinarily rapid economic recovery that catapulted it into great economic power status for the first time

- A replacement for the League of Nations, the **United Nations**, was established and proved somewhat more effective than its predecessor in providing a forum for peaceful resolution of disputes

- The inhuman treatment of the Jews and other minorities and the brutality of the Germans in Russia and the Japanese in China left a permanent mark of disgrace on those societies. The need to guard against man's capacity to do evil was rendered self-evident

THE COLD WAR

In 1946 Churchill described an **Iron Curtain** dividing Europe between the Soviet controlled East and the free West. The West formed a military alliance, the North Atlantic Treaty Organization (**NATO**). The US policy developed to counter the Soviet threat was called "**containment**," constant counter-pressure to the expansive pressure of the USSR.

CAUSES OF THE COLD WAR

- The Soviets had been excluded from the secret of the Atomic bomb and feared the West might use it unilaterally while they had yet to acquire the technology. In part, the bomb dropped on Hiroshima was a message to the USSR that the West was prepared to use nuclear weapons if necessary to preserve freedom (a message sent at the cost of the Japanese)

- Stalin was both paranoid and ambitious to conquer all of Europe and Asia

- Fear developed in the West about superior Russian missile technology.

- The communist and capitalist ideologies were both aggressive, based on the assumption of total moral ascendancy

- The Russians saw their control of Germany and Poland in particular and Eastern Europe in general as a reasonable strategy to prevent a repeat of the German/Austrian attacks of 1914 and 1941. The West saw a Communist empire in the making

- The West feared Communist parties might win elections in France and Italy, which would lead to an overthrow of democracy and alliance with the Soviet Union. Many resistance heroes during the war were communists, and they did well in elections afterwards

- Stalin was not the only one suffering from paranoia. The West saw signs of a vast Communist conspiracy around the world once Mao achieved power in China—nearly half of humanity was now under red rule. The **Korean War** (1950–53) reinforced conspiracy theories

- The Soviets remained bitter about the failure of the US and UK to launch a second front in Europe in 1942 and 1943, which would have relieved some of the German pressure. The assumption was that the West wanted the stuffing knocked out of the Soviet Union

- The West was horrified by the brutality of Stalin's rule

- Communists were horrified by the racism inherent in White domination of the American political system and European imperialism

- The **Marshall Plan** (1947), even though offered to the Soviets, was seen as a plot to bribe Europeans with American wealth

- The **Berlin Blockade** (1948–49) was an attempt to push the West out of Germany (US response of "airlift")

- **NATO** (1949) was seen by communists as an offensive alliance preparing to attack Russia

- The **Warsaw Pact** was seen in the West as a Soviet offensive alliance preparing to invade Western Europe

- In the end, enormous wealth generated by economic growth throughout all classes in the West was rightly seen by the Communist leaders as a mortal danger to the long-term survival of Communism

THE POST WAR WORLD

Ironically, the Cold War and the spread of nuclear weapons (first to Britain, then Russia, France, and China) created the idea of mutually assured destruction (MAD), which prevented another general war so long as no accidents or another Hitler came on to the scene. Only the **Cuban Missile Crisis** of 1962 seemed to bring the Cold War to a near hot one. Nevertheless, everyone was aware of possible doom. Competition even included war for medals at the Olympic Games.

"THE 60's"

During the 1960's much cultural innovation and protest against traditional values arrived, largely as a product of pressure from youth, especially college aged students. Everything from the ascent of "the Beatles" to the Civil Rights movement in the American South to the world crisis evoked by the Vietnam War played a role. Clothes, music, political rhetoric, and social structure all changed. Some see the "60s" rebellion as an uprising by privileged youth against boredom, security, and the lack of existential challenge in the post-war capitalist boom. This was clearly not the case in Belfast or Selma, however.

SOVIET UNION

- Stalin died in 1953 and his successor, Nikita **Khrushchev** not only condemned his brutality and began to dismantle the gulags but also tried to establish links with the West

- Khrushchev's failed agricultural policy and the perception that he was the loser in the Cuban Crisis led to his overthrow in 1963

- Khrushchev's successor, Brezhnev, was more brutal and less innovative but also interested in links with the West.

- The Soviets succeeded in reducing infant mortality, spreading education, and achieving more equality. The successes of their Space Program and military prowess distracted attention from the failure of food production and the underlying weakness of the economy

GREAT BRITAIN

- Atlee's Labour Party won power in 1945 and proceeded to nationalize major industries, provide more educational opportunities, and establish the National Health Service (free medical care)

- Structural weaknesses in the economy, loss of world markets, and continued high spending on military forces suitable to its pre-war stature slowed recovery from the war.

- Powerful labor unions, class conflict, and loss of status as a great power left Britain weakened and by the 1970s the country was in turmoil

FRANCE
- The Fourth Republic staggered to a collapse in the mid-1950s humiliated by the loss of empire, and the on-going conflict in Algeria.

- De Gaulle was recalled to power and imposed a new constitution with a strong president—the **Fifth Republic**.

- The Gaullist, center-right party dominated until student and worker uprisings in 1968 drove the General from power

GERMANY
- **Konrad Adenauer** and Ludwig Erhard led the Federal Republic into the respectable circle of nations and produced an economic "miracle" of recovery. Germany rapidly became the most powerful economy in Western Europe and stayed on a democratic course

ITALY
- Became a republic in 1946. The Christian Democrats under De Gasperi staved off the Communists, rebuilt the economy, joined NATO, moved towards economic strength for the first time since unification

EAST GERMANY
- The most depraved and unhappy of the Soviet satellites under the crude and craven rule of Stalinists. Berlin Wall built in 1961 to stop everybody from leaving

POLAND
- Unrest in 1956 led to a lessening of harsh communist policies under Wladyslaw Gomulka.

- The Solidarity workers' movement began to erode Communist authority and legitimacy, as did the activities of the Polish **Pope John Paul II**

HUNGARY
- Open revolt in 1956 led by Imre Nagy suppressed violently by Russian invasion

CZECHOSLOVKIA
- **"Prague Spring"** followed by Soviet "invasion" and suppression of reform 1968

DECOLONIALIZATION

GREAT BRITAIN
Great Britain withdrew from India in 1947 and two warring states, Muslim Pakistan and Hindu India emerged. The independence movement had been led by Gandhi and Nehru. Britain gave up its African colonies in the 1950s and 60s.

THE NETHERLANDS
The Dutch left Indonesia in 1949.

FRANCE
The French fought against a Communist insurgency in Vietnam led by Ho Chi Minh unsuccessfully and were forced to withdraw in 1954. A war in Algeria dragged on until 1961. Loss of the rest of the empire followed.

UNITED STATES
The USA gave independence to the Philippines in 1946.

PORTUGAL
The Portuguese resisted the loss of their empire until 1975 which led to severe political disruption at home

BELGIUM
As in the 19th century, the worst suffering due to colonialism occurred in the Belgian Congo, where European rule had always been at its most depraved, and the African successor governments were no better. The legacy of Belgian rule in Rwanda, where the most terrible racial violence since World War II broke out in 1994, was equally appalling.

SUEZ CRISIS
The disastrous intervention by the British and French at Suez in 1956 in which they attempted to resist Egypt's nationalization of the canal was condemned both by the USA and the USSR and discredited remaining imperialist impulses.

SOUTHERN AFRICA
In South Africa, a post-colonial white regime established *apartheid* and brutally repressed African peoples. It cut its links with Great Britain, as did the White supremacists in Rhodesia. A peaceful transition of power in South Africa was not arranged until 1991.

CAUSES OF THE RAPID EUROPEAN RETREAT FROM EMPIRE

- Effective leadership of independence movements by native leaders

- Exhaustion of European powers by the war

- Pressure from the USA to decolonize and threatened withdrawal of aid if they did not

- Spread of education and nationalist aspirations in Africa and Asia

- The British defeat at Singapore by the Japanese convinced colonial peoples they could defeat the Europeans

- Cold War diplomatic and propaganda requirements and the West's realization that it must live up to its own declared values relating to freedom and democracy

- Realization that many colonies cost more than they were worth

INTERNATIONAL COOPERATION

The Bretton Woods Agreement (1944) provided for new currency and banking arrangements, and led to the International Monetary Fund (IMF) and the World Bank. These aided economic recovery and later helped developing nations. The UN established many agencies to promote world health, refugees, education, and children.

THE MIDDLE EAST

During the First World War, the British had attempted to win support against the Ottomans and from Jews in the US and Germany by issuing the **Balfour Declaration** in 1917, which promised support for a Jewish national homeland. Once in control of Palestine, the British did not hinder Jewish immigration, but they also did not help the Zionists. After the war the British were too weak to continue to hold on to their empire and much sympathy for the Jews had been engendered around the world due to the **Holocaust**. The creation of the state of Israel in 1948 was welcomed by many Europeans.

The Arabs, however, viewed this event with horror and bitterness that has never been assuaged. Repeated wars have ensued. The Europeans have tried to balance their need for oil (which comes largely from Arab states), and their support for democracy in Israel, which has a largely European Jewish population. The irreconcilable differences in the Middle East were exploited during the Cold War, led to a huge surge in terrorism, use of oil as a political weapon by the producing states (OPEC) that ignited serious inflation and economic downturns during the 1970s in the West. The terrorist Palestinian movement, the **PLO**, was led by Yasser Arafat.

THE EUROPEAN UNION

Jean Monnet of France worked quickly after the war to establish an economic system that would tie Germany, France, and the Benelux countries so tightly together that integration would make future war impossible. The European Coal and Steel Union was the result of this work (1952). Later more economic links and more countries were included leading to the **Treaty of Rome** in 1957 which established a six-nation free trade area, the **European Economic Community** (**EEC**) or Common Market. In 1967 the next step was to begin a movement towards political union, which led to the European parliament at Strasbourg and the rise of the European Community (EC). A treaty of **European Union** was signed at Maastricht in 1991 (**EU**). This organization now regulates laws, issues passports, and has established a common currency (**euro**). Some countries such as Denmark and Britain have been reluctant followers. Sweden came in late, and Norway not at all. Many of the former Soviet states entered the Union in 2004 and afterwards.

THE WELFARE STATE

After the war most Western democracies committed heavily to reforms to equalize society in all its basic functions: the workplace, parenthood, medical care, education, recreation, vacations, and housing. Government care from "cradle to grave." This was paid for by heavy taxation that at some levels could reach over 90%. Inheritance taxes also increased. However, after many initial successes, governments found that nationalizing some industries made them inefficient and over reliant on subsidies, so privatization began to restore them to the controls of the marketplace. Also, very high taxation tended to drive businesses elsewhere and throttle entrepreneurship and dynamism on the job. Most countries have been forced to retreat when the price of the welfare state became too high to allow capitalism to flourish.

INTELLECTUAL CURRENTS

- Existentialism, especially associated with Camus (d. 1960) and **Sartre** (d. 1980), in the tradition of Nietzsche and Kirkegaard, painted a bleak picture of the human condition, we are alone and "condemned to be free". They emphasized taking action.

- Organized religion weakened further, and regular religious attendance diminished to a tiny minority in most Western countries.

- Deconstructionists focused on the biases and class and cultural assumptions in the texts detached from the creative force of artists.

- Increasing tolerance for homosexuals.

- **Postmodernism** in the arts embraced contemporary popular and commercial culture.

- Rock dominated the music scene and homogenized culture.

- **Vatican II** (1962) liberalized Catholic practice and theology. Latin mass abandoned. **John Paul II** (1978) charted a more conservative course. The first non-Italian elected to the Papacy in modern times. His Polish origins made him an influential force in the breakdown of Soviet power in Eastern Europe.

- Artists' and composers' visions of their role in society were fragmented and chaotic. Styles proliferated, many eschewed beauty, realism was reviled, primitivism, cacophony, and abstraction prevailed. The desire to shock became rampant.

- Television and radio largely devoted themselves to popular culture. Professional athletics became big business.

- Big science was well funded, and research universities produced many breakthroughs in medicine, biology, and physics. **DNA** was identified at Cambridge (1952) and slowly decoded. Organ transplants became possible. The "pill" transformed sex life. "Dolly" the sheep cloned. Human genome mapped.

- Social science became more influential and respected.

WOMEN'S LIBERATION

Women built on the achievements of earlier **feminists** and the work of authors such as **Simone de Beauvoir** (*The Second Sex*, 1949) made the case that discrimination against women went far deeper that political and legal issues. Women had accepted their fate too passively. Women were encouraged to enter into the workforce in much larger numbers and to demand equal wages and rights to promotion. The work at home must be more equally divided. Special account needed to be taken of the impact of motherhood on careers and marriages. Leadership roles in politics and business were slow to come, but progress was made. Mediterranean cultures found it harder to adjust, and conservatively interpreted Islam remained a major impediment.

IMPORTANT DEFINITIONS AND IDENTIFICATIONS

- Konrad Adenauer
- Allies
- Clement Atlee
- Atomic bomb
- Axis
- Balfour Declaration
- Simone de Beauvoir
- Berlin Blockade
- Bretton Woods Agreement
- Winston Churchill
- "containment"
- Cuban Missile Crisis
- DNA
- Dunkirk
- Charles de Gaulle
- euro
- European Economic Community (EEC)
- European Union (EU)
- Existentialism

- Feminism
- Fifth Republic
- Germany First
- Hiroshima
- Adolf Hitler
- Holocaust
- Iron Curtain
- Pope John Paul II
- Nikta Khrushchev
- Korean War
- Lend-Lease
- Mao Zedong
- George Marshall
- Marshall Plan
- Jean Monnet
- Benito Mussolini
- NATO
- Nuremburg Trials
- Pearl Harbor
- PLO

- Postmodernism
- Potsdam
- Prague Spring
- RADAR
- Treaty of Rome
- Franklin Roosevelt
- Jean Paul Sartre
- Singapore
- Stalingrad
- Suez Crisis
- Tito
- Harry Truman
- Truman Doctrine
- United Nations
- Vatican II
- Vichy
- Warsaw Pact
- Welfare State
- Women's Liberation
- Yalta

IMPORTANT DATES

*1939 Outbreak of Second World War

1940 Fall of France
Battle of Britain

1941 Invasion of Russia
Pearl Harbor

1942 Battle Stalingrad

1944 Normandy Invasion (D-Day)

*1945 End of Second World War
Hiroshima

1957 Treaty of Rome

1968 French political turmoil
Youth Revolt

CHAPTER 11
MULTIPLE-CHOICE QUESTIONS

Questions 1.1–1.3 refer to the "welfare state" illustrated below on the cover of a 1944 official pamphlet.

1.1 This pamphlet produced by the British Government in 1944 placed emphasis on what aspect of the welfare state?

   (A) Free education at universities
   (B) Building a classless society
   (C) Self-insurance to pay for benefits
   (D) Cradle to grave benefits from the state

1.2 The programs listed in this pamphlet can be characterized in which of the following ways?

   (A) The opening round of welfare benefits in Britain
   (B) Further development of a program already in place
   (C) The first welfare state established in Europe
   (D) Free health care for all

1.3 The benefits promised in this program were the result of which of the following?

   (A) The triumph of socialism in Britain during the Second World War
   (B) The revival of the Liberal Party in the 1930s
   (C) The conversion of the Conservative Party to socialist principles
   (D) Compromise worked out in a wartime coalition government

175

Questions 2.1–2.3 refer to US—USSR relations during the Cold War illustrated by the photograph of the 1959 "kitchen debate" in Moscow reproduced below.

2.1 Premier Khruschev and Vice President Nixon debated at an exhibition of American products in Moscow in 1959. What was the mostly likely topic of their debate?

(A) The hours laborers worked in the USSR vs. USA
(B) The ability to travel freely outside the USSR
(C) How clean American houses were
(D) Availability and prices of consumer goods

2.2 Soviet communism failed most visibly in what area compared with the West?

(A) The space race
(B) Production of nuclear weapons
(C) Increase in the standard of living
(D) Provision of adequate and affordable health care

2.3 Premier Khruschev ran into serious difficulties and was eventually lost power due to what event?

(A) Sending Russian missiles to Cuba
(B) Attacking China
(C) Denouncing Stalin
(D) Setting up a new system of slave labor

Question 3.1–3.3 refer to the document below.

A new situation has been created in Poland as a result of her complete liberation by the Red Army. This calls for the establishment of a Polish Provisional Government which can be more broadly based than was possible before the recent liberation of the Western part of Poland. The Provisional Government which is now functioning in Poland should therefore be reorganized on a broader democratic basis with the inclusion of democratic leaders from Poland itself and from Poles abroad.

This Polish Provisional Government shall be pledged to the holding of free and unfettered elections as soon as possible on the basis of universal suffrage and secret ballot. In these elections all democratic and anti-Nazi parties shall have the right to take part and to put forward candidates.

"Yalta Agreement", J. Stalin, Franklin D. Roosevelt, Winston S. Churchill, 1945

3.1 What actually happened in Poland after the Second World War came to an end?

(A) The USSR undermined attempts to carry out the pledges it made at Yalta and seize control of the country
(B) Poland became a democracy
(C) The Polish monarchy was restored
(D) Poland was divided in half between Germany and the USSR

3.3 Which of the following Communist countries in Eastern Europe did not follow the directives coming from the USSR but successfully charted an independent course?

(A) East Germany
(B) Hungary
(C) Bulgaria
(D) Yugoslavia

3.2 What gave Stalin influence in Poland to set the course there?

(A) The threat of using nuclear weapons
(B) The presence of the Soviet army of occupation
(C) The Poles asked Stalin to take over
(D) The USA and Great Britain ceased to be allies

Questions 4.1–4.3 refer to the 1944 sculpture by Picasso entitled "Man and Lamb" illustrated below.

1958-155-1 For Condition Report Only

4.1 This sculpture of a man with a lamb by Picasso completed in 1944 is emblematic of which of the following?

    (A) Celebration of the heroism of ancient civilizations
    (B) The agony of the human condition in the mid-twentieth century
    (C) Concerns over the environment and global warming
    (D) The Papacy of Pius XII

4.2 Picasso's masterpiece "Guernica", completed a few years earlier, was concerned about what issue?

    (A) The Spanish Civil War
    (B) World War I
    (C) The Great Depression
    (D) The failures of modern art

4.3 Modern artists increasingly adopted what style?

    (A) Impressionism
    (B) Realism
    (C) Abstractionism
    (D) Romanticism

Questions 5.1–5.3 refer to the statistical table below.

Aircraft Production of the Powers, 1940–1945

	1940	1941	1942	1943	1944	1945
USA	12,804	26,277	47,836	85,898	96,318	49,761
USSR	10,565	15,735	25,436	34,900	40,300	20,900
UK	15,049	20,094	23,672	26,263	26,461	12,070
UK Emp.	1,100	2,600	4,575	4,700	4,575	2,075
Total	39,518	64,706	101,519	151,761	167,654	84,806
Germany	10,247	11,776	15,409	24,807	39,807	7,540
Japan	4,768	5,088	8,861	16,693	28,180	11,066
Italy	1,800	2,400	2,400	1,600	—	—
Total	16,815	19,264	26,670	43,100	67,987	18,606

5.1 What is the most important thing that a historian can learn from the data presented above?

(A) The United States was a great economic power
(B) The British Empire made a vital contribution to victory
(C) The Allies possessed overwhelming economic superiority over the Axis
(D) Italy was unprepared for a major war and should not have participated

5.2 Proportionate to its size and population, which country produced the largest number of aircraft 1940–45?

(A) Germany
(B) Japan
(C) UK
(D) USA

5.3 Part of the reason why Germany failed to produce enough munitions during the Second World War was its

(A) Inefficient use of labor
(B) Insufficient supplies of coal
(C) Small size
(D) Inability to persuade Spain to become an ally

SHORT-ANSWER QUESTIONS

Question 1

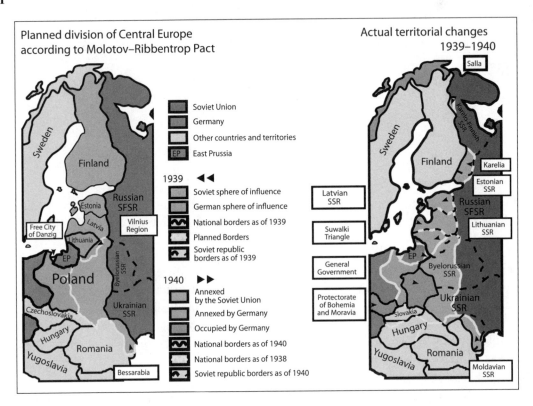

The map above shows Poland at the beginning of the Second World War in September 1939. Using the map and your knowledge of European History answer the following questions (A, B, and C).

A) Identify and explain ONE of the reasons why Hitler invaded Poland in 1939.
B) Identify and explain ONE of the reasons why Stalin invaded Poland in 1939.
C) Identify and explain ONE of the reasons why Stalin made a non-aggression pact with Hitler in the summer of 1939.

Question 2

"VERY WELL, ALONE"

" *So our poor old Empire is alone in the world.*"
" *Aye, we are—the whole five hundred million of us.*"

The two cartoons above published in June and July 1940 appeared after the surrender of France to Hitler, which left Britain the sole European power at war with Germany (the USSR did not enter the war until June 1941 and the United States until December 1941). Using the cartoons and your knowledge of European history answer the questions below (A and B).

A) Identify and explain the contradictory views expressed in the two cartoons.
B) Identify and explain TWO factors that contributed to British victory in the Second World War.

CHAPTER 12

CONTEMPORARY EUROPE

THE COLLAPSE OF COMMUNISM *1989–1991

The Cold War rumbled on with ups (*détente*) and downs. Space and arms races frightened everyone. Cuba, Vietnam, and Afghanistan were the most notable open points of conflict. The Prague Spring in 1968, was put down by a Soviet invasion, and the **Solidarity Movement** led by Lech Walesa in Poland besmirched the reputation of the Russians around the world and at home in ways previous protest movements had failed to do.

CAUSES OF THE COLLAPSE OF COMMUNISM

- Russia stagnated and drifted during Brezhnev's last years and the deaths in rapid succession of his two immediate successors from old age were embarrassingly symbolic of atrophy

- Communist ideology was wrong about human motivation. The system lacked incentives, deterred entrepreneurship, and failed to produce enough food due to collectivized agriculture

- **Centralized planning** of the economy proved impractical over the long run (could be effective during wars or to achieve specific tasks (**space race**). Failure to produce consumer goods became increasingly corrosive as it became obvious that the West excelled in the production of automobiles and blue jeans for the masses

- The Russian birthrate was declining and that of ethnic minorities rising. The latter would soon outnumber the former in total population and many were restive under Russian rule.

- Deep nationalistic aspirations were a serious danger especially when combined with the revival of Islamic faith in the southern regions

- The invasion of Afghanistan (1979) bogged down in a military morass that devoured resources and became extremely unpopular at home

- *Détente* between China and the USA (1972) weakened the notion of monolithic communism and the USSR felt threatened

- Conquered peoples in the Baltic republics and Eastern Europe were pressing for freedom

- The cost of competing with Western military technologies, especially "Star Wars", which threatened to make the USA invulnerable to a nuclear attack, was getting beyond the capacity of the USSR to pay

- Middle class professionals and managers were increasingly resentful of their exclusion from decision making

- The invention of photocopiers and videotape players made it impossible to control the dissemination of censored material

- **George Orwell's** *Animal Farm* and *1984* (1949) had made it difficult for communist propagandists to convince educated people that totalitarian rule had any redeeming value

- **Solzhenitsyn's** documentation of the history of repression destroyed any remnants of moral authority the Soviet Union retained

- Housing was totally inadequate.

- The new leader, **Mikhail Gorbachev** (1985–1991) instituted reforms (*glasnost*—openness; *perestroika*—decentralization of the economy) that did not go far enough and antagonized the old guard. He still believed in communism

- Gorbachev was not prepared to use violence and repression to preserve Soviet rule in Eastern Europe and withdrew his support for the troglodyte leaders of the East German regime

- Hungary opened its borders with Austria, which allowed safe access for escape from East Germany. The trains began to fill

- Elections in Poland and the "velvet" revolution in Prague led by **Vaclav Havel** destroyed the underpinnings of communist power in the East

- The **Berlin Wall** was demolished

The failed *coup* attempt against Gorbachev in 1991 destroyed the credibility of the old leadership, and placed the dynamic, if erratic, **Boris Yeltsin**, who denounced the Communist Party, in power

OUTCOMES OF THE COLLAPSE OF COMMUNISM
- The Cold War came to an end

- Russia went into a deepening economic and demographic crisis from which it has not recovered. It is propped up only by rising energy prices

- Russia took faltering steps towards democracy and the free market

- **Gorbachev** was ousted and held responsible for Russian loss of prestige and empire

- Baltic states gained independence; East and West Germany reunified

- Czechoslovakia, Hungary, Romania, Bulgaria, Albania and Poland gained freedom

- Czechoslovakia broke into the Czech Republic and Slovakia

- Yugoslavia broke apart in the 1990s. The resulting civil wars produced independent states of Serbia, Bosnia, Croatia, Slovenia, Kosovo, Montenegro, and Macedonia. The US and European states intervened militarily. Racial cleansing took place with mass murders

- Ukraine, Moldova, and Belarus broke away from Russia and took important military and economic assets with them. Fears of "loose nukes" have so far proved ungrounded. All three have suffered political setbacks, and a Communist remnant still rules Belarus as a dictator

- Islamic republics in the south and Georgia and Armenia in the Caucasus also gained independence

- A radical decline in the already poor standard of living took place in Russia during the 1990s. There has been some improvement since then. Alcoholism rose dramatically, and the average age of mortality dipped fast

- Civil war and terrorism in **Chechnya**

- Land reform finally enacted (2002) but has made slow progress

- Government control over the press has returned and **Vladimir Putin** appears to be establishing a proto-fascist regime

- The United States became the only superpower; with China in the wings

EUROPE AFTER THE COLD WAR

GREAT BRITAIN
- Britain emerged out of its economic and social crisis of the 1970s with a yank of the neck by Prime Minister **Margaret Thatcher** (1979–90). She crushed the unions and Argentina (Falklands War). She reversed economic decline and changed the spirit of the nation. However, her policies caused deep antagonism and ideological blindness induced her fall

- The success of the Conservatives led to the remaking of the Labour Party (**New Labour**) by **Tony Blair**, who renounced socialism as the fundamental principle of the party

- In the late 1990s Blair led the movement for **devolution** (parliaments for Scotland and Wales), helped tame the Northern Irish crisis, and moved towards greater integration with Europe while continuing a special relationship with Washington

- Blair's alliance with George Bush in the Iraq War brought New Labour into disrepute followed by the economic crash of 2008

- In the 2010 election a "hung Parliament" led to the formation of a coalition between the Conservative and Liberal Parties with David Cameron as Prime Minister. He has tried to move the Tories leftwards on social issues and impose economic austerity to reduce the budget deficit

- The Conservative Party remains divided on membership in the **European Union** (**EU**). Britain never joined the European currency (euro)

- The royal succession was made gender blind in 2013 and the monarchy experienced near deification in the 60th year of the reign of the immensely popular Elizabeth II, the only surviving major public figure in Europe from the Second World War era and increasingly influential as head of the **Commonwealth** (former countries from the Empire)

- Scotland voted to stay within the UK (2014)

FRANCE

- The Gaullists were defeated in 1981 by the Socialists under **François Mitterrand**. He proved to be a moderate reformer, worked effectively on European integration, and cooperated with a **Gaullist** prime minister (*cohabitation*).

- The Gaullists regained the presidency in 1995. Although the communists and some neo-fascists were largely marginalized, fringe groups in profound disagreement with the existing constitution remain prevalent.

- France led the resistance to **George Bush's** policy of **war in Iraq**

- Gaullists lost the presidency to Socialist François Holland in 2012.

RUSSIA

- **Yelstin** failed to make effective economic reforms which led to further economic and political crises. He allowed many valuable state assets to be sold off cheaply, which created a small group of very rich businessmen called the "oligarchs"

- **Vladimir Putin** elected President in 2000 initially restored a sense of purpose and order. He has made some effective reforms and finally pushed through the right to buy and sell agricultural land. He was at first cooperative with the West while Russia was weak, but he is a former KGB agent with no time for a free press and also a deeply committed nationalist. It is also increasingly clear he is criminally corrupt

- The weakness in Ukraine offered a chance to regain some territory. Will this policy of expanding the borders continue? Who else is under threat? The Baltic states? Belarus and Moldova? Poland?

- Democracy is disappearing

- The economy survived due to rising energy prices (exports of gas and oil bring revenues to the state and the economy) The rest of the economy remains weak, and the price of oil is going down

GERMANY

- Chancellor **Helmut Kohl** organized reunification in 1990. This proved costly and produced a less happy marriage than expected. The East's economy was so bad that even the dynamism of the West has struggled to achieve prosperity and repair the damage of 45 years of misrule

- The socialist Chancellor Schröder charted a newly independent foreign policy and saw the EU as a counterbalance to US power

- **Angela Merkle** (born and raised in the East) has been an exceptionally strong and skilful leader. Under her administration the German economy has remained the strongest in Europe and Germany is now the dominant power in the **EU**

- Berlin again became the capital of Germany after 50 years of the West being centered at Bonn

ITALY

- Serious terrorist outbreaks in the 70s dissipated. The economy prospered, but the lengthy rule of the **Christian Democrats**, kept in power because the only alternative was Communism, led to widespread corruption in the political system. Finally alternative parties have gained office

- Silvio Berlusconi's tenure as Prime Minister (intervals between 1994–2011) was that of a half clown and half incompetent. He faces numerous criminal charges and may yet end in prison

- The Italian economy stagnated in recent years and the national deficit sky-rocketed. No long-term solution is in sight

YUGOSLAVIA

- Ethnic antagonisms re-emerged after Tito's death in 1980. The upheavals elsewhere in the Balkans unleashed civil war

- Croatia and Slovenia became independent in 1991

- The worst fighting took place in Bosnia. The UN and NATO intervened in 1994. Serbian leader **Slobodan Milosevic** continued to foster ethnic trouble and terror until overthrown after **NATO** bombing in 1999–2000. He was put on trial for war crimes at The Hague

THE FIRST AND SECOND IRAQ WARS

In 1991 Iraq attacked Kuwait and Israel. A Western/Japanese coalition led by the USA freed Kuwait and punished **Iraq** in the Gulf War, but the latter continued as a rogue state. Russian weakness made it possible for the West to become more aggressive in attacking Iraq, but liberal ideologies and questionable evidence about the threat posed by Saddam Hussein weakened support for further battles. US and Britain invaded Iraq again in 2003 and toppled regime. This plunged the country into a chaotic stew of sectarian violence that made many question whether any advance had been made over the previous regime. Europeans will be very skeptical about following the United States into further adventures. Does this mark the end of the Western alliance? Cooperation in the overthrow of the dictator of Libya suggests perhaps not.

SOCIAL MORES

The lives of ordinary Europeans have been greatly transformed in recent years. Divorce has become common and unmarried childbirth routine. One-parent families proliferate and in most two-parent families both parents worked outside the home. Manufacturing jobs have declined, and more and more people work in the service or technology sectors. Small farms are disappearing. More and more people go on to higher education. Drug use proliferated. Concern about "dumbing-down" of education arose. Toleration of deviance from traditional social norms became widespread in Western Europe, though not in the East. Spain and Ireland, once bastions of religious conservatism, recently enacted laws sanctioning gay marriage.

RELIGION

The Roman Catholic Church, once so influential in Southern and Eastern Europe has declined radically in influence as it became increasingly out of step either with the secularization of society (says the Church leadership) or the humane values of modern civilization (say many ex-followers). In his last years **Pope John Paul II** fell ill and was unable to provide leadership. His successor Benedict XVI (the first German Pope) was a rigid conservative. On his retirement, the first Pope from South America, Francis, was elected in 2013. He faces a two front crisis. The first is the failure of the Church hierarchy adequately to address a gigantic scandal of sexual abuse by priests that reached frightful proportions in Ireland but also affected many other countries. The costs in legitimacy and money have been huge. The second is how to reconcile the conservative social views of the expanding membership in Africa, Asia, and South America with the far more liberal views of followers in Europe and North America. The hierarchy seems paralyzed about how to address issues such as married priests, female priests, birth control, homosexuality, and use of condoms to prevent the spread of HIV/Aids. Church attendance is now in single digits in once universally Catholic countries such as Italy and not a single priest was ordained in Ireland in 2012. Even in South America the Church faces challenges from evangelical Protestant ministries.

PROBLEMS CONFRONTING EUROPE TODAY

- How to confront deeply conservative social and religious practices of **Islamic immigrants** who now constitute as much as one in ten (or more) of the Western European population with advanced views of much of the native population on sex, gender, free speech, the law, etc. This problem has led to political assassinations and terror in countries once thought immune to such divisions such as the Netherlands and Denmark

- How to protect against and eliminate **jihadi terrorism**

- How to reconcile the nationalist aspirations of people in Catalonia, the Basque county, Scotland, Northern Ireland and other pockets of minority populations with the modern nation states as they presently exist

- The rising popularity of extremist political groups, including **neo-facists**

- How to cope with a continued flow of new immigrants and refuges fleeing to Europe to avoid war, poverty, and persecution

- How to educate the population to live and work in a post-industrial economy

- How to manage the information economy and the Internet which have transformed business, recreation, education, and all forms of technology.

- How to address the increasingly threatening aspects of **global warming** without damaging current employment and prosperity

- How to manage the grotesque disparity between the rich and poor in the world

- How to cope with what may be a long-term crisis of capitalism reflected in the collapse in 2008 and rising inequality in the distribution of wealth

- How to rectify the crisis in the euro zone precipitated by the 2008 troubles and the too rapid admission of countries not yet ready to regulate their economies into the **EU** (Greece, Cyprus, etc.) and the serious deficit problems in Italy, Spain, Ireland and elsewhere. What role is the exceptionally powerful Germany going to play vis a vis the less powerful France and Britain both of which still aspire to leadership roles.

- What to do when the North Sea Oil runs out

- How to cope with Russia, still a great nuclear power that has not found its feet economically or politically. Is Vladimir Putin, a corrupt oligarch, a searcher for electoral popularity to sustain his rule at home, or a sinister figure with the aspirations of a Mussolini or even a Hitler?

- A demographic crisis faces Europe. Many populations are not replacing themselves. How will fewer and fewer workers and consumers fund an economy that can support a growing elderly population that lives longer and longer due to modern medicine

- To admit or not to admit Islamic Turkey to the EU

- Volcano eruptions in Iceland nearly brought trans-Atlantic air traffic to a halt for weeks in (2010). Vulcanologists predict further and maybe more extreme episodes of eruptions in the near future

- To stick with nuclear power (France is the most dependent) or not? Both the crisis after the tsunami in Japan and the continuing problems of dealing with radioactive waste bedevil the system

- What to do if Iran gets nuclear weapons and threatens to use them?

- Can the **EU** survive? Many people resent the bureaucratic interference of Brussels. Some fear it as an engine of German dominance. Others see the political system as unwieldy. Many fear diminished national autonomy. Developing a universal financial policy and foreign policy has proved elusive at best.

- How will Europe align itself with the emergent great economic and military power in China. Will NATO remain a meaningful organization or even survive in the long-term. What will relations be with the United States?

IMPORTANT DEFINITIONS AND IDENTIFICATIONS

- Berlin Wall
- Tony Blair
- George Bush
- Centralized planning
- Chechnya
- Christian Democrats
- Commonwealth
- *Détente*
- Devolution
- euro
- European Union (EU)
- Gaullist Party

- *Glasnost*
- global warming
- Mikhail Gorbachev
- Vaclav Havel
- Iraq Wars
- Islamic immigration
- Jihadi terrorism
- Pope John Paul II
- Helmut Kohl
- New Labour
- Angela Merkle
- Slobodan Milosevic

- François Mitterrand
- NATO
- Neo-fascists
- George Orwell
- *Perestroika*
- Vladimir Putin
- Solidarity Movement
- Alexander Solzhenitsyn
- space race
- Margaret Thatcher
- Boris Yeltsin

IMPORTANT DATES

1979   Thatcher Prime Minister in Great Britain

*1989**   disintegration of the Soviet empire begins

1991   Gorbachev ousted

2008   Financial crisis

CHAPTER 12
MULTIPLE-CHOICE QUESTIONS

Questions 1.1–1.3 refer to the passages below written by two contemporary historians.

For it is as a warrior, determined to impose her version of faith and truth on her enemies, that [Prime Minister Margaret Thatcher] will go down in history, and that was precisely why she was so politically successful: she was a figure of her time, benefiting from the deep social divisions and anger of the 1970s. But since 2008 it has become increasingly evident that she did not lay the foundations for a prosperous Britain. Indeed, her approach to the major political and economic questions—much of which was inherited by the succeeding Labour government—has left Britain in deep trouble.

Margaret Thatcher's supreme achievement, as even her opponents now admit, was to blow away the stale winds of decline. By the time she left office, Britain was unquestionably a more open, dynamic, entrepreneurial and colourful society than it had been in the 1970s. Taxes were lower, strikes were down, productivity growth was much improved and far from fleeing Britain, as they had once threatened to do, foreign investors were now queuing to get in.

Dominic Sandbrook, author of *The Battle for Britain*, 1974–1979, 2013

1.1 Why is Margaret Thatcher such a controversial figure among historians?

(A) She let Britain decline into poverty and chaos
(B) She wanted to turn the Cold War hot
(C) She renounced the special relationship with the United States
(D) She took radical steps to implement her economic philosophy

1.2 What is the key point of disagreement between the historians in these passages?

(A) Thatcher's long-term economic policy
(B) The war in the Falkland Islands
(C) Thatcher's relationship with Germany
(D) Thatcher's impact on culture

1.3 Mrs. Thatcher was leader of the Conservative Party, but she was noted for which of the following?

(A) Opposition to the monarchy
(B) Refusal to use force to defend the national interest
(C) Being the first female prime minister
(D) Cutting government spending by half

Questions 2.1–2.3 refer to the fall of the Berlin Wall in 1989 illustrated below.

2.1 The wall built in 1961 that divided East and West Berlin was intended for what purpose?

(A) As a response to the Cuban Missile Crisis
(B) West Germany wanted to take a step away from unification
(C) Too many East Germans were fleeing to West Berlin
(D) The Russians wanted to defend themselves against invasion

2.2 What factor contributed the most to bringing down the Berlin Wall in 1989.

(A) The ugly appearance depressed tourism
(B) It was replaced by one further back in East Germany.
(C) It was no longer needed once the Cold War was over
(D) East Germans found a new exit to the West through Hungary making the Wall inoperable

2.3 The collapse of Soviet rule in Eastern Europe took place for all the following reasons EXCEPT.

(A) Military victory over West Germany by Russian forces
(B) The election of a new Soviet leader who refused to use military force to hold on to the Soviet Empire
(C) The puppet dictators working for the Russians lost legitimacy
(D) The allure of the freedom and material plenty in the West

Questions 3.1–3.3 refer to the document below.

Nonetheless, the key issue—politically, strategically, and morally—underlying the security of the "safe areas" (which were supposed to be protected by UN forces) was the essential nature of "ethnic cleansing." As part of the larger ambition for a "Greater Serbia," the Serbs set out to occupy the territory of the enclaves [of Muslim Bosnians]; they wanted the territory for themselves. The civilian inhabitants of the enclaves were not the incidental victims of the attackers; their death or removal was the very purpose of the attacks upon them. The tactic of employing savage terror, primarily mass killings, rapes, and brutalization of civilians, to expel populations was used to the greatest extent in Bosnia and Herzegovina, where it acquired the now-infamous euphemism of "ethnic cleansing." The Bosnian Muslim civilian population thus became the principal victims of brutally aggressive military and para-military Serb operations to depopulate coveted territories in order to allow them to be repopulated by Serbs.

"The Fall of Srebrenica: An Assessment", Report of the Secretary-General of the United Nations, 1999

3.1 What might have led the United Nations to fail to protect Muslim Bosnians from massacres by Serbs?

(A) They did not have the support of world leaders to prevent genocide
(B) The Chinese vetoed any action to help the Bosnians
(C) The victims were Muslims
(D) They did not realize until afterwards what was going on

3.2 When it became obvious that the Serbian government would use any means to oppress minority peoples, what action did NATO and the United States take?

(A) Bombed Belgrade until they stopped
(B) Invaded Serbia with ground troops
(C) Ignored the crisis in the former Yugoslavia
(D) Allowed the Russians to invade

3.3 One of the most common sources of political violence within states in the 1990s was?

(A) Disputes over federal vs. local control of civil law
(B) Religious differences
(C) Meddling by neighboring powers
(D) Struggles between communists and liberals

Questions 4.1–4.4 relate to the statistical table below.

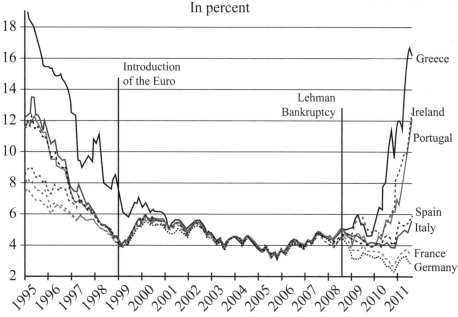

INTEREST RATES ON 10-YEAR GOVERNMENT BONDS
In percent

4.1 The data in the graph above indicates which of the following about the euro crisis 2009–2011?

  (A) The wide range of effects of the crisis in different countries
  (B) The euro was highly successful in lowering interest rates over the long term
  (C) Greece was the biggest winner in the euro crisis
  (D) The British made a mistake in not joining the euro

4.2 High interest on government bonds

  (A) Has a positive effect on an economy
  (B) Has a negative effect on an economy
  (C) Has no effect on an economy
  (D) Promotes national pride

4.3 The data in the graph above demonstrates which of the following?

  (A) Europe has little impact on the global economy
  (B) The Euro Zone is protected from the impact of events outside Europe
  (C) The Euro is the dominant force in the global economy
  (D) The interconnectedness of the global economy

4.4 Rising interest rates in Greece, Ireland, and Portugal between 2009 and 2011 were caused by which of the following?

  (A) Deficit spending by governments that got out of control
  (B) Too little was spent by the governments to stimulate the economy
  (C) Careful management of the economies by those governments
  (D) Could be easily addressed by more government spending

Questions 5.1–5.3 refer to the following passage.

In retrospect, the Millennium marked only a moment in time. It was the events of September 11 that marked a turning point in history, where we confront the dangers of the future and assess the choices facing humankind. It was a tragedy. An act of evil. From this nation, goes our deepest sympathy and prayers for the victims and our profound solidarity with the American people. We were with you at the first. We will stay with you to the last.

Be in no doubt: Bin Laden and his people organized this atrocity. The Taliban aid and abet him. He will not desist from further acts of terror. They will not stop helping him. Whatever the dangers of the action we take, the dangers of inaction are far, far greater.

The action we take will be proportionate; targeted; we will do all we humanly can to avoid civilian casualties. But understand what we are dealing with. Listen to the calls of those passengers on the planes. Think of the children on them, told they were going to die. Think of the cruelty beyond comprehension as amongst the screams and the anguish of the innocent, those hijackers drove at full throttle planes laden with fuel into buildings where tens of thousands worked. They have no moral inhibition on the slaughter of the innocent.

There is no compromise possible with such people, no meeting of minds, no point of understanding with such terror. Just a choice: defeat it or be defeated by it. And defeat it we must.

Tony Blair, Prime Minister of Great Britain, speech, Oct. 2, 2001

5.1 According to Tony Blair what is the most serious problem confronting the UK and USA after "9/11"?

(A) Religious fanaticism
(B) The attitude of the European Union
(C) Incompetent leadership by President George Bush
(D) The advantage the Russians might take of the situation

5.2 The European allies of the United States that were members of NATO did which of the following after "9/11"?

(A) Were reluctant to do anything
(B) Ignored the event
(C) Invaded Afghanistan with the US forces
(D) Tried to persuade President Bush to attack Iraq

5.3 Why was Prime Minister Blair anxious to act in concert with President George W. Bush in Afghanistan and Iraq?

(A) To protect British interests in the Far East
(B) Win popularity at home
(C) Maintain the special relationship with the USA
(D) Separate himself from the European Union

SHORT-ANSWER QUESTIONS

Question 1

Using your knowledge of European history answer the question below (A and B).

A) Identify and explain TWO of the difficulties confronting European countries in integrating recently arrived immigrants into established society.

B) Identify and explain ONE way the Europe will be permanently changed by the diversification of previously largely homogenous populations and cultures.

SAMPLE EXAMINATIONS

THE DOCUMENT-BASED QUESTION [THE DBQ]

This is the best part of the examination. It consists of one essay question based on five to seven historical documents counting twenty-five percent of the exam score with an hour to write your answer. Take time to read over the documents, which may consist of quotations (from letters, diaries, newspapers, speeches, or diary entries), statistical tables, graphs, maps, cartoons, paintings, photographs, or other materials and to outline your answer. To do well you have to understand how to analyze historical documents and evaluate the point of view or biases of the authors or creators of the material. You have to be able to develop a thesis, synthesize a variety of ideas, and write coherently. It is also important to connect your analysis to the historical events or themes under consideration. You need to bring to bear your knowledge acquired from the course to your answer. Taking into consideration the constraints of time and place, the document-based question successfully simulates what a historian does in practice. The more accurate you are in bringing in outside knowledge, the more successful you will be.

As you go through the documents, ask the five "W" questions: who, what, where, when, why? Why have the examiners put this document in the collection? What does it contribute? Can I connect it with another document? Is it a primary or secondary document? Should I take it literally or is it sarcastic or ironic in tone? What is the social, economic, and political background of the author of the document? Is the document intended for public consumption or is it a private letter or diary entry never intended to be seen by outsiders? Is it polemical or a reluctant admission of truth running counter to the interests of the author? What is the point of view or bias of the author? Are gender or nationality likely to affect the author's outlook? Be alert to the dates of the documents. Is there change over time in the course of the set? Explicitly include your answers to these questions in your analysis.

The examiners are looking for a unified essay with a thesis. They expect an introduction, an argument based closely on the documents, and if time allows a conclusion. You must have a thesis that addresses all parts of the question and does not simply repeat the question. You must back up the thesis convincingly with evidence drawn from all of the documents. You must demonstrate in as many cases as possible that you understand the point of view of the document. State this explicitly.

In the introduction restate the question in your own words to show that you understand it. Notice the command words in the question. Are you asked to discuss, to analyze, to assess, to compare? Make sure you do what is asked, not what you want. Make sure you answer all parts of the question. Good students can come to grief when they forget to answer all parts of the question. State your thesis clearly in the introduction.

In the body of the essay establish your thesis. Identify patterns in the documents. Group several documents together. Do not catalogue the documents in a laundry list. Do not go over the historical background already provided in the question. This is not an exercise in regurgitation. The readers have the documents right in front of them as they grade your exam. Do not waste time stating the obvious. The readers are interested in your analysis not in re-reading the documents in correct numerical order as paraphrased by you. If you find yourself going over each document in numerical order, stop! Put them in an order that fits your thesis. Assess the quality of the evidence; analyze and explicitly state the point of view of the authors. Mention every document. Do not over generalize. Note changes in opinion over time if that is explicit or implicit in the documents. Note nuances of language.

Incorporating outside information in support of the thesis argument not included in the documents is now a required element for this essay. The topics will be well known, so this should not be too difficult. Bring in names, events, trends that you have studied in the textbook or in class. This also helps place your argument in the context of broader regional, national, or global processes. That also is a requirement for this essay.

Avoid using your own biases and opinions or standards to judge historical controversies. For example do not use feminist, anti-abortionist, civil rights, anti-communist ideas to analyze women's suffrage, population expansion, slave trade issues, or Bolshevism. Keep your personal political, social, and religious views to yourself. Try to be as impartial and objective as possible.

Use a few quotations, if appropriate, but do not quote at length. Always identify the documents that you quote or cite. The best method is to abbreviate and put them in parentheses - for example "(docs. 2, 3, and 7)", but NEVER, NEVER, NEVER refer to a document solely by its number. Always begin by identifying the author or source ("as General von Preussen said" [Doc. 4], "as the graph on population decline demonstrates" [Doc 7], "as the cartoon poking fun at the capitalist class reveals" [Doc. 1], and etc.).

Write a conclusion if you have time. The conclusion should not repeat the essay over again. Try to place the question in a new context, connect it with other historical events. Is there a lesson to be learned? This will help you fulfill the requirement that you synthesize the argument by extending your thesis beyond its initial statement, or connecting the topic to other historical periods, geographical areas or circumstances, or drawing on ideas or methods from different fields or disciplines in support of the argument.

Practice is vital. You should go over sample questions in class. Do this first verbally, analyzing documents and developing theses as part of a discussion. Then write some essays without time restraints. (The number of documents has been reduced in the new exam format, but the skills tested are the same as in the older DBQs. If your teacher has copies of old exams, use the old DBQs to practice). Finally, practice in a one-hour time limit.

The College Board releases actual answers written by students on previous years document-based questions. Ask your teacher to see these so that you can compare your work to that of your peers, and see what scores they received.

In the heat of the moment, you may easily forget to do the things listed above. I have a simple mnemonic device that students find helpful. You may want to develop a better one of your own. Mine is based on the word for a French roll - BAGET(TE), with an O added at the end suggesting an Italian touch.

B is for bias—make sure you analyze for point of view.

A is for all—try to use all the documents.

G is for group—group documents together when you can

E is for evaluate—that is to analyze not just regurgitate.

T is for thesis—make sure you have one.

O is for outside information

If you write BAGETO at the top of your paper and remember to follow those rules, you should write an excellent essay.

SAMPLE QUESTION

DOCUMENT-BASED QUESTION (55 minutes)

Directions: Write a well-integrated essay that does the following:

- Has an appropriate thesis that directly addresses all parts of the question
- Supports the thesis with evidence from all or all but one of the documents AND your knowledge of European history beyond/outside the documents.
- Analyzes a majority of the documents in terms of such features as their intended audience, purpose, point of view, format, argument, limitations, and/or social context as appropriate to the argument.
- Places the argument in the context of broader regional, national, or global processes.

1. Analyze the various factors that led France to become a state bent on military conquest 1789-1815.

<u>Document 1</u>

Source: film poster, 1938

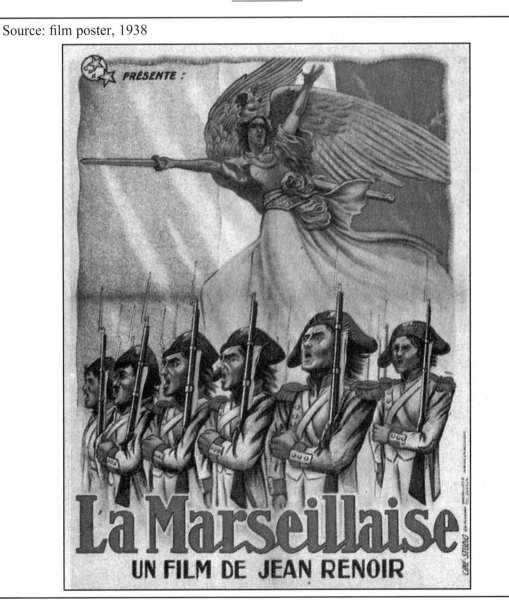

Document 2

Source: Letter from Monseron de l'Aunay to the Marquis de Condorcet, *Journal de Paris*, 28 December 1789

You send me alarming news from our sugar islands, principally from Saint Domingue [in the Caribbean]. The inhabitants of that island may all be currently being held at knife point by the Negroes in revolt. Half of France would be plunged into sadness and misery if the income from the islands was lost. Our eternal rival [Britain], whose ambitious policies may be having them underhandedly sharpen their swords, smile at our misfortunes and, beneath this horrible rubble, foresee the scepter of their world-wide domination that no human force would be able to take from them.

Document 3

Source: Address to the King from the National Assembly, 29 November 1791

These preparations for hostilities and these threats of invasion require weapons that absorb immense sums. Sire, it is your role to make [the German princes threatening invasion] stop. It is your role to address these foreign powers with a language worthy of the King of the French People. France shall view them as nothing less than enemies. Sire, everything, your interest, your dignity, the glory of the outraged nation, calls for some other language than that of diplomacy. Let your declaration be underscored by the movement of forces that have been entrusted to you, so that the nation is aware of who are enemies and who are friends. With these bold steps, we shall recognize the defender of the Constitution.

Document 4

Source: Letter from Thomas Jefferson to William Short, 3 January 1793

The Nation was with [the Revolutionaries] in opinion, for however they might have been formerly for the constitution framed by the first assembly, they were come over from their hope in it, and were now generally Jacobins. In the struggle which was necessary, many guilty persons fell without forms of trial, and with them some innocent. [The deaths of the innocent] I deplore as much as anybody, and shall deplore some of them to the day of my death. But I deplore them as I should have done had they fallen in battle. It was necessary to use the arm of the people, a machine not quite so blind as balls and bombs, but blind to a certain degree. … The liberty of the whole earth was depending on the issue of the contest, and was ever such a prize won with so little innocent blood? Rather than it should have failed, I would have seen half the earth desolated.

Document 5

Source: Napoleon Bonaparte on the *Coup d'État* 10 November 1799

The Council of Elders summoned me; I answered its appeal. A plan of general restoration had been devised by men whom the nation has been accustomed to regard as the defenders of liberty, equality, and property; this plan required examination, calm, free, exempt from all influence and all fear. Accordingly the Council of Elders resolved upon the removal of the Legislative Body to Saint-Cloud; it gave me the responsibility of disposing the force necessary for its independence. I believed it my duty to my fellow citizens, to the soldiers perishing in our armies, to the national glory acquired at the cost of their blood, to accept the command. The Councils assembled at Saint-Cloud; republican troops guaranteed their security from without, but assassins created terror within. Several deputies of the Council of Five Hundred, armed with stilettos and firearms, circulated threats of death around them.

Document 6

Source: Benjamin Constant, *The Spirit of Conquest and Usurpation*, 1814

Had France remained at peace, her peaceful citizens, her idle warriors would have observed the despot, would have judged him, and would have communicated their judgments to him. Truth would have passed through the ranks of the people. Usurpation would not have long withstood the influence of truth. Thus Bonaparte was compelled to distract public attention by bellicose enterprises. War flung onto distant shores that part of the French nation that still had some real energy. It prompted the police harassment of the timid, whom it could not force abroad. It struck terror into men's hearts, and left there a certain hope that chance would take responsibility for their deliverance: a hope agreeable to fear and convenient to inertia. How many times have I heard men who were pressed to resist tyranny postponing this, during wartime till the coming of peace, and in peacetime until war commences!

Document 7

Size of European Armies 1756-1814			
	1756	1789	1812/14
France	330,000	180,000	600,000
Britain	200,000	40,000	250,000
Austria	200,000	300,000	250,000
Prussia	195,000	190,000	270,000

THE LONG ESSAY QUESTION

This section of the exam contains a long essay. You will have 35 minutes to write the essay that counts fifteen percent of the exam. You will be offered a pair of essays from which you will choose one to answer.

Do not pick the question that seems so broad that you can bull your way through. The examiners will be looking for specific data in that answer, and if the data is not there, you will not get a good score

Practice makes perfect. The way to learn to write essays is to write a lot of them. Going over previous years thematic questions and answering them verbally is also helpful. Making lists of the causes and consequences of the great events of European history is also a good way to review. (The outline included in this review book will help you with this task.) You should have at you finger tips the causes of the French Revolution, the consequences of the Reformation, etc. It also does not hurt to know the provisions of the great treaties such as Westphalia or Versailles.

Analyze the question. What is it really asking? Pay special attention to the command words such as "analyze" or "describe" (which mean very different things). Answer all parts of the question. That sounds like advice to a simpleton, but I assure you brilliant essays are written by very able students that get poor scores because one of the instructions in the question was neglected. If a question asks you to talk about before and after some event, do both. If you are asked about 17th century France, do not talk only about Louis XIV, who reigned during the second half of the century. Henry IV, Richelieu, Mazarin, and the Fronde, all of who preceded him, require mention as well. If you are asked to talk about the factory system and the domestic system, do not write only about factories.

Develop a thesis. This is hard to do in 35 minutes. It can be a quite simple one, but some organizing idea is necessary to give the essay coherence and make it stand out. It must also address all parts of the question. Write an introduction that restates the question in your own words. This forces you to be alert to the whole question. Place the issue in its historical context. Then state your thesis, an argument about which reasonable people may disagree. Try to grab the reader's attention.

In the body of the essay use specific, vivid, and effective examples to back up your thesis. Be logical. Acknowledge any major arguments that can be made against your case. You must demonstrate that you know about the topic. The answer must be meaty and well-documented. Link your specific evidence directly to the thesis. Draw on at least one category of analysis (e.g. social, economic, political) beyond those mentioned in the question, or connect the topic to other historical periods, geographical areas, or circumstances, or bring in analysis from a different discipline or method of study.

Every good essay in real life has a conclusion. In a 35 minute format you will probably not have much time to do this. At all costs avoid repeating your points in the last paragraph. If you are doing this, it must be because you had too little knowledge of the question and the reader will assume that is the case. Try to end by answering the question, "So what?" Nothing gives an argument more force than a good answer to that question.

Proof read if you have time. Amazing errors slip past you in the heat of writing. The clearer your handwriting the better. If you cross something out, do so thoroughly.

Spell key names and terms correctly. Writing about Napoleon "Bonepert" instead of "Bonaparte" creates distinct unease in the reader's mind. Much will be forgiven in terms of style and spelling, but confusing Louis XIV with Louis XVI will not be. Also, do not write Queen Elizabeth "the" I (the numerals of monarchs follow the name immediately without a "the") nor speak about "peasants" in 19th century England (members of the working classes in England were proletarians who owned nothing of value: agricultural laborers in the countryside and workers in the cities. "Peasants" in France or Germany did not live in cities and though often wretchedly poor possessed certain rights or even owned small bits of property). Erroneous use of the word "peasant" to describe workers in England is an example of what will set off alarm bells in the graders' heads. It is not a mere usage error but demonstrates a fundamental historical misunderstanding.

You may be witty but not flippant. Make sure the reader is laughing with you and not at you. Hindsight has a way of making us feel superior towards the people of the past. Try to remember to put yourself in their places and you will sound less patronizing. Applying the word "stupid" to Wilhelm II of Germany, for example, is not a good idea. He made grave errors of judgment, but he was by no means an unintelligent man. Also avoid overly familiar relations with the great. Florence Nightingale should not be called "Flo" or even Florence nor Napoleon I "Nappy".

Try to use simple and direct language; avoid jargon. Use the active voice and the past tense. Keep track of your thesis at all times. Avoid wild generalizations. Nothing causes more rapid deterioration in your reputation in the grader's eyes than a statement such as "all rulers are stupid." The words "never," "always," "all," etc. are dangerous and almost never accurate. "Perhaps" and "probably" can sound wishy-washy but are usually more appropriate and safer.

Remember that writing is a process of selection. You are selecting ideas and facts from a huge mass of information and you are selecting words to make your other selection process vivid, lively, and persuasive. Keep it simple. Be creative. Do not repeat yourself. Good luck!

SAMPLE QUESTIONS

1. Compare and contrast European imperialism in the 17th century and the 19th century.

2. Was one nation more responsible than the others for the outbreak of the First World War in 1914?

SAMPLE EXAMINATION ONE

SECTION I, Part A

Time—55 minutes

55 Questions

Directions: Each of the questions or incomplete statements below is followed by either four suggested answers or completions. Select the one that is best in each case and then fill in the appropriate letter in the correspoinding space on the answer sheet.

Questions 1.1–1.3 relate to the 1819 image of an imaginary British treasure chest containing valued historical documents.

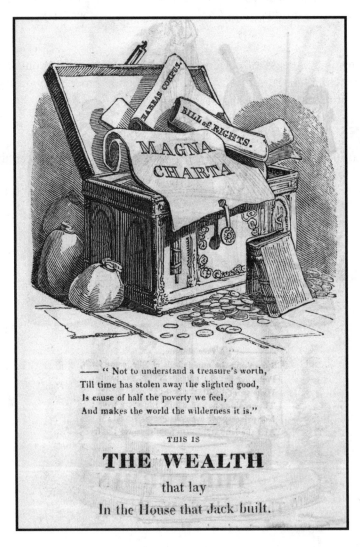

—— " Not to understand a treasure's worth,
Till time has stolen away the slighted good,
Is cause of half the poverty we feel,
And makes the world the wilderness it is."

THIS IS

THE WEALTH

that lay

In the House that Jack built.

1.1 The image above depicts which of the following?

(A) The royal Treasury of England in 1640
(B) Important constitutional rights gained by the British between 1215 and 1689
(C) The content of the essentials of the curriculum in British secondary schools in 1560
(D) The rights granted to the Thirteen Colonies in 1774 to avoid a revolution

1.2 Habeas Corpus was the foundation of individual freedom in the English-speaking world because?

(A) It established Roman Law as paramount in Britain
(B) Guaranteed no taxation without representation
(C) Gave votes to women
(D) Protects against arbitrary arrest and punishment

1.3 The documents in the treasure test made Britain in the 18th and 19th centuries

(A) A backward and "unmodern" country
(B) Equal to Germany and France in the rights granted citizens
(C) The most oppressed state in Europe
(D) The freest state in Europe

Questions 2.1–2.3 refer to the statistical table below.

COMPARATIVE EUROPEAN REAL WAGES, 1250–1809

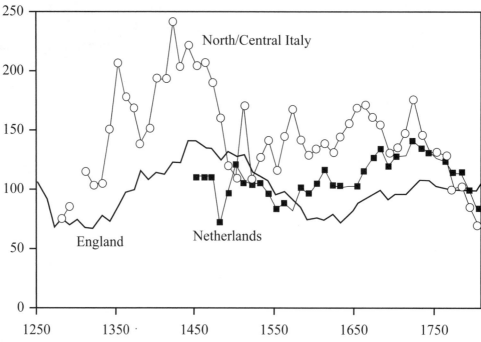

(Real wages are a measure of how many units of a standard bundle of goods laborers could buy with one day's earnings adjusted for inflation)

2.1 The most dramatic development indicated by the data in this graph is which of the following?

(A) The consistent superiority in wealth of Holland over England
(B) Widespread poverty in England
(C) The impact of the success of the Dutch East India Company on the wealth of Holland
(D) The wealth generated in Northern Italy during the Renaissance

2.2 What does the data in the graph tell us about the impact of the Industrial Revolution?

(A) The superior wealth of England made it the most likely to industrialize
(B) Italy and Holland were better off than England at the beginning of the Industrial Revolution
(C) Italy sustained success despite not industrializing
(D) Commerce sustained wealth better than industry during the early stages of the Industrial Revolution

2.3 What does the data tell us about the impact of the Wars of Religion on European real wages?

(A) Italy was hit the hardest
(B) Holland was hit the hardest
(C) England was hit the hardest
(D) Had little effect

Questions 3.1–3.4 refer to the list of incentives by the modern historian Gregory Clark (2007) and a response by another historian, Robert Allen (2008).

Incentives of Medieval versus Modern England

Economic desiderata (positives)	1300	2000
Low tax rates	Yes	No
Modest social transfers	Yes	No
Stable money	Yes	No
Low public debt	Yes	No
Security of property	Yes	Yes
Security of the person	?	Yes
Social mobility	Yes	Yes
Free goods markets	Yes	Yes
Free labor markets	Yes	Yes
Free capital markets	Yes	Yes
Free land markets	Yes	No
Rewards for knowledge creation	?	Yes

Gregory Clark, *A Farewell to Alms: A Brief Economic History of the World*, 2007

Gregory Clark's list of "economic desiderata" is not an adequate analysis of good institutions. States made many contributions—some intentionally, others not—to economic development. In the eighteenth century, the British state created an empire, which sustained the demand for British manufacturing and provided capital to finance it, provided canals and turnpikes, and operated a system of poor relief that improved [and] underpinned an industrial labor force. In the nineteenth century, governments in Europe and North America built infrastructure, created mass education, and enacted tariffs.

Robert C. Allen, "A Review of Gregory Clark's *A Farewell to Alms*," 2008

3.1 The "incentives" referred to in Clark's table were to promote what activity?

(A) Democracy
(B) Empire building
(C) Economic growth
(D) A stable political order

3.2 On which of the following points about England in the eighteenth century are Gregory Clark and Robert C. Allen likely to agree?

(A) It was in decline
(B) It was growing at too fast
(C) It was unlikely to grow rapidly
(D) It was a successful state

3.3 The debate between Gregory Clark and Robert C. Allen prompted by this table related to which of the following?

(A) The industrial revolution
(B) Demographic change
(C) Banking and finance
(D) Agricultural production

3.4 Robert C. Allen uses what historical technique to challenge Gregory Clark's assumptions?

(A) Questioning the reliability of his data
(B) Providing other evidence that Clark neglected
(C) Citing other historians who disagree with Clark
(D) Questioning the usefulness of Clark's data

Questions 4.1–4.3 refer to issues in Eastern Europe in the 17th and 18th centuries illustrated in the maps reproduced below.

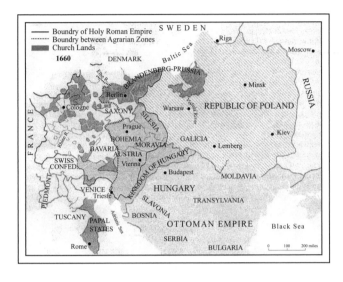

4.1 The fact that the "agrarian zone" line follows the same path on both maps indicates which of the following did not change?

(A) West of the line mainly rice and corn were cultivated

(B) East of the line serfdom continues to be the source of agricultural labor

(C) Serfdom extended West of the line to the French border

(D) East of the line most agricultural production was related to animal husbandry

4.2 All of the following changes occurred in the period between 1660 and 1795 EXCEPT.

(A) Poland was partitioned between Prussia, Russia, and Austria

(B) Prussia acquired part of Poland and all of Silesia, doubling its size

(C) The Austrian Empire expanded into the Balkans at the expense of the Ottomans

(D) Bavaria conquers all of southern and central Germany

4.3 The maps demonstrate that which of the following changes took place in the borders of Russia between 1660 and 1795?

(A) Gained access to the Baltic and Black seacoasts

(B) Lost control over Poland

(C) Drove the Ottomans out of the Balkans

(D) Gained control over the Straits giving them access to the Mediterranean

Questions 5.1–5.3 refer to the statistical graph below.

TRADE AROUND THE CAPE OF GOOD HOPE, 1500–1800

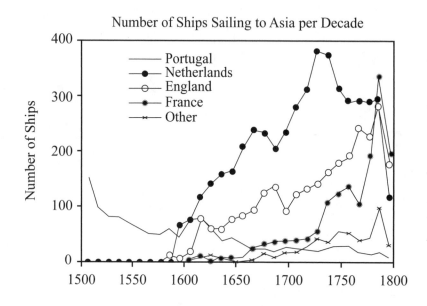

5.1 What strategic advantage over its rivals did the Dutch possess in trade with Asia during this period?

(A) Ports on the Atlantic
(B) Control over India
(C) Control over the Cape of Good Hope
(D) Access to the Baltic

5.2 What might account for the fact that even though Portugal opened the sea trade route to Asia it did not sustain its predominance?

(A) Lost a war with England
(B) Was preoccupied by trade in the Mediterranean
(C) Was dominated by its larger neighbor Spain
(D) Lost its overseas empire to France

5.3 Why did the Dutch lose their preeminence in the Asia trade at the end of the eighteenth century?

(A) Conquest by Britain
(B) Conquest by France
(C) They turned their attention to the Baltic
(D) They lost their colonial possessions in the East Indies

Questions 6.1–6.3 refer to Erasmus of Rotterdam painted in 1523 by Hans Holbein reproduced below.

6.1 All of the following are true about this portrait of Erasmus EXCEPT.

(A) The realistic portrayal of his face reflects the artistic style of the 16th century
(B) He is portrayed in the simple dress of a member of the clergy
(C) He is surrounded by the lavish decoration suitable to his wealth and noble rank
(D) He is portrayed with the pen and paper suitable to his life as a humanist

6.2 Erasmus was best known as

(A) A Christian humanist who stayed loyal to the Roman Catholic Church
(B) A radical cleric who launched the Great Schism
(C) The priest who married Henry VIII to his second wife after the divorce with Catherine of Aragon
(D) A Protestant reformer in league with Zwingli

6.3 In his writings and teaching Erasmus was noted for

(A) Placing humanism above Catholicism
(B) Praising Luther for his break with Rome
(C) Attacking abuses in the Catholic Church
(D) Avoiding discussion of political and social issue

Questions 7.1–7.3 refer to the following passage.

As a young man raised in Spain, King Philip II of Spain was treated with all deference and respect which seemed due to the son of the greatest emperor, Charles V, whom Christendom had ever had, and to the heir to such a number of realms and to such grandeur. As a result of this education, when the king left Spain for the first time and visited Flanders (the Spanish Netherlands), passing on his way through Italy and Germany, he everywhere made an impression of haughtiness and severity, so that the Italians liked him but little, the Flemish were quite disgusted with him, and the Germans hated him heartily. But when he had been warned above all by his father, that his haughtiness was not in place in a prince destined to rule over a number of nations so different in manners and sentiment, he altered his manner and everywhere exhibited such distinguished mildness and affability that no prince ever surpassed him in these traits.

In the king's eyes no nation is superior to the Spaniards. It is among them that he lives, it is they that he consults, and it is they that direct his policy; in all this he is acting quite contrary to the habit of his father.

> Venetian Ambassador to Madrid, diplomatic report, 1559

7.1 To which of the following might Philip's bias in favor of Spain have contributed?

    (A) His denunciation of papal authority
    (B) His conversion to Protestantism
    (C) War with the Ottoman Empire
    (D) The Dutch Revolt

7.2 Why might a Venetian look on Philip II with suspicion?

    (A) Venice and Spain were commercial rivals in the Mediterranean
    (B) Philip planned to invade Venice
    (C) Venice was allied with Elizabeth I of England
    (D) Venice was Protestant

7.3 Charles V decided to divide his empire into two pieces, Germany and Austria was given to his brother Ferdinand and Spain, the Netherlands, and the overseas colonies to his son Philip. What was the Emperor's main reason for making this division?

    (A) Ferdinand ruled the Protestant lands and Philip the Catholic ones once it was clear the Reformation could not be ended
    (B) The empire was too large and unwieldy to be ruled by one monarch
    (C) Philip was known to hate the Germans
    (D) The Germans refused to elect Philip Holy Roman Emperor

Questions 8.1–8.4 refer to the following passage.

After the King awoke the grand chamberlain was called and those who had what was called the *grandes entrées*. The chamberlain drew back the bed curtains. That was the time to speak to the King, if anyone had anything to ask him; in which case the rest stood aside. The same officer gave him his dressing gown; immediately after, other privileged courtiers entered, and then everybody, in time to find the King putting on his shoes and stockings.

The King, wishing to retire said goodnight with an inclination of the head. Then commenced what was called the *petit coucher*, at which only the specially privileged remained. They did not leave until he got into bed. It was a moment to speak to him.

He liked splendour, magnificence, and profusion in everything: you pleased him if you shone through the brilliancy of your houses, your clothes, your table, your equipages. Thus a taste for extravagance and luxury was disseminated through all classes of society; causing infinite harm, and leading to general confusion of rank and to ruin.

As for the King himself, nobody ever approached his magnificence. His buildings, who could number them? At the same time, who was there who did not deplore the pride, the caprice, the bad taste seen in them? He built nothing useful or ornamental in Paris, except the Pont Royal, and that simply by necessity.

The Duke de Saint-Simon, courtier at Versailles, *Memoirs of the Reign of Louis XIV*, (written in the 1740s but not published until later)

8.1 What might have motivated Saint-Simon to be critical of King Louis XIV?

(A) Desire to be the king himself
(B) Republican sympathies
(C) He was a Protestant and the king a Catholic
(D) The king made the nobility bend to his will

8.2 For what purpose did Louis XIV build the palace of Versailles?

(A) As a private retreat away from the nobility
(B) To remove himself from popular pressure of the mob in Paris
(C) To save money spent on his personal pleasure
(D) As a new space for the Estates General

8.3 Why might the king allow courtiers such intimate glimpses of his getting up in the morning or going to bed at night?

(A) He had no idea about privacy
(B) He wanted them under his direct observation
(C) He liked company
(D) He feared assassination

8.4 One of the greatest challenges to Louis early in his reign was a

(A) war with Russia
(B) Huguenot rebellion
(C) middle class revolt
(D) rebellion of the nobility

Questions 9.1–9.4 refer to the following passage.

I came to believe that the four following rules would be found sufficient, always provided I took the firm and unswerving resolve never in a single instance to fail in observing them.

The first was to accept nothing as true which I did not evidently know to be such.

The second, to divide each of the difficulties I examined into as many parts as may be required for its adequate solution.

The third, to arrange my thoughts in order, beginning with things the simplest and easiest to know, so that I may then ascend little by little, as it were step by step, to the knowledge of the more complex.

And the last, in all cases to make enumerations so complete, and reviews so general, that I should be assured of omitting nothing.

I then proceeded to consider, in a general manner, what is requisite to the truth and certainty of a proposition. Having found one—*I think, therefore I am*—which I knew to be true and certain, I thought that I ought also to know in what this certainty consists; I judged that I could take as being a general rule, that the things we apprehend very clearly and distinctly are true.

René Descartes, *Discourse on Method*, 1637

9.1 How did this statement made by Descartes challenge medieval ways of thinking?

(A) Embraces faith in a supreme arbiter
(B) Draws on Classical Greek thinking
(C) Demands empirical evidence
(D) Relies on philosophy not mathematics

9.2 Descartes wanted to advance knowledge by what means?

(A) Bursts of inspiration
(B) Being methodical
(C) Relying on the Great Chain of Being
(D) Build on the work of other scientists

9.3 In what area of study did Descartes concentrate?

(A) Mathematics
(B) Astronomy
(C) Biology
(D) Geology

9.4 Descartes greatest contribution to the modern world was?

(A) Building the first modern observatory
(B) Looking to the New World for inspiration for new ideas
(C) Sweeping away traditional beliefs
(D) Identifying the Jesuits as the greatest advancers of knowledge

Questions 10.1–10.4 refer to the following passage.

At first sight, no doubt, the monopoly of the great commerce of America naturally seems to an acquisition of the highest value. The dazzling splendour of the object, however the immense greatness of the commerce, is the very quality which renders the monopoly of it hurtful.

The immense debts contracted in the late wars were contracted in defense of America.

The expense of the peace establishment of the colonies was, before the commencement of the present disturbances, very considerable, and is an expense if no revenue can be drawn from the colonists ought certainly to be saved altogether. But countries which contribute neither revenue nor military force towards the support of the empire, cannot be considered as provinces. They may perhaps be considered as appendages, as a sort of splendid and showy equipage of the empire. But if the empire can no longer support the expense of keeping up this equipage, it ought certainly to lay it down.

Adam Smith, *The Wealth of Nations*, 1776

10.1 What was the most important reason why Adam Smith objected to the possession of a colonial empire?

(A) He was an advocate of free trade
(B) He believed in mercantilism
(C) He saw strategic and geopolitical considerations as more important than defense costs
(D) He thought wars against native Americans immoral

10.2 Mercantilism was an economic theory that advocated what principle?

(A) Colonies are of no benefit to the mother country
(B) The greatest benefit of colonies is derived from trade between colonies of different countries
(C) Colonies benefit the homeland by excluding other countries from the profits of trade
(D) Peace is to be sought at any cost

10.3 In Adam Smith's view the British colonies in North America should be made to pay for their own defense through

(A) Developing more natural resources such as gold mines
(B) Increasing trade
(C) Making peace with the Spanish and French
(D) Taxing the colonists for the costs of protecting them

10.4 Which colonies where the most profitable for the British throughout the 18th century?

(A) Virginia
(B) The New England colonies
(C) The West Indies islands
(D) Florida

Questions 11.1–11.4 refer to the following passage.

At the Council meeting with King William I July 23, 1866 after the defeat in battle of the Austrian army I declared it to be my conviction that peace must be concluded on the Austrian terms, but I remained alone in my opinion; the King supported the military majority. I thereupon set to work to commit to paper the reasons which in my opinion spoke for the conclusion of peace; and begged the King, in the event of his not accepting the advice for which I was responsible, to relieve me of my functions as chief minister if the war were continued.

We had to avoid wounding Austria too severely; we had to avoid leaving behind in her any unnecessary bitterness of feeling or desire for revenge; we ought rather to reserve the possibility of becoming friends again with our adversary of the moment, and in any case to regard the Austrian state as a piece on the European chessboard and the renewal of friendly relations with her as a move open to us. If Austria were severely injured, she would become the ally of France and of every other opponent of ours; she would even sacrifice her anti-Russian interests for the sake of revenge on Prussia.

Prince Otto von Bismarck, *Reminiscences*, 1898

11.1 What did Bismarck hope to achieve through fighting a war with Austria in 1866?

(A) The destruction of the Habsburg dynasty
(B) War with Russia in the Balkans in order to remove the Ottoman Empire from Europe
(C) Defeat by Austria would force King William I to agree to Bismarck's plans
(D) Victory over Austria would remove them as a rival for control over a united Germany

11.2 What other great power threatened to block Bismarck from achieving German unification?

(A) Italy
(B) France
(C) Great Britain
(D) The United States

11.3 What other state or states stood in the way of Bismarck's plan for a united Germany?

(A) Poland
(B) Sweden
(C) South German states
(D) The Netherlands

11.4 What were Bismarck's plans in the long run after German unification?

(A) Make an alliance with Austria to hold the balance of power in central Europe
(B) Make an alliance with Russia as a counterweight to Austria
(C) Make an alliance with Britain to protect its overseas empire
(D) Make an alliance with the Ottoman Empire to seize Africa

Questions 12.1–12.3 refer to the poem below.

> Fair Greece! Sad relic of departed worth!
>   Immortal, though no more; though fallen, great;
> Who now shall lead thy scattered children forth,
>   And long accustomed bondage uncreate?
> Not such thy sons who whilome did await,
>   The hopeless warriors of a willing doom,
> In bleak Thermopylae's sepulchral strait—
>   Oh! Who that gallant spirit shall resume,
> Leap from Eurotas' banks, and call thee from the tomb?
>
> Spirit of Freedom! When on Phyle's brow
>   Thou sat'st with Trasbulus and his train,
> Couldst thou forebode the dismal hour which now
>   Dims the green beauties of thine Attic plain?
> Not thirty tyrants now enforce the chain,
>   But every carle can lord it o'er thy land;
> Nor rise thy sons, but idly rain in vain,
> Trembling beneath the scourge of Turkish hand,
>   From birth till death enslaved; in word, in deed, unmanned.

Lord Byron, "Childe Harold's Pilgrimage", 1812–18

12.1 Which of the following terms best characterizes the style of poetry in the above passage written by Lord Byron?

(A) Baroque
(B) Romantic
(C) Victorian
(D) Impressionist

12.2 Byron makes reference to which of the following in his poem?

(A) The British attack on the Crimean peninsula
(B) The Greek alliance with Austria
(C) The Turkish imposition of the Muslim religion in Greece
(D) The Greek war of independence from the Ottoman Empire

12.3 Which of the following was true about Lord Byron?

(A) He died trying to swim the Dardanelles
(B) He died serving in the Greek forces rebelling against Turkish rule
(C) He was also the author of *Frankenstein*
(D) He was Lord Castlereagh's brother

Questions 13.1–13.4 refers to the following passage.

We have nationalized the Egyptian Suez Canal company. When Egypt granted the concession to Ferdinand de Lesseps in the 1860s it was stated in the concession between the Egyptian Government and the Egyptian company that the company of the Suez Canal is an Egyptian company subject to Egyptian authority. Egypt nationalized this Egyptian company in 1956 and have declared freedom of navigation will be preserved.

But the imperialists became angry. Britain and France said Egypt grabbed the Suez Canal as if it were part of France or Britain. The British Foreign Secretary forgot that only two years ago he signed an agreement stating the Suez Canal is an integral part of Egypt.

Egypt declared she was ready to negotiate. But as soon as negotiations began threats and intimidations started.

By stating that by succeeding, Abdel Nasser would weaken Britain's stand against Arab nationalism, British Prime Minister Anthony Eden is in fact admitting his real objective is not Abdel Nasser as such but rather to defeat Arab nationalism and crush its cause. Eden speaks and finds his own answer.

Gamel Abdel Nasser, President of Egypt, speech, September 15, 1956

13.1 President Nasser was seen as a threat by Prime Minister Eden for which of the following reasons?

(A) He was threatening to introduce democracy in Egypt
(B) He was attempting to arose all African states to demand independence
(C) He had requested Britain to return all Egyptian antiquities
(D) He was an exponent of Arab nationalism who might ally with the USSR

13.2 What steps did Britain and France take in response to Nasser's nationalization of the Suez Canal in 1956?

(A) Invaded the Canal Zone with military force to retake control of the Canal.
(B) Negotiated a settlement satisfactory to all parties
(C) Took no action
(D) Arranged for the United Nations to take over the Canal Zone

13.3 The United States intervened in the Suez Crisis in order to

(A) Overthrow the Nasser regime
(B) Help Israel
(C) Remove British and French forces
(D) Block an invasion by the USSR

13.4 In retrospect the Suez Crisis of 1956 appears to have been which of the following?

(A) A decisive propaganda victory for the Soviet Union in the Cold War
(B) The last gasp of old-style European imperialism
(C) Eden's greatest moment as Prime Minister
(D) Forged a new alliance between France and Britain

Questions 14.1–14.4 refer to the career of Mohandes Gandhi, illustrated below, and his role in freeing India from British rule.

14.1 This photograph of Mohandas Gandhi, the leader of the independence movement against British rule in India conveys what about the man?

(A) He was a simple and ineffectual man easily outwitted by the British
(B) He was an uneducated peasant who led fellow agricultural laborers to freedom
(C) He was a guerilla fighter who did not wear a uniform while he led an armed struggle in the jungles of India
(D) He was a shrewd lawyer and propagandist trying to portray himself as a victim of British oppression

14.2 Although Gandhi's most important mission was to achieve India's independence, he was also deeply concerned about which of the following?

(A) Border wars with China
(B) Gaining absolute power for himself
(C) Lifting the masses out of poverty
(D) Industrializing India

14.3 Gandhi's greatest contribution to India other than gaining independence was which of the following?

(A) Making the weaving of beautiful cotton cloth a national pastime
(B) Creating an enduring democracy
(C) Unification of the whole country in one state
(D) Planning a national rail network

14.4 Prime Minister Winston Churchill despised Gandhi and made denigrating remarks about him in public. What motivated the antagonism?

(A) He was prejudiced against Muslims
(B) He objected to India becoming a democracy
(C) He saw brown skinned people as inferior to whites
(D) He hated Gandhi's alliance with the Soviet Union

Questions 15.1–15.3 refer to the following passage.

The kept woman—wife or mistress—is not freed from the male just because she has a ballot paper in her hands; while today's customs impose fewer constraints on her than in the past, such negative licenses have not fundamentally changed her situation; she remains a vassal, imprisoned in her condition. It is through work that woman has been able, to a large extent, to close the gap separating her from the male; work alone can guarantee her concrete freedom. The system based on her dependence collapses as soon as she ceases to be a parasite; there is no longer need for a masculine mediator between her and the universe. The curse on the woman vassal is that she is not allowed to do anything; so she stubbornly pursues the impossible quest for being through narcissism, love, or religion. It is also understandable that a shop girl, and office worker, or a secretary should not want to give up the advantages of having a male to lean on. I have already said that it is an almost irresistible temptation for a young woman to be part of a privileged caste when she can do so simply by surrendering her body; she is doomed to have love affairs because her wages are minimal for the very high standard of living society demands of her; if she settles for what she earns, she will be no more than a pariah: without decent living accommodations or clothes, all amusement and even love will be refused her.

Simone de Beauvoir, *The Second Sex*, 1949

15.1 What did de Beavoir see as the fundamental disadvantage suffered by women in 1949?

(A) Less education than men
(B) Lower wages than men
(C) Fewer skills than men
(D) Legal restrictions against women

15.2 What would de Beauvoir say about allowing women to vote?

(A) It changed everything
(B) It changed nothing
(C) It was vital to women's progress
(D) Men would vote more frequently than women

15.3 The most important achievements of feminism in the post-1945 world were?

(A) More equality in the home and workplace
(B) Divorce and property law
(C) Suffrage
(D) Authority over children

Questions 16.1–16.3 relate to the statistical table below.

Total GNP and per capita GNP of the Powers in 1950
(in 1964 dollars)

	Total GNP	Per Capita GNP
USA	381 billion	2536
USSR	126	699
UK	71	1393
France	50	1172
West Germany	48	1001
Japan	32	382
Italy	29	626

16.1 What does the data in this table suggest about the members of NATO vs. the Soviet Union?

(A) The USSR was able to dominate Europe easily
(B) The Western Alliance included only strong economies
(C) Capitalism produced stronger economies than communism
(D) Japan and Italy had already recovered their pre-war strength

16.2 What does this table suggest about West Germany?

(A) Its recovery from the Second World War was painfully slow
(B) It was already strong enough to threaten the Soviet Union again
(C) Its recovery from the Second World War was very rapid
(D) It was the weakling of the West

16.3 Why was the per capita GNP for the Soviet Union in 1950 and later such an important piece of data?

(A) It gives a good indication of Soviet military preparedness
(B) It was a good indicator of the Soviet economy's failure to provide a comparable standard of living to Western countries
(C) It was a good indicator of its leadership over the Warsaw Pact counties under its control
(D) It was a result of the setbacks of the two world wars from which Russia never really recovered

SAMPLE EXAMINATION ONE

SECTION I, Part B

Time—50 minutes

4 Questions (Short Answer)

Directions: Read each question carefully and write your responses in the corresponding boxes on the free-response answer sheet.

Use complete sentences; an outline or bulleted list alone is not acceptable. You may plan your answers in this exam booklet, but only your responses in the corresponding boxes on the free-response answer sheet will be scored.

Question 1:

In histories of empire the sound and fury of the ideological battlefield are rarely absent for long. For many of those who have written (and still write) about empire, there has been a missionary purpose. It springs from a deep sense of moral unease about the impact of empire, and often from the presumption that the worst ills of our time can be traced to its influence. Such authors believe imperial history should set out to show that an imperial mentality was deluded and false and deeply immoral. Historians should strip away the nostalgia that still colours our image of empire and reveal the imperial assumptions that still pervade Western thinking about non-Western peoples. Indeed for some Western historians, it remains *de rigueur* to insist that for them empire was 'evil'.

John Darwin, *Unfinished Empire: The Global Expansion of Britain*, 2012.

Based on this quotation from a modern historian and your knowledge of European history answer the questions (A, B, and C) below.

A) Identify and explain ONE example of a social or economic development historians of the views John Darwin describes would use as evidence of the "evil" of European imperialism.

B) Identify and explain ONE example of a cultural development historians of the views John Darwin describes would use as evidence of the "evil" of European imperialism.

C) Identify and explain ONE aspect of imperialism that could be cited to counter the argument that it was "evil".

Question 2:

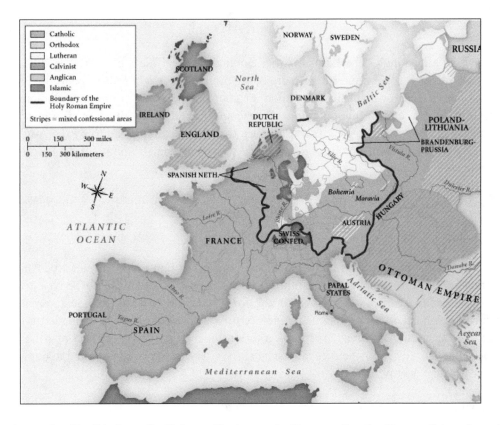

The map shows the distribution of religious allegiances in Europe after the Peace of Augsburg in 1555. Using the map and your knowledge of European history answer questions (A, B, and C) below.

A) Identify and explain ONE reason why northern Europe had fragmented into three distinct Protestant communions by 1555.
B) Identify and explain ONE long-term religious problem left unresolved by the Augsburg settlement of 1555.
C) Identify and explain ONE long-term political problem left unresolved by the Augsburg settlement of 1555.

Question 3:

Mercantilism is a term used to describe the predominant economic thinking of the 17th century concerning trade and relations with other countries. Using your knowledge of European history answer parts A and B below.

A) Identify and explain TWO examples of mercantilist thinking about trade and economic growth.
B) Identify and explain ONE major drawback or defect in mercantilist thinking.

Question 4:

Source 1:

On February 5, at a meeting of the British, American and Soviet Chiefs of Staff, the Russians pointed out that several divisions of German troops were being brought back across Europe to the Eastern Front. The Russians then asked for a substantial Allied air attack on German communications in the Berlin-Leipzig-Dresden region, and for the bombing of these specific cities, as a matter of urgency, to prevent the German reinforcements moving eastwards against them. This was agreed to by the Anglo-American Chiefs of Staff, and instructions given for a series of Anglo-American bombing raids. Dresden was to be one of the targets.

Sir Martin Gilbert, *Churchill: A Life*, 1993

Source 2:

It seems to me that the moment has come when the question of bombing German cities simply for the sake of increasing the terror, though under other pretexts, should be reviewed. Otherwise we shall come into control of an utterly ruined land. We shall not, for instance, be able to get housing materials out of Germany for our own needs because some temporary provision would have to be made for the Germans themselves. The destruction of Dresden remains a serious query against the conduct of Allied bombing. I am of the opinion that military objectives must henceforward be more strictly studied in our own interests rather than that of the enemy.

Prime Minister Winston Churchill, memorandum to the British military Chiefs of Staff, March 28, 1945

The modern historian Sir Martin Gilbert, official biographer of Winston Churchill, and the memorandum written by Churchill himself soon after the event discuss the bombing of the German city of Dresden, a cultural icon, in February and March 1945, which resulted in the deaths of 35,000 or more civilians. Using the quotations above and your knowledge of European history answer the questions below (A, B, and C).

A) Identify and explain ONE of the reasons for the strategic bombing of German cities by the Allies in the Second World War.

B) Identify and explain ONE reason why bombing Dresden in particular was considered necessary in 1945.

C) Identify and explain ONE reason why the two accounts above seem to contradict each other about the reasons for bombing Dresden.

SAMPLE EXAMINATION ONE

SECTION II, Part A

Total Time—55 minutes

Question 1 (Document-Based Question)
Suggested reading period: 15 minutes
Suggested writing period: 40 minutes

Directions: Write a well-integrated essay that does the following:

- Has an appropriate thesis that directly addresses all parts of the question
- Supports the thesis with evidence from all or all but one of the documents AND your knowledge of European history beyond/outside the documents.
- Analyzes a majority of the documents in terms of such features as their intended audience, purpose, point of view, format, argument, limitations, and/or social context as appropriate to the argument.
- Places the argument in the context of broader regional, national, or global processes.

---

1. Analyze the views about women in Great Britain since the eighteenth century.

<u>Document 1</u>

Source: Jonathan Swift, "The Furniture of a Woman's Mind", 1727

> A set of phrases learn'd by rote;
> A passion for a scarlet coat;
> When at a play to laugh, or cry,
> Yet cannot tell the reason why;
> Never to hold her tongue a minute,
> While all she prates has nothing in it;
> Whole hours can with a coxcomb sit,
> And take his nonsense all for writ;
> Her learning mounts to read a song,
> But half the words pronouncing wrong;
> Has every repartee in store
> She spoke ten thousand times before.
> ****
> If chance a mouse creeps in her sight,
> Can finely counterfeit a fright;
> So sweetly screams, if it comes near her,
> She ravishes all hearts to hear her.
> Can dexterously her husband tease,
> By taking fits whene'er she please;
> By frequent practice learns the trick
> At proper seasons to be sick;
> Thinks nothing gives one airs so pretty,
> At once creating love and pity.

Document 2

Source: Caroline Sheridan Norton, *The Separation of Mother and Child by the Law of "Custody of Infants," Considered*, 1838

The custody of legitimate children, is held to be the right of the Father *from the hour of their birth*: to the utter exclusion of the Mother, whose separate claim has no legal existence, and is not recognized by the Courts. No circumstance can modify or alter this admitted right of the father: though he should be living in open adultery, and his wife legally separated from him on that account.

Surely in this country, where hatred of all oppression is made a national boast, where if a master were to strike his footboy, an action would lie for assault and damages—where even offensive and violent language subjects a man to a penalty; in this country, and at this time, when all liberal opinions are encouraged and fostered, it is a strange and crying shame, that the only despotic right an Englishman possesses is to wrong the mother of his children!

Document 3

Source: Mrs. John Sandford, *Women in Her Social and Domestic Character*, 1837

A really sensible woman feels her dependence. She does what she can, but she is conscious of inferiority, and therefore grateful for support. She knows she is the weaker vessel.

Nature has assigned her a subordinate place, as well as subordinate powers; and it is far better that she should feel this, and should not arrogate the superiority of the other sex, whilst she claims the privileges of her own.

Want of judgment is, indeed, one of the most common defects in female character, and it is in discernment, rather than in capacity, that the inferiority of women consists. It is where judgment is required that she is most apt to fail. …

A woman must be domestic. Her heart must be at home. She must not be on the look-out for excitement of any kind, but must find her pleasure as well as her occupation in the sphere which is assigned to her.

Document 4

Source: John Stuart Mill, *The Subjection of Women*, 1869

Ever since there have been women able to make their sentiments known by their writings (the only mode of publicity which society permits them), an increasing number of them have recorded protests against their present social condition: and recently many thousands of them, headed by the most eminent women known to the public, have petitioned Parliament for their admission to the parliamentary suffrage. The claim of women to be educated as solidly, and in the same branches of knowledge, as men is urged with growing intensity, and with a great prospect of success; while the demand for their admission into professions and occupations hitherto closed against them becomes every year more urgent.

Document 5

Source: Punch, Jan. 30, 1901

JUSTICE.

Document 6

Source: Report of the War Cabinet Committee on Women in British Industry, 1919

In some munitions factories the men's work was almost entirely carried out by women.

The main fact with regard to the teaching profession in the war is that towards making good the loss of 22,000 men teachers, some 13,000 women were drawn into the service. The temporary displacement will probably accelerate the change in the proportion of the two sexes engaged which had been going on for some years before the war.

As an indirect result of the war and of the grant of the parliamentary suffrage to women some new professions are being opened to them. In January, 1918, the Society of Incorporated Accountants and Auditors obtained permission from the Chancery Court to alter their articles of association so as to permit of the admission of women as members. In March, 1918, a Bill to admit of women qualifying as Barristers and Solicitors passed the House of Lords.

Document 7

Source: Enoch Powell, Speech in the House of Commons, March 26, 1975

Why refuse to recognize that there is an immense gradation, infinitely subtle, of the differences in the carrying out of a whole range of jobs according to whether it is a man or a woman who does so? This depends not only upon the nature of the job but upon the period of time for its performance—whether it is a matter of a short time, a year or a career which is envisaged—and varies almost invisibly with the changes in society, with the changes in qualifications and with the changes in industry. …

The Bill is a denial of the infinite differentiation of jobs and of those best fitted to perform them, … the differentiation of sex is all-pervasive and, in relation to different jobs and functions in society, confers—now in one direction, now in the other—more or less advantage and benefit on the way in which they are performed. Yet here is a Bill which sets out to eliminate the effects of that differentiation except where it is total or absolute. This is a defiance of reality.

SAMPLE EXAMINATION ONE

SECTION II, Part B

Question 2 or Question 3 (Long Essay)

Suggested writing period: 35 minutes

Directions: Choose EITHER question 2 or question 3. You are advised to spend 35 minutes writing your answer..

In your response you should do the following.

- · State a relevant thesis that directly addresses all parts of the question.
- · Support your argument with evidence, using specific examples.
- · Apply historical thinking skills as directed by the question.
- · Synthesize the elements above into a persuasive essay.

---

2. The Catholic Reformation was both a success and a failure. Analyze the reasons for both.

3. Analyze the factors that made England the first fully industrialized nation by 1850.

SAMPLE EXAMINATION TWO

SECTION I, Part A

Time—55 minutes

55 Questions

Directions: Each of the questions or incomplete statements below is followed by either four suggested answers or completions. Select the one that is best in each case and then fill in the appropriate letter in the correspoinding space on the answer sheet.

Questions 1.1–1.3 refer to the timeline below.

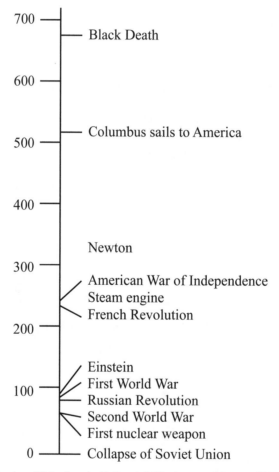

"The Scale of Modernity" *David Christian, Maps of Time 2005*

1.1 The data displayed in this timeline suggests which of the following?

(A) The acceleration in number of great events as the years progress towards the present
(B) Isaac Newton made a greater contribution to science than Albert Einstein
(C) All of the events listed are linked
(D) Nothing of importance occurred between the voyages of Columbus and the discoveries of Newton

1.2 The selection of events included in the timeline suggests which of the following?

(A) Europe remains the dominant power in the world
(B) The threat of a pandemic has receded into the past
(C) All events are linked together
(D) Wars are the most prevalent factors of change

1.3 Which among the following is the most significant item not included in the timelime over the last 300 years?

(A) The War of the Austrian Succession
(B) The publication of Charles Darwin's *On the Origins of Species*
(C) The Crimean War
(D) The publication of Aldous Huxley's *Brave New World*

Questions 2.1–2.3 relate to the graph below.

English Laborers Real Wages, 1209–1809

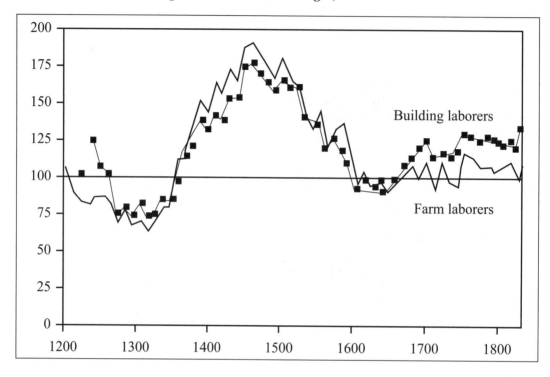

(Real wages are a measure of how many units of a standard bundle of goods laborers
could buy with one day's earnings adjusted for inflation)

2.1 The event that had the largest effect on driving
wages higher between 1209 and 1809 was?

(A) The Industrial Revolution
(B) The Black Death (Plague)
(C) The Civil War
(D) The Anglo-Dutch Wars

2.2 The cost of the American War of Independence
(American Revolution) had which of the
following effects on real wages?

(A) Created a small rise
(B) Created a dramatic rise
(C) Lowered
(D) Had little or no effect

2.3 A debate among historians about the impact of
the Industrial Revolution on wage laborers 1800–
1850 has reached a consensus that the standard of
living did which of the following in this period?

(A) Rose
(B) Fell
(C) Stayed the same
(D) Rose and then fell

Questions **3.1–3.4** relate to the two palaces illustrated below.

3.1 El Escorial on the left built by Philip II of Spain (1563–84) and Versailles built by Louis XIV of France (1664–1710) are often seen as representative of the two monarch's characters. These can be summarized respectively as follows.

(A) Cowardly and negligent
(B) Austere and flamboyant
(C) Uninterested in work and lazy
(D) Loved war and hated war

3.2 Which of the following is the most accurate description of the attitude towards religion of the builders of these palaces?

(A) Tolerant and accepting of Protestantism
(B) They largely ignored religion
(C) They decided policy on the basis of what benefited them and used religion as an excuse to conceal their real motives
(D) Devout and faithful

3.3 These palaces can also been seen to illustrate Philip's and Louis's views on monarchy.

(A) The ruler was God's anointed representative on earth
(B) Monarchs needed to negotiate as equals with elected representatives of the people
(C) Dynastic interests were unimportant
(D) War should never be conducted against fellow monarchs

3.4 Many monarchs in the 18th century took Versailles as a model to be copied for their own palaces. Why?

(A) They wanted to avoid the mistakes of Philip II
(B) Stone was cheaper than brick to build with
(C) Louis epitomized the reign of an ideal monarch
(D) International Style architecture had become fashionable

Questions 4.1–4.3 refer to the statistical table below.

Combined Yield Ratios [from one bushel of seed] of Wheat, Rye, and Barley, 1600–1820

Period	Zone I	Zone II	Zone III	Zone IV
1600–49	6.7	—	4.	4.0
1650–99	9.3	6.2	4.1	3.8
1700–49	—	6.3	4.1	3.5
1750–99	10.1	7.0	5.1	4.7
1800–20	11.1	6.2	5.4	—

Zone I: England, Low Countries
Zone II: France, Spain, Italy
Zone III: Germany, Switzerland, Scandinavia
Zone IV: Russia, Poland, Czechoslovakia, Hungary

4.1 What can the data set above tell us about the economic history of Europe?

(A) The most advanced commercial economies were also the most agriculturally productive
(B) Serfdom probably had no significant effect on crop yields
(C) Climatic conditions made a huge difference in productivity
(D) Geography played no role in determining crop yields

4.2 High crop yields were most likely to affect which of the factors listed below?

(A) The political structure of a country
(B) The likelihood of expansion overseas
(C) The height of military recruits
(D) Encouragement of scientific research

4.3 Which of the following factors was most likely to have the most impact on increased agricultural output?

(A) Political stability
(B) Number of peasants per acre
(C) Soil temperature
(D) Field rotations

Questions 5.1–5.3 refer to the following passage.

Presuming that the English path was the only road to freedom, historians have assumed that representative institutions, such as the English Parliament, were the people's sole defense against a ravenous, absolutist state. They have portrayed the monarchs of continental Europe robbing their downtrodden subjects and riding roughshod over property and liberty. So ingrained is this distinctly English view of early modern state building that much of it passes for common sense. The notion that those who are freest are taxed least does not hold up in the light of comparative history. If we compare the rates of taxation in Spain, France, England, and the Netherlands, we find that in the absolutist states, Spain and France, taxation was relatively light. In the end, representative institutions, not absolute monarchy, proved superior in revenue extraction. Liberty was a necessary precondition for the emergence of a strong state, a state of wealth and power.

P. T. Hoffman and K. Norberg, *Fiscal Crises, Liberty, and Representative Government, 1450–1789*, 1994

5.1 The historians Hoffman and Norberg believe the most important factor in building a modern estate was?

(A) A strong military
(B) The ability to tax heavily
(C) Full democracy
(D) Far-seeing leaders

5.2 What does Hoffman and Norberg criticize in the interpretations of other historians?

(A) Seeing elected legislatures as a defender of the individual against the power of the state
(B) Seeing monarchy as an outmoded and old-fashioned method of government
(C) Believing that France and Spain were less efficient than England in raising taxes
(D) Believing that dictatorship could not be modern or efficient

5.3 Historians now criticize the idea that the development of democracy in Britain was the inevitable outcome of possessing Parliament, a representative body, from early in is history. On what grounds might they question the inevitability of a democratic outcome?

(A) Parliament was not democratic at first
(B) Other countries also had elected legislatures
(C) Women were excluded from Parliament until 1918
(D) Parliament possessed a hereditary upper chamber

Questions 6.1–6.3 refer to the following passage.

When they come home from being married, the wife is set at the upper end of the table, and the husband next unto her; they fall then to drinking till they bee all drunke, they perchance have a minstrel or two, and two naked men, which led her from the Church daunce naked a long time before all the companie. When they are wearie of drinking, the bride and the bridegrome get them to bed, for it is in the evening always when any of them are married: and when they are going to bedde, the bridegrome putteth certain money both golde and silver, if they have it, into one of his boots, and then sitteth down in the chamber, crossing his legges, and then the bride must plucke off one of his boots, which she will, and if she happen on the boote wherein the money is, she hath not onely the money for her labor, but is also at such choyse, as she need not ever from that day forth to pul off his boots.

One common rule is amoengst them, if the woman be not beaten with the whip once a weeke, she will not be good, and therefore they looke for it orderly, & the women say, that if their husbands did not beate them, they should not love them.

Anthony Jenkinson, English traveler in Russia, 1557

6.1 How would you characterize Jenkinson's opinion of Russian society?

(A) Very similar to English society
(B) More old fashioned and refined than England
(C) Barbaric and alien
(D) In advance of Western Europe

6.2 The religious traditions of Russia would have seemed alien to English observers. What faith did the Russians practice?

(A) Lutheranism
(B) Roman Catholicism
(C) Eastern Orthodoxy
(D) Calvinism

6.3 One of the reasons other than religion that separated Russian society from the rest of Europe?

(A) It was cut off from much influence from the Renaissance
(B) Warfare was constant
(C) No trade routes were established with the West
(D) Peasants controlled the government

Questions 7.1–7.3 refer to the following passage from a play.

SGANARELLE. Is this the patient?

GÉRONTE. Yes, I have but one daughter; and I would never get over it if she were to die.

SGANARELLE. Do not let her do anything of the kind. She must not die without a prescription of the physician.

GÉRONTE. She has become dumb, without our having been able till now to discover the cause….

SGANARELLE. (Turning to the patient) Give me your hand. (To Géronte) The pulse tells me that your daughter is dumb.

GÉRONTE. Sir, that is what is the matter with her; ah! Yes, you have found it out at the first touch.

SGANARELLE. Of course! We are great physicians, we know matters at once. I hit the nail on the head from the first, and I tell you that your daughter is dumb.

GÉRONTE. Yes, but I should like you to tell me whence it arises.

SGANARELLE. Nothing is easier; it arises from loss of speech. Our best authorities will tell you that it is because there is an impediment in the action of the tongue. Aristotle on this subject says a great many clever things. My advice is to put her to bed, and make her, as a remedy, take plenty of bread soaked in wine.

GÉRONTE. Why so, sir?

SGANARELLE. Because there is in bread and wine mixed together a sympathetic virtue which produces speech. Do you not see that they give nothing else to parrots, and that, by eating it, they learn to speak?

GÉRONTE. That is true. Oh! The great man! Quick, plenty of bread and wine.

Molière, *A Doctor in Spite of Himself,* 1666.

7.1 What in the opinion of the French playwright Molière was the state of medical knowledge in 1666?

(A) Very deep and useful
(B) Limited
(C) Poor
(D) Useless

7.2 How likely was Molière's opinion of physicians typical of the general population?

(A) Physicians were seen as very helpful
(B) People were skeptical of their value but consulted them
(C) Physicians were actively scorned
(D) Most people did not have an opinion

7.3 The real breakthrough for modern medicine in terms of being able to treat a wide range of diseases and conduct internal surgery came with advances in which of the following?

(A) Anatomy in the 16th century
(B) The microscope in the 17th century
(C) Chemistry in the 18th century
(D) Biology in the 19th century

Questions 8.1–8.3 refer to the following passage.

Article VII, sec. 1: By the unanimous consent of His Imperial Majesty the Emperor and of all the Estates of the Empire, it has been found good that the same right or privilege which all the other Imperial constitutions, the religious peace, the present public treaty, and the settlement of grievances contained therein, accord to the Catholic Estates and subjects and to those of the Lutheran faith, be also accorded to those who call themselves the Reformed [Calvinists].

Treaty of Westphalia, 1648

8.1 Article VII of the Treaty enforced what major change?

(A) Privileged Roman Catholics over Protestants
(B) Rejected the Protestant Reformation
(C) Recognized Calvinism as a legitimate religion
(D) Granted the Emperor supreme power in Germany

8.2 The Treaty of Westphalia was also important for what other provision?

(A) Acknowledging the emergent European state system for the first time
(B) Freeing the serfs
(C) Recognizing England and Russia as coequal with Austria, Spain, and the Netherlands
(D) Liquidating the German aristocracy

8.3 The Treaty of Westphalia brought an end to the Thirty Years' War (1618–48). The outcome of that war was

(A) A triumph for Spain
(B) Inconclusive for most participants
(C) Brought France to its knees
(D) Raised Russia to the front rank of powers

Questions 9.1 to 9.3 refer to the following passage.

I take the first opportunity that has been given to us, to acquaint you with our disconsolate situation in this solitary waste of creation. Our passage … was tolerably favourable; but the inconveniences since suffered for want of shelter, bedding &c. are not to be imagined by any stranger. Notwithstanding all our presents, the savages continue to do us all the injury they can, which makes the soldiers' duty very hard, and much disaffection among the officers. I know not how many people have been killed. As for the distresses of the women, they are past description those who have young children are quite wretched. Kangaroo are like mutton, but much leaner; and here is a kind of chickweed so much in taste like our spinage, that no difference can be discerned. In short, everyone is so taken up with their own misfortunes, that they have no pity to bestow on others. All our letters are examined by an officer; but a friend takes this for me privately. The ships sail tonight.

Woman convict, letter from Botany Bay, Australia, 1788

9.1 What may make this account of the first convicts "transported" as punishment to Australia particularly reliable?

(A) It is an eyewitness account
(B) The author is not critical of the authorities
(C) The letter was not inspected by a censor
(D) It was written by a woman

9.2 Why did the British state employ transportation of convicts to Australia as a punishment in the eighteenth century?

(A) A rapidly rising crime rate filled all the prisons
(B) They did not put women in prison
(C) No guards were needed
(D) It was a cheap method of colonization

9.3 Which of the following statements best describes the Botany Bay colony?

(A) A disastrous failure that had to be abandoned due to starvation
(B) Led to the establishment of modern Australia
(C) Remained unimportant
(D) Was wiped out by the aboriginal inhabitants

Questions 10.1–10.3 refer to the following passage.

The torture of a criminal during the course of his trial is a cruelty consecrated by custom in most nations. It is used with an intent either to make him confess his crime, or to explain some contradictions into which he had been led during his examination, or discover his accomplices, or for some kind of metaphysical and incomprehensible purgation of infamy, or, finally, in order to discover other crimes of which he is not accused, but of which he may be guilty.

No man can be judged a criminal until he be found guilty; not society take from him the public protection until it has been proved that he has violated the conditions on which it was granted. What right, then but that of power, can authorize the punishment of a citizen so long as there remains any doubt of his guilt? Besides, it is confounding all relations to expect that pain should be the test of truth, as if truth resided in the muscles and fibers of a wretch in torture. By this method the robust will escape, and the feeble be condemned.

Marquis di Beccaria, *Essay on Crimes and Punishments*, 1764

10.1 The author of this passage is making use of which of the following while making his argument?

(A) Historical reasoning
(B) Analytical reasoning
(C) Intuitive reasoning
(D) Theological dogma

10.2 Which of the following terms best describes the Marquis di Beccaria?

(A) Politician
(B) Humanist
(C) *Philosophe*
(D) *Zietgeist*

10.3 Subsequent reforms advocated within the criminal justice systems of Western Europe in the nineteenth century included which of the following?

(A) Punishment of children in a way that was different than adults
(B) Use of the electric chair for capital punishment
(C) Increase the use of the pillory
(D) Shorten prison sentences

Questions 11.1–11.3 refer to the following passage.

One opinion pervaded the whole company [at dinner], that they are on the eve of some great revolution in the government: that every thing points to it: the confusion in the finances is great; with a deficit impossible to provide for without the [calling of the Estates] General of the kingdom, yet no ideas formed of what would be the consequence of their meeting: no minister existing, or to be looked to in or out of power, with such decisive talents as to promise any other remedy than palliative ones: a prince on the throne, with excellent dispositions, but without the resources of a mind that could govern in such a moment without ministers: a court buried in pleasure and dissipation; and adding to the distress, instead of endeavouring to be placed in a more independent situation: a great ferment amongst all ranks of men, who are eager for some change, without knowing what to look to, or to hope for: and a strong leaven of liberty, increasing every hour since the American revolution; altogether form a combination of circumstances that promise e'er long to ferment into motion.

Arthur Young, *Travels in France*, 1787

11.1 What major cause of the French Revolution did Arthur Young neglect to mention in his list?

(A) The British invasion of France
(B) A series of bad harvests in the 1780s
(C) War with Spain
(D) Economic competition with the Netherlands

11.2 Arthur Young was an Englishman. How might his nationality have effected his views of France in 1787?

(A) He believed things were better than they really were
(B) He believed things were worse than they really were
(C) Admiration for the French monarchy
(D) Belief the French government was inferior to the British

11.3 Aspirations to achieve a governmental system similar to the British one was held by which social group in France before the Revolution?

(A) The nobility
(B) The clergy
(C) The royal family
(D) The peasants

Questions 12.1–12.3 refer to the rise of modern consumer culture exemplified by the illustration of the *Bon Marché* department store in Paris illustrated below.

12.1 The emergence of the department store in the later nineteenth-century suggests which of the following is true?

(A) The consolidation of goods due to the expansion of railway networks
(B) Old stores continued under new names
(C) The price of goods rose making large stores profitable
(D) The growth of commerce due to mass markets make goods more affordable

12.2 Among other things department stores did which of the following?

(A) Provided a safe space for women to meet outside the home
(B) Sold only hand-crafted products
(C) Formed a club space used by men to smoke and play cards
(D) Attracted mainly working-class men looking for cheap goods

12.3 Consumerism became an increasing part of nineteenth and twentieth-century life because?

(A) The increased rate of finished goods manufactured in China and India lowered prices
(B) Small specialty shops made it easy to find goods
(C) The religious revival of the nineteenth century encouraged people to pursue material happiness
(D) Goods proliferated in quantity at lower and lower prices

Questions 13.1–13.2 refer to the following passage.

Like other tyrannies, the tyranny of the majority was at first, and is still, vulgarly, held in dread, chiefly as operating through the acts of the public authorities. But reflecting persons perceive that when society itself is the tyrant—society collectively, over the separate individuals who compose it—its means of tyrannizing are not restricted to the acts which it may do by the hands of its political functionaries. Society can and does execute its own mandates. It practices social tyranny more formidable than many kinds of political oppression. Protection, therefore, against the tyranny of the magistrate is not enough; there needs protection also against the tyranny of the prevailing opinion and feeling; against the tendency of society to impose, by other means than civil penalties, its own ideas and practices as rules of conduct on those who dissent from them.

John Stuart Mill, *On Liberty*, 1859

13.1 Into what category of nineteenth-century political opinion does John Stuart Mill best fit?

(A) Conservative
(B) Revolutionary
(C) Liberal
(D) Marxist

13.3 Mill was a strong advocate of which of the following?

(A) War with France
(B) Women's suffrage
(C) Overthrow of Queen Victoria
(D) Imperialism in Africa

13.2 With which statement would Mill have been most likely to agree?

(A) Autocracy is the best form of government
(B) Aristocracy is a good counterweight to middle class opinion
(C) Democracy can be a form of tyranny
(D) Socialism guarantees individual rights

Questions 14.1–14.3 refer to the Women's Suffrage movement in England illustrated in the 1913 poster reproduced below.

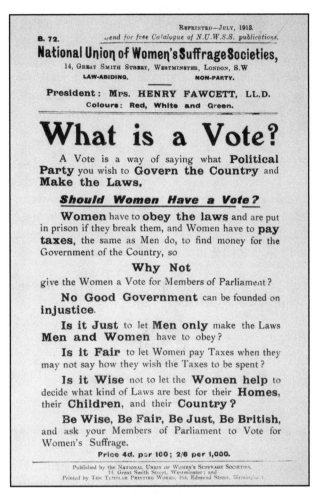

14.1 The arguments listed on the poster make an appeal to which of the following?

(A) The fundamentals of socialist theories of equality
(B) Marxist doctrines of dialectical materialism
(C) The ideas of the Enlightenment expressed by Rousseau
(D) British traditions and rights

14.2 The arguments listed on the poster were intended to separate Mrs. Fawcett's organization from

(A) Men who supported women's suffrage
(B) Nationalists who wanted war with Germany
(C) Militant Suffragettes who used violence
(D) The Trades Union movement

14.3 What impact did the First World War (1914–18) have on the suffrage movement?

(A) Led Parliament to grant suffrage to women immediately to gain their support in the war
(B) Had no impact on the suffrage movement
(C) The vote was given to women who served in the armed forces
(D) Made it impossible not to grant suffrage after the war due to women's contributions to victory

Questions 15.1–15.3 refer to the passage below.

It has long been the policy of successive British governments to work towards the realization of self-government in India. In pursuance of this policy an increasing measure of responsibility has been devolved on Indians and today the civil administration and the Indian Armed Forces rely to a very large extent on Indian civilians and officers. In the constitutional field the Acts of 1919 and 1935 passed by the British Parliament each represented a substantial transfer of political power. In 1940 the Government recognized the principle that Indians should themselves frame a new constitution for a fully autonomous India, and in the offer of 1942 they invited them to set up a Constituent Assembly for this purpose as soon as the war was over.

His Majesty's government desire was to hand over responsibility to authorities established by a constitution approved by all parties in India in accordance with the Cabinet Mission's plan, but unfortunately there is at present no clear prospect that such a constitution and such authorities will emerge. The present state of uncertainty is fraught with danger and cannot be indefinitely prolonged. His Majesty's government wish to make it clear that it is their definite intention to take the necessary steps to effect the transference of power into Indian hands by a date not later than June 1948.

It is therefore essential that all parties should sink their differences in order that they be ready to shoulder great responsibilities which will come to them next year.

Clement Attlee, British Prime Minister, speech in the House of Commons Feb. 20, 1947

15.1 The independence of India from British rule can be characterized as

  (A) The transfer from an imperial dictatorship to a indigenous dictatorship
  (B) Seamless and easy to achieve quickly
  (C) The result of an armed revolution
  (D) The outcome of a sequence of steps toward self-government

15.2 The uncertainty "fraught with danger" that Attlee mentioned referred to what difficulty?

  (A) Inability of Muslims and Hindus to agree on a united single state of India after British rule ended
  (B) Gandhi's death which left India without its greatest moral and political leader
  (C) The refusal of the independent princely states to cooperate in the unification of the country
  (D) The threat of intervention by the military forces of the Soviet Union

15.3 Britain moved towards decolonialization of most of its empire from 1947 onwards because?

  (A) Because Winston Churchill was out of office after 1945.
  (B) The British were economically weak after World War II
  (C) They were following the example of the United States in the Philippines
  (D) They wanted to concentrate on holding onto Africa

Questions 16.1–16.3 refer to the Middle East region after the Second World War illustrated in the map below.

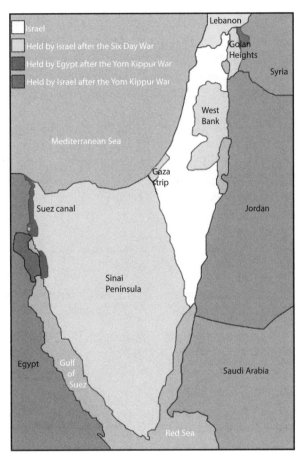

16.1 The Middle East was a region of significance to European states because?

(A) Further colonies were acquired there after the Second World War
(B) Hostility between Israel and the Arab States intertwined with the Cold War
(C) The rise of Jordan threatened European interests
(D) The Egyptians gave up control of the Suez Canal

16.2 Weaker European relations with some Arab states after the Second World War threatened which of the following?

(A) The flow of oil imports
(B) Relations with the United States
(C) Relations with China
(D) Access to the Suez Canal

16.3 Some analysts predicted the Middle East was a tinder box with the potential to provoke the Third World War because?

(A) The USSR and the USA took different sides there during Arab-Israeli wars
(B) Egypt's desire for hegemony in Africa
(C) Saudi Arabia's fear of Israeli attack
(D) Israel's hostility to Turkey

Questions 17.1–17.3 refer to the following passage.

I can't construct a scenario where the Axis could have won the Second World War. In fact, the "Axis" is itself a misnomer because it contained a failed Italian Fascist state, which became a German auxiliary, and the Japanese who were fighting their own war and had no interest in co-ordinating grand strategy. So really we're talking about Germany, and Germany simply did not have the industrial depth to wage a protracted war against the coalition that was likely to be ranged against it.

There is a myth that Germany was on the cusp of defeating the Soviet Union, but every attempt to turn the war in the east into a close-run thing is just not plausible. In key weapons systems such as tanks, artillery and general munitions the Soviets were out-producing Germany throughout the war, despite huge losses in the beginning. The German generals knew that if you couldn't defeat the Soviet Union quickly then you couldn't defeat it at all, and even in the third week of August 1941, General Halder was writing: "Uh-oh, they're still coming".

Joe Maiolo, author of *Cry Havoc: The Arms Race and the Second World War, 1931–41*, 2013

17.1 The passage above challenges the interpretation of historians who have written that which of the following was true?

(A) Either side could have won the Second World War
(B) The Axis was always going to lose the war
(C) The Russians were too strong for the Germans
(D) The intervention of the Japanese was key to German's loss of the war

17.2 This historian would agree that which of the following forces determines the outcome of history?

(A) Political
(B) Ideological
(C) Economic
(D) Nationalism

17.3 Adolf Hitler was a failure as a military leader because?

(A) He invaded Russia a year too early
(B) He made an alliance with Japan
(C) He let the Italians dominate the Axis alliance
(D) He failed to understand the underlying balance of world power

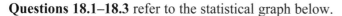

Questions 18.1–18.3 refer to the statistical graph below.

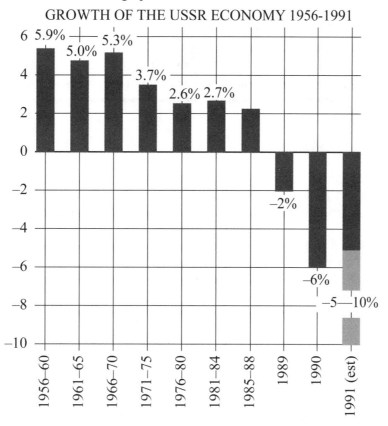

GROWTH OF THE USSR ECONOMY 1956-1991

18.1 Which of the following statements is true about the above graph?

  (A) The Soviet economy was always in negative growth

  (B) The Soviet economy never grew at a rate greater than the rest of Europe

  (C) The Soviet Economy went into a tailspin in the 1970s

  (D) Gorbachev's reforms were unable to slow the decline

18.2 The fundamental problem of the Soviet economy was which of the following?

  (A) It tried to combine capitalism and communism

  (B) Too much money was spent on the space race

  (C) Command economies cannot respond to infinite numbers of variables

  (D) A series of incompetent finance ministers made too many mistakes

18.3 Great dissatisfaction among the Soviet people was evoked by what aspect of the economy?

  (A) Failure to produce sufficient armaments
  (B) Inability to trade with foreign countries
  (C) Not enough consumer goods
  (D) Too much concentration on the car industry

SAMPLE EXAMINATION TWO

SECTION I, Part B

Time—50 minutes

4 Questions (Short Answer)

Directions: Read each question carefully and write your responses in the corresponding boxes on the free-response answer sheet.

Use complete sentences; an outline or bulleted list alone is not acceptable. You may plan your answers in this exam booklet, but only your responses in the corresponding boxes on the free-response answer sheet will be scored.

Question 1:

Important discoveries in the field of science during the sixteenth and seventeenth centuries reshaped mankind's knowledge of the universe. Using your knowledge of European history answer the questions (A, B, and C) below.

A) Many historians identify the "Scientific Revolution" as a major turning point in Western history. Identify and explain which ONE of the following developments was the most significant discovery.

   • Andreas Vesalius's (1514–64) advancements in medical knowledge
   • Tycho Brahe's (1546–1601) astronomical observations
   • Francis Bacon's ideas about a "scientific method"
   • Isaac Newton's (1642–1727) work in physics

B) Some historians argue against the view that the discoveries mentioned above constitute a "revolution". Identify and explain ONE argument that can be made against the idea of a "Scientific Revolution".

C) Identify and explain ONE way that the Scientific Revolution contributed to the Enlightenment.

Question 2:

In every country it always is and must be the interest of the great body of the people to buy whatever they want of those who sell it cheapest. Every individual endeavors as much as he can both to employ his capital in support of commerce and manufacturing, and by directing that industry in such a manner as its produce may be of the greatest value, he intends only his own gain. He is in this led by an invisible hand to promote an end, which was not part of his intention. By pursuing his own interest he frequently promotes that of society more effectively than when he really intends to promote it.

Adam Smith, *An Inquiry into the Nature and Causes of the Wealth of Nations*, 1776

The quotation above comes from the seminal work on economics that became the foundation of modern capitalism. Adam Smith was the greatest and most influential economist of the Enlightenment. Based on this quotation and your knowledge of European history answer the questions below (A and B).

A) Identify and explain TWO ideas that constitute the basis of "Classical Economics", of which Adam Smith is considered the greatest exponent.

B) Identify and explain ONE way in which Adam Smith's thought can be considered compatible with the spirit of the Enlightenment.

Question 3:

The familiarity with the sickness and death constantly present in the crowded and unwholesome districts, appears to re-act as another concurrent cause in aggravation of the wretchedness and vice in which they are plunged. Seeing the apparent uncertainty of the morrow, the inhabitants really take no heed of it, and abandon themselves with the recklessness and avidity of common soldiers in a war to whatever gross enjoyment comes within their reach.

> Edwin Chadwick, *Report on the Condition of the Labouring Population of Great Britain*, 1843

Based on your understanding of European history and the extract from the report on the condition of the urban poor in England in the 1840s answer the following questions (A and B).

A) Identify and explain TWO aspects of urbanization that affected rural inhabitants moving to industrial cities in the nineteenth century in a positive way.
B) Identify and explain ONE aspect of urbanization that affected rural inhabitants moving to industrial cities in the nineteenth century in a negative way.

Question 4:

Source 1:

Churchill's vision of what might happen in the event of Britain failing to win can be seen in terms of reference that he gave his Chiefs of Staff on 26 May, when he asked them to say what situation would arise in the event of 'terms being offered to Britain which would place her entirely at the mercy of Germany'. But what grounds were there for supposing that Germany's terms would necessarily be extremely harsh and brutal? Were there no grounds for supposing that Hitler might be disposed to pay handsomely to avoid the perilous task of a sea and airborne invasion?

John Charmley, *Churchill: The End of Glory*, 1993

Source 2:

Had Hitler won the Second World War we would be living in a different world. His aim was to dominate Europe and most of European Russia—and make or force Britain and Russia and the United States to accept such a German victory. [But] the man in Hitler's way was Churchill. At the time there *were* reasons for a British government to at least ascertain whether a temporary compromise with Hitler was at all possible. Churchill, however, said no. Even the first cautious moves would mean stepping on a slippery slope; he was right.

John Lukacs, *Five Days in London May 1940*, 1999

When Winston Churchill became Prime Minister of Great Britain in May 1940 his country stood alone in Europe in defiance of Hitler. The modern historians John Charmley and John Lukacs disagree about his decision to fight on. Using the quotations above and your knowledge of European history answer the uestions below (A, B, and C).

A) Identify and explain ONE factor Churchill took into account in making his decision not to negotiate with Hitler.
B) Identify and explain ONE factor that may have contributed to the disagreement between the accounts by Charmley and Lukacs.
C) Identify and explain ONE reason Churchill may have feared Hitler more than Stalin.

SAMPLE EXAMINATION TWO

SECTION II, Part A

Total Time—55 minutes

Question 1 (Document-Based Question)
Suggested reading period: 15 minutes
Suggested writing period: 40 minutes

Directions: Write a well-integrated essay that does the following:

- Has an appropriate thesis that directly addresses all parts of the question
- Supports the thesis with evidence from all or all but one of the documents AND your knowledge of European history beyond/outside the documents.
- Analyzes a majority of the documents in terms of such features as their intended audience, purpose, point of view, format, argument, limitations, and/or social context as appropriate to the argument.
- Places the argument in the context of broader regional, national, or global processes.

1. Analyze the responses to the proposal to reform the British electoral system in 1832.

Document 1

Borough constituency electorates in the unreformed House of Commons	
1–100 electors	77 borough seats
101–300 electors	36 borough seats
310–1,000 electors	46 borough seats
1,000 plus electors	43 borough seats

Document 2

Source: William Cobbett, radical journalist, *Cobbett's Political Register*, newspaper, 1816.

With what indignation must you hear yourselves called the Rabble, the Mob, the Swinish Multitude .... As to the cause of our present miseries, it is the enormous amount of the taxes, which the government compels us to pay for the support of its army, its placemen, its pensioners, etc. and for the payment of the interest on the debt.... The remedy consists wholly and solely of such a reform in the Commons or People's House of Parliament, as shall give to every payer of taxes a vote at elections, and as shall cause the Members to be elected annually.

Document 3

Source: Viscount Althorp, Whig MP*, letter to a political ally, J. C. Gotch, 1821.

I am not afraid of those who attempt to stir up trouble amongst the poor, for they have no power to do any harm, but I am very much afraid of the excuse they will give to those who wish to establish despotism, and I really and sincerely believe such a design is in existence. No man can now gravely assert that the House of Commons have any pretensions to say that they express the feelings of the country. If there is a grain of English spirit left petitions for reform of Parliament will come from every parish in the kingdom.

* Member of the House of Commons

Document 4

Source: Viscount Milton, Whig MP, "Address on the Corn Laws", pamphlet, 1825.

The landed gentlemen of England ought to be at the head of everything liberal, and prepared to sacrifice their own interests to promote the general welfare of the country. Was it for them to use their power to pass tariffs through Parliament in order to enrich themselves at the expense of their fellow subjects? He blushed for the order to which he belonged when he thought of the Corn Laws and the arguments used in the House of Commons to maintain them. We stand on a noble eminence; we occupy a station in the public eye, which has been conceded to us by the affections and by the favour of successive generations. Let us beware how we teach men to scan too minutely the value of our claims and the reasonableness of their favour.

Document 5

Source: Sir Robert Peel, Conservative MP, speech in the House of Commons, 1831

It is triumphantly asked, will you not trust the people of England? Do you charge them with disaffection to the monarchy and to the constitution under which they live? I answer, that without imputing disaffection to the people, or a deliberate intention on their part to undermine the monarchy, or to destroy the peerage, my belief is, that neither the monarchy nor the peerage can resist with effect the decrees of a House of Commons that is immediately obedient to every popular impulse, and that professes to speak the popular will.... I have been uniformly opposed to reform on principle, because I was unwilling to open a door which I saw no prospect of being able to close.

Document 6

Source: Thomas Babington Macaulay, Whig MP and historian, speech in a debate in the House of Commons, 1831.

We exclude from all share in the government vast masses of property and intelligence—vast numbers of the middle classes—those who are most interested in preserving tranquillity and who know best how to preserve it. We do more. We drive over to the sin of revolution those whom we shut out of power. The happiness of the people cannot be promoted by a form of government in which the middle classes place no confidence.

Document 7

Source: J. L. Marks cartoon

SAMPLE EXAMINATION TWO
SECTION II, Part B
Question 2 or Question 3 (Long Essay)
Suggested writing period: 35 minutes

Directions: Choose EITHER question 2 or question 3. You are advised to spend 35 minutes writing your answer..

In your response you should do the following.

- State a relevant thesis that directly addresses all parts of the question.
- Support your argument with evidence, using specific examples.
- Apply historical thinking skills as directed by the question.
- Synthesize the elements above into a persuasive essay.

2. Why were Europeans able to achieve economic and political control over many non-European peoples between 1450 and 1750?

3. Can Karl Marx be considered the last philosophe of the Enlightenment?

APPENDIX

Page 70

The John Bacon Family, c.1742-43... Devis, Arthur (1712-87) Credit: Yale Center for British Art, Paul Mellon Collection, USAPaul Mellon Collection/Bridgeman Images

Page 71

"Map 7.2: The Rise of Prussia, 1648-1720", from A HISTORY OF MODERN EUROPE: FROM THE RENAISSANCE TO THE PRESENT, THIRD EDITION by John Merriman. Copyright © 2010, 2004, 1996 by John Merriman. Used by permission of W. W. Norton & Company, Inc.

Page 73

©SSPL/Science Museum / The Image Works

Page 98

From: *The Age of Manufactures, 1700-1820: Innovation, and Work in Britain*, 2nd ed., Maxine Berg, Copyright (© 1994) and Routledge, London, reproduced by permission of Taylor & Francis Books UK.

Page 99

Maps of Time: An Introduction to Big History, by David Christian, © 2011 by the Regents of the University of California. Published by the University of California Press.

Page 97

From an original work by Norman Davies, copyright © Norman Davies 1997.

Page 125

William Simpson (artist, 1823–1899) E. Walker (lithographer, lifespan unknown, working for Day & Son) Publishers: Paul and Dominic Colnaghi, London; Goupil & Cie, Paris; Otto Wiegel, Leipzig. Restoration by Adam Cuerden

Page 126

© The British Library Board found in Linda Colley Taking Stock of Taking Liberties, British Museum, London, 2008, British Library referenced BL, 1911-14 LON MLD5 NPL.

Page 138

Gregory Clark. *A Farewell to Alms: A Brief Economic History fo the World.* © 2007 Princeton University Press. Reprinted by permission of Princeton University Press.

Page 139

Hafiz Abdul Karim; Queen Victoria by Hills & Saunders © National Portrait Gallery, London

Page 161

David Low / Solo Syndication

Page 162

From STORM OF STEEL by Ernst Junger, translated by Michael Hofmann, copyright 1920, © 1961 by J. G. Cotta'sche Buchhandlung Nachfolger GmbH, Stuttgart; translation copyright © 2003 by Michael Hofmann. Used by permission of Penguin Classics, an imprint of Penguin Publishing Group, a division of Penguin Random House LLC.

Page 175

© The British Library Board. Found in Linda Colley, *Taking Stock of Taking Liberties*, British Library, London, 2008, reference BL, 1899.ss.18 (74).

Page 176

AP Images

Page 178

© 2015 Estate of Pablo Picasso / Artists Rights Society (ARS), New York.

Page 179

"Table 34: Aircraft Production of the Powers, 1939-1945" from THE RISE AND FALL OF THE GREAT POWERS: ECONOMIC CHANGE AND MILITARY CONFLICT FROM 1500 TO 2000 by Paul Kennedy, copyright © 1987 by Paul Kennedy. Used by permission of Random House, an imprint and division of Penguin Random House LLC. All rights reserved.